Trinity and Humanity

'Colin Gunton helped shape contemporary theology by inspiring and shaping many young scholars: he did this by his passion as much as he did it by his methodology and dogmatic conclusions. In this welcome survey of Gunton's theology, Uche Anizor attentively captures not only the content, but also the energy behind Gunton's work. Even when Gunton falls short, and he does at times, there remains so much to learn from him. Thankfully, Anizor's volume will help us not forget the mark this joyful and yet restless theologian left.'

– *Kelly M. Kapic, Professor of Theological Studies,*
Covenant College, USA

'Colin Gunton, one of the leading theologians of his generation, memorably once said that everything looks different in light of the Trinity. This book, which demonstrates exactly how and why that is so, is a must read for all who believe that the doctrine of the Trinity is the central Christian doctrine which shapes all others. What makes this book an important theological resource is the fact that the author discusses the full range of Gunton's thought extending from the Trinity to creation, reason and revelation, ecclesiology, Christology, atonement, Pneumatology and more, while carefully providing his own very helpful and insightful critical responses. This is accomplished without in the least undercutting the author's desire to encourage readers to return to Gunton's own writings in order to learn afresh how theology, which takes divine freedom seriously as the basis for human freedom, can and should be done today. Whether one agrees or disagrees with Colin Gunton or does a little of both, one certainly will learn a great deal both from this book and from Gunton's own voluminous writings on a variety of important theological themes.'

– *Paul D. Molnar, Professor of Systematic Theology,*
St. John's University, Queens NY, USA

Trinity and Humanity

An Introduction to the Theology of Colin Gunton

Uche Anizor

Copyright © 2016 Uche Anizor

First published 2016 by Paternoster
Paternoster is an imprint of Authentic Media Limited
PO Box 6326, Bletchley, Milton Keynes, MK1 1GG, UK
authenticmedia.co.uk

The right of Uche Anizor to be identified as the Author of this Work has been asserted by him in accordance with the Copyright, Designs and Patents Act 1988.

All rights reserved. No part of this publication may be reproduced, stored in a retrieval system, or transmitted in any form or by any means, electronic, mechanical, photocopying, recording or otherwise, without the prior permission of the publisher or a licence permitting restricted copying. In the UK such licences are issued by the Copyright Licensing Agency, Saffron House, 6–10 Kirby St, London, EC1N 8TS.

British Library Cataloguing in Publication Data

A catalogue record for this book is available from the British Library

ISBN: 978-1-84227-8543
e-book: 978-1-78078-335-2

Unless otherwise noted, Scripture quotations are taken from the Holy Bible, New International Version Anglicised Copyright © 1979, 1984, 2011 Biblica
Used by permission of Hodder & Stoughton Ltd, an Hachette UK company
All rights reserved.
'NIV' is a registered trademark of Biblica UK trademark number 1448790.

Scripture quotations marked (ESV) are taken from the ESV Bible (The Holy Bible, English Standard Version), copyright © 2001 by Crossway, a publishing ministry of Good News Publishers. Used by permission. All rights reserved.

Cover Design by Pete Barnsley (CreativeHoot)
Printed and bound by CPI Group (UK) Ltd., Croydon, CR0 4YY

To Gregg Allison and my former professors at
Southern Seminary,
who were among the first to make theology
exciting for me

Contents

Preface	xi
Acknowledgements	xiii
Abbreviations	xv

1 Theology and the Theologian: An Introduction — 1
A Prolegomena to Theology — 5
Conversation Partners — 15
On Reading Gunton: Major Motifs — 22
The Structure of the Book — 23

2 Persons in Communion: The Triune God and the Divine Attributes — 25
Polemics against Process Theology — 25
Early Soundings in Barth's Theology — 29
Augustine as Foil, or The Woes of the West — 33
Towards a Fully Trinitarian Theology — 38
On Persons and Particularity — 41
'The Difference the Trinity Makes' — 43
Conclusion — 50

3 'It Is Very Good': Creation, Providence and Human Personhood — 54
Platonizing Creation: A Historical Sketch — 54
Triune Creation: Its Basic Shape — 63
The Being of the World — 65
On Providence — 68
On Human Being — 71
Conclusion — 77

4	**The Knowledge of Faith: Reason, Revelation and Scripture**	**82**
	Faith and Reason	82
	A Theology of Revelation	88
	A Stronger Doctrine of Scripture	94
	Conclusion	98
5	**The Logic of Divine Saving Love: Jesus Christ**	**102**
	Issues in Christological Method	102
	The Eternally Begotten One	113
	In the Likeness of Sinful Flesh	116
	Conclusion	120
6	**Metaphors and Atonement: The Work of Christ**	**124**
	On Metaphor	124
	Atonement in Three Metaphors	127
	Atonement and the Triune God: Towards a Theology of Reconciliation	138
	Conclusion	143
7	**The Real and Ideal Community: The Church**	**147**
	In Search of an Ontology	147
	The Transcendent Spirit and the Church	152
	The Church's Christ-Shaped Orientation	155
	The Humanity and Eschatology of the Church	156
	The Sacraments	158
	Conclusion	162
8	**Perfecting Cause and Perfected End: The Spirit and Last Things**	**167**
	Problems in Pneumatology	168
	The Spirit in the Economy	170
	The Eternal Spirit	176
	The End of All Things	179
	Conclusion	184

9	**A Concluding Commendation**	**187**
	Theology as Conversational and Creative	188
	Theological High Points	192
	Recommended Reading	199
	Bibliography	201
	Endnotes	216

Preface

My first encounter with Colin Gunton was as a Master of Divinity student skimming through his *Christ and Creation*. While I couldn't make heads or tails of what I was reading – which was no fault of Gunton's – it appeared to me a strange new world of theology. During my years of doctoral studies, while I was making early forays into Barth's theology, I looked for something of a critical guide as I made my way through the labyrinth. Gunton became that guide (though, of course, not a perfect guide). One summer, I decided to read through as many of Gunton's works as I could. In the process, I slowly forgot about Barth (the chief reason I was reading Gunton in the first place) and became increasingly enamoured with the style of theology in which I was being immersed. Here was constructive theology. Here was confident theology. Undoubtedly taking his cues from Barth, Gunton's theology evinced a conviction that the Christian faith not only had an internal coherence and beauty, but that it possessed the resources for addressing the most important questions within and without the church. It was chiefly from him that I got a taste of the excitement and possibilities of theology. This book is a small tribute to a theologian I never met, but who influenced my love for systematic theology. One need not, and I do not, follow Gunton at every turn – as will be evident in the critical comments at the end of each doctrinal chapter – but in his work there is a restlessness and hope, a groping after the truth and implications of the gospel, that should be a feature of all good evangelical theology. With respect to the purpose of this volume, I'll make two additional comments. First, I intend this book as an overview to those who have heard of Gunton but have had only minimal or no exposure to his thought. Second, it will hopefully be a starting point for those interested in delving into one or another aspect of his theology. I attempted to synthesize almost everything he has written on a particular doctrine, while being sensitive to developments where I noticed them. My synthesis or sensitivity to development will certainly not satisfy all, but I hope I am faithful to my subtitle by providing an *introduction* to this important theologian.

I would like to give special thanks to my LA 'Inklings' group – Bob Lay, Jeremy Treat, Charlie Trimm, Hank Voss and Isaac Voss – for their feedback and sharpening of several chapters of this book. Thanks to Jordan Barrett for encouragement as well as careful critique of some chapters. To Matt Jenson, thank you for taking time during the busiest part of the semester to give very constructive feedback on several sections. To Andy Draycott, I'm grateful for close editing of one of my chapters. I am also indebted to Talbot School of Theology for allowing me to take a research leave that freed me to write several chapters, and to Biola University for providing a time-release grant that further lightened my teaching load. To Chad Duarte, thank you for putting some finishing touches on the book with your work on the notes and bibliography. Without the help of good friends and colleagues this project would still be in progress. Finally, thank you to my wife, Melissa, who provided constant prayer and encouragement to me during the process of writing a book on a theologian she may never read; and to my kids, Zoe, Eli and Ezra, thanks for being excited about your dad writing a book, even though you don't quite yet grasp what that means.

Uche Anizor
September 2015

Acknowledgements

Portions of Chapter 4 appear as 'The Problem and Promise of Mediation: Gunton on Barth and the Doctrine of Scripture', *Scottish Bulletin of Evangelical Theology* 33 (2015). Used by permission.

Portions of Chapter 7 appear as 'A Spirited Humanity: The Trinitarian Ecclesiology of Colin Gunton', *Themelios* 36.1 (2011): pp. 26–41. Used by permission.

Abbreviations

CD	Karl Barth, *Church Dogmatics* (4 vols; ed. and trans. G.W. Bromiley and T.F. Torrance (London: T&T Clark, 2009)
IJST	*International Journal of Systematic Theology*
JTS	*Journal of Theological Studies*
NZSTh	*Neue Zeitschrift für Systematische Theologie und Religionsphilosophie*
SJT	*Scottish Journal of Theology*

1

Theology and the Theologian: An Introduction

'Not since John Henry Newman,' writes theologian Stephen Holmes in an obituary, 'has an English theologian generated such a school of followers.'[1] What is it about this man that attracted such devotion and exercised such an influence? By his own account, Colin Ewart Gunton would have seen himself as simply one particular person from a particular place with a particular set of relationships with a particular vocation in God's world – little more than that. He was born on 19 January 1941 in Nottingham, England, where he was also raised.[2] Among the early privileges he cites is his parents' devotion to church ministry, as well as the exposure he had to Scripture and the great works of literature. He attended Nottingham High School, where he was exposed to the Greek and Latin classics, which opened him up to the craft of writing.

Gunton entered university at Hertford College, Oxford, where he continued in his love for the classics, as a student in the 'Greats' (or Classics) course, with some interest in philosophy. He then entered Mansfield College, Oxford, to read theology, completing his MA in 1967 before entering doctoral work in theology. He recalls his transition from interest in philosophy towards a passion for theology as being triggered by contact with (surprisingly) John A.T. Robinson's *Honest to God*, a modernist classic. Of this influential volume he writes: '[T]he book provided an introduction to the excitement of theology – to a feeling that here are indeed questions to be engaged of far greater weight and depth than the often ahistorical orientation and often essentially trivial concerns of much of the philosophy in whose mysteries . . . I was being initiated.'³ Decisive influences would come later, but this was a starting point.

For his doctoral work, Gunton intended to write on Alfred North Whitehead's influence on later process theologians – Hartshorne, Cobb and Ogden – but was encouraged in a different direction by his doctoral supervisor, Robert Jenson. Rather than focusing solely on process thought, Jenson had Gunton place Hartshorne in conversation with Barth, as there were some illuminating similarities and differences between the two.⁴ Many of the themes, emphases and concerns found in this early work would reverberate throughout Gunton's career; he would merely enrich them rather than leave them behind. For example, his close reading of Barth would provide the foundations of a Trinitarian theological orientation that he would carry with him to his last days.

After two years of doctoral work, in 1969, he received a teaching post in the philosophy of religion at King's College, London. In the early years of teaching, he taught the history of Western philosophy, which exposed him to a wide swath of important thinkers and issues. He would remark that these years helped shape convictions regarding the necessity of a proper doctrine of creation for addressing perennial issues in philosophy, such as the battle between empiricism and rationalism. Ten years after his initial appointment, he became King's' first Lecturer in Systematic Theology (1980), and then Professor of Christian Doctrine (1984). These were the beginnings of many fruitful years at King's College. He would complete two monographs on Christology (*Yesterday and Today* and *Christ and Creation*) and one on rationality in conversation with Enlightenment philosophy (*Enlightenment and Alienation*). From 1983 to 1988 he was invited to be a part of the British Council of Churches Study Commission, an ecumenical group charged with studying the nature of Trinitarian theology. These gatherings proved formative because they exposed him more deeply to Eastern Orthodox theology, particularly the Cappadocians through John Zizioulas. The Trinitarian thought of the East left an indelible mark on Gunton and would further deepen his commitment to developing a fully Trinitarian theology – but a particular brand of it. Another significant contribution to those fruitful years was the addition of Christoph Schwöbel to the King's faculty. He quickly became a collaborator with Gunton in ways both formal and informal, most notably in the establishment of the Research Institute in Systematic Theology. The Institute, which consisted largely of regular Tuesday gatherings, one-day conferences and biannual international conferences, became a hotbed of theological activity, attracting the brightest scholars and students from around the world and producing important collections of essays (most of which were edited by Gunton).[5] Many of Gunton's writings would first be reviewed and refined by graduate students and colleagues at these meetings, something he acknowledges in footnotes throughout his works.

Other career highlights include the invitation to give the prestigious and long-standing Bampton Lectures at his alma mater in 1992, out of which came his most celebrated volume, *The One, the Three and the Many*. He also co-founded and co-edited one of the finest theology journals, the *International Journal of Systematic Theology*, while also being a co-editor for the eminent *Neue Zeitschrift für Systematische Theologie und Religionsphilosophie*. He became the head of the Department of Theology and Religion at King's from 1994 to 1997, and would go on to receive honorary doctorates from the universities of London, Aberdeen and Oxford.

While the academy loomed large in his life and in a very important sense Gunton was an academic theologian, he loved his family – both immediate and churchly. He was married to Jennifer (Jenny) at a young age, and they had four children – Carolyn, Christopher, Jonathan and Sarah. He was also a devoted minister of his local church. While finishing doctoral work, he was ordained in the United Reformed Church, a small denomination formed through the union of English Presbyterians, English, Scottish and Welsh Congregationalists, and members of the Churches of Christ. Although he served well in this (moderately) Reformed denomination, how Gunton himself could be identified as Reformed is not always obvious. He saw himself as a dissenter, a Nonconformist, and he was this way even in his church affiliation. As a theologian and churchman, he was ecumenically minded, congregationally oriented, and eclectic in terms of influences. Apart from some commendations of features of Calvin and Owen, and a strong Reformed-like commitment to the centrality of hearing Scripture (and God's word therein) in congregational life, his place within the Reformed tradition seemed tenuous or at least complex – especially in his critiques of its perceived preoccupation with the predestination of individuals.[6] Election, instead, is temporal and eschatological, not pre-temporal and protological; it has more to do with vocation than destinies. Election takes place in history as the Spirit gathers together a community that anticipates in its life the future perfection of all things. The Spirit is the God who elects and perfects the human community and the created order.[7] Rather than viewing his leanings as 'Reformed', long-time friend Bruce McCormack concludes: 'Gunton's theology is better characterized as a kind of older (pre-Roman) Catholicism. He was in many ways a throwback to the second century.'[8] Gunton served Brentwood United Reformed Church in Essex, a small congregation, as an associate minister for twenty-eight years, preaching at least monthly (among other things). Stephen Holmes recalls Gunton saying on more than one occasion: 'You can always tell when a theologian has stopped preaching; their work loses something vital.'[9] Preaching was vital for the life of *this* theologian. In the end, however, it is not inappropriate to see Gunton as an academic theologian. It is to this task that he gave his intellectual energies and for which he will be remembered. He died unexpectedly on 6 May 2003, leaving behind family, students and devotees, friends, admiring colleagues, and a legacy as the most important English theologian of the second half of the twentieth century.[10] A closing quote from Holmes:

> Colin was the most intellectually able British theologian of his generation by some distance; this judgement seems to me simply incontrovertible. Many others were more politically-skilled and so prospered better in the university environment; some had better judgement on what and when to publish and so produced a more even corpus of work; a few

– not many, if any! – might have had a better grasp of the breadth and the detail of the theological tradition; but in terms of sheer theological ability, Colin comfortably outstripped them – us – all.[11]

A Prolegomena to Theology

Perhaps to better understand the man Colin Gunton, it is critical to explore his understanding of the discipline to which he devoted most of his career. Outlining his prolegomena may seem contrary to his own intentions. Robert Jenson notes that in the first volume of Gunton's unfinished and unpublished dogmatics 'prolegomena as such disappear completely'. He goes on: 'The epistemological topics usually taken up as prolegomena are simply absorbed into material dogmatic sections.' Gunton is 'anti-traditional', not wishing to give epistemological issues the independent attention and governing influence common in modern theologies.[12] Anti-traditionalism notwithstanding, an examination of his reflections on the nature of systematic theology is warranted by the sheer volume of occasional writings Gunton produced on this and related issues. Moreover, he saw prolegomena as necessary in theology's self-reflective engagement with church and culture. Thus, in a number of writings, he attempts to give rough outlines and definitions of systematic theology. For example, he describes it as 'the articulation of the truth claims of Christianity, with an eye to their internal consistency, on the one hand; and, on the other, to their coherence with Scripture, the Christian tradition and other truth – philosophical, scientific, moral and artistic'.[13] Though not his only description,[14] this provides a helpful entrée to what might be called his prolegomena, his understanding of the discipline and task of theology. Two key features form the core of his approach.

First, theology seeks to articulate Christian truth claims. Truth for the Christian has everything to do with the one who declared, 'I am . . . the truth' (John 14:6). Truth is thus christologically focused, centring on the gospel as the announcement of God's work of creation and redemption in Jesus. 'Systematic theology's distinctive character,' Gunton writes, 'derives from its responsibility for articulating the meaning and implications of the church's claims for the truth of the Christian gospel.'[15] The truth with which we are concerned cannot, therefore, be merely propositional (though it is that), but rather makes claims on one's life. Jesus 'the truth' is also 'the way' and 'the life'; he calls for a response from all who hear. Because truth concerns this Jesus, it is self-involving or, rather, what Gunton calls 'other-involving' – that is, it brings people into a new relationship with God.[16] This suggests that while theology is an intellectual discipline, it is not so exclusively.

Second, systematic theology is concerned with being, well, systematic. Every discipline seeks to be systematic in the sense that it proceeds according to some rational order. When this term is applied to theology, it can be (and has been) construed in at least two ways: with a strong conception of 'system' or a mild one. The first option, characterized by such diverse figures as Origen, Spinoza, Kant, Hegel and Schleiermacher, tends to 'treat Christianity as containable in a complete and logically watertight system'.[17] The drive in this model is towards comprehensiveness – a perfectly coherent and logically consistent system that explains the totality of truth, Christian and otherwise. Gunton contends that this tendency towards 'over-systematization' often fails to recognize the limits on system inherent in Christian teaching, such as the nature of God and the fallenness and finitude of humanity, sometimes imposing an order or system on truths that are resistant to systematization.[18] A second way of being systematic is to have an awareness of the interconnections between various tenets of the Christian faith. Irenaeus (along with Anselm and Coleridge, among others) is set forth as a chief example of this form, since he was able 'to perceive connections between truths, and to know which belongs to which'. Moreover, quoting Brunner's characterization of Irenaeus approvingly, Gunton writes: 'No other thinker was able to weld ideas together which others allowed to slip as he was able to do.'[19] What makes the second-century theologian commendable is that he did all this without attempting to build a unifying, all-encompassing system;

he displays what Gunton calls 'a free and open unity' in his systematic thought.[20] Being systematic in theology, according to Gunton, involves at least two criteria: (1) there must be consistency of some sort among the various doctrines, so that theology does not allow for proper contradictions; (2) there must be an awareness of the relationship between the content of theology and the contents of Scripture, tradition and the 'truths' of the broader culture.[21] This second criterion must be given more detailed attention, specifically for theology's relation to each of these sources of knowledge.

Systematic theology and Scripture

According to Gunton, systematic theology is Christian only insofar as it engages in a conversation, one in which the first word is spoken by an authority, Scripture in this case. The Bible is central to the theological task because it speaks a word that shapes human reality in the most fundamental way, chiefly by mediating the Word made flesh in a unique manner. Following Calvin's teaching that reality cannot be rightly discerned apart from Scripture, Gunton writes: 'Scripture, accordingly, is that without which certain things may not be said. It is the necessary but not sufficient condition for theology's being Christian.' The Bible is the 'earthen vessel' through which God presents Jesus Christ, who engenders certain forms of ecclesial life, one of which is systematic theology. Thus, without Scripture there is no Christian community, and without this worshipping community theology loses its *raison d'être*.[22] Scripture is authoritative for theology primarily because of this function it performs in the church. Secondarily, the Bible exercises its authority by prescribing the material with which the theologian must work. For example, the main themes (of creation, humanity, sin, salvation, eschatology, etc.), the form in which they must be handled (e.g. creation by one God versus pantheism), and the appropriate human response, are all given to the theologian.[23] Scripture thus sets boundaries and creates the conditions within which theology can and must operate.

Yet, more needs to be said of the relation of the Bible to systematic theology. A common understanding of the systematic task is to summarize and synthesize the whole of the Bible's teaching on this or that matter. Gunton, however, is careful to undercut any pretensions to capture the whole of the Bible's teaching. All theology, he asserts, is partial, provisional and contextual. Several things follow from this statement. First, given the nature of God and the limits of the human mind, attaining *the* biblical message is a 'chimera'. Second, it is the Spirit that enables the reaffirmation of the biblical faith in particular historical and cultural forms, as is needed for the times. Third, the particularity of theological expression does not negate the truth that some relatively comprehensive '*summae*' do a better job than others at approximating the wholeness of the biblical message. Yet even full-blown systematic theologies omit important items and may be incorrect on areas that are included. Fourth, the relation between contemporary theological articulation and the concepts, ideas, commands and narratives of the Bible is indirect and takes many forms. Theologians must make judgements on how to relate the various aspects of Scripture and bring them to contemporary expression; there is no one straightforward path from biblical text to systematic theological restatement. All these comments lead to one final consideration that has to do with the work of the Spirit on the theologian. Gunton frames this concern as a question: 'May we not say that the theologian should be free to emphasize now one dimension of the manifold message, now another, and to develop a concept beyond the limits of its meaning in the source from which it is drawn – as in the case of the image of God, perils and mistakes being admitted?' One of the Spirit's ministries is to grant humanity freedom, not autonomy, but liberty to live out and express the truth within the limits set by God and, in this case, by Scripture.[24] The same Spirit who gives the Scriptures to the theologian in the first place frees him or her to bring to expression its message for the good of God's people. The one who inspires the book inspires the reader as well.[25]

Systematic theology, dogma and tradition

Gunton lays out the relationship between dogma and theology with the use of a handy metaphor, writing: '[S]o far as the relations of dogma to theology are concerned, dogma is that which delimits the garden of theology, providing a space in which theologians may play freely and cultivate such plants as are cultivable in the space which is so defined.'[26] We spoke earlier of the boundaries set by Scripture; here we observe that dogma contributes to or even mediates Scripture's boundaries. The theologian is a gardener with only certain plants to cultivate within a limited space, yet he or she is at liberty to make the garden as useful and beautiful as individual skill and the Spirit enables. Freedom within limits, play within borders – this characterizes the theologian's tension. 'Dogma' refers to the authoritative teachings of the church, its attempt to capture or summarize the gospel and other divine mysteries in human words, usually propositional in form and 'universally' affirmed.[27] Dogma performs what Gunton calls an 'intermediate measure' between Scripture and the theologian: by summarizing the teaching of Scripture in a way that neither stifles creativity nor permits boundless plurality, it provides the context for a theologian's work.[28]

The possibility of theological creativity, particularly as it takes concrete form in church tradition, brings to the surface an additional dimension of the theologian's relationship to dogma. According to Gunton, the theologian's task

> is to question not only whether the Church has been too enthusiastically creative, but whether the results of such creativity can be seen to cohere with other articles of the faith as they have been accepted and handed down within the process of tradition. That is to say, part of theology's systematic task is to examine the coherence of different dogmatic expressions, not only with Scripture but with one another.[29]

Theologians are to assess the church's theological creativity not merely in terms of apparent scriptural fidelity, but also with respect to the coherence between the 'novel' dogmatic expression and other articles of faith. Churches must ever make decisions concerning whether new dogmatic formulations, arising from particular cultural challenges, express the same gospel. In that light, the theologian is not merely bounded by – thus indirectly related to – dogma. Rather, Gunton concludes, 'the theologian is *directly* involved in dogma as one putatively learned enough in both historical and systematic theology to be able to consider the broader context within which dogmatic formulation takes shape, and so to assist the Church as a whole to make informed decisions'.[30] While the theologian plays within the bounds of the garden, he or she is also involved in ensuring the legitimacy of those very boundaries.

This discussion raises the issue of the development of doctrine within the church of Christ – an issue to which Gunton devoted some attention early in his career. He develops his views in conversation with Barth, whose repudiation of what is called the 'deposit theory' of development sets the stage for Gunton. This theory is characterized by the belief that the 'truths of revelation' were once and for all delivered to the church, infallibly and complete. The dogmatic task, and thus the theologian's relationship to the past, is to repeat, repackage and elucidate these truths in ever-changing situations. 'The theologian,' Gunton writes, 'can say the same things better, but no more.'[31] Barth (and Gunton in agreement) rejects this view on one simple ground: it denies the freedom of God in his revelation, the freedom to say more about himself than we know at present. Truth, and thus dogma and theology, has an eschatological dimension. This being the case, Gunton concludes: 'The final truth belongs to the future: because of this we are not freed from further enquiry.' Theologians do not just repeat the past as if past knowledge and formulations are all that can be had. There is ever the possibility, in the light of God's freedom, that theology is able to say something that has not been said before.[32]

What is most promising in Barth's theology is this orientation towards the future. However, Gunton questions whether Barth follows his instincts far enough, asking if the latter has truly moved beyond the deposit theory, or merely repeated it with a different conceptuality. In Barth's view, revelation does not come in the form of some static deposit, but rather as the repeated event of God's self-presentation, authoritatively witnessed in Scripture and paradigmatically displayed in Jesus Christ. In revelation, revelatory events of the (biblical) past are brought into the present. But does not this orientation to past revelation resemble the deposit theory? Gunton observes:

> The deposit is different, but it remains a deposit: a series of events, with the Jesus event the paradigm case and epistemological key, about which we can learn more and more not so much by deduction, as in the old model, but this time by induction – certainly an improvement, but scarcely revolutionary in its implications. The treasure is, as it were, scattered about the biblical field: we know what to look for, and there is always the chance that we may unearth another piece of the well-known coin. But it is another piece of the same or very similar coin, rather than anything new.[33]

Both views of the development of doctrine are 'excessively backwards-looking', so that there is no expectation of new knowledge. 'In each case,' according to Gunton, 'everything significant has happened already.'[34] What is needed, and what seems lacking in Barth, is the biblical emphasis on the Spirit as the one who brings eschatological realities into the present.[35] According to Scripture, it is the Spirit of truth who makes known what is to come (John 16:13), is described as a first instalment or 'deposit' of future blessing (2 Cor. 1:22), and enables the church to make innovations in its outreach (e.g. book of Acts). The Spirit opens the church to the possibilities of the future, enabling it to do and say greater things than were done and said in the past (John 14:12), all in anticipation of the end. Thus, theology is not a slave to the past. Instead, taking direction from the past, the theologian strains, under the direction of the Holy Spirit, towards the open future, recognizing that every formulation is provisional and subject to God's judgement.[36] Rather than viewing doctrinal development in terms of progress – which often connotes a modern contempt for the past – Gunton prefers the term 'enrichment' over 'development'. The theologian's aim, in this light, is to draw from the past and, in doing so, enrich it, not merely move beyond it. Whether one has enriched the tradition or distorted it will ultimately be determined in the *eschaton*.[37]

Systematic theology, philosophy and culture

One of the driving forces behind Christian theology is its encounter with prevailing culture and particularly its attendant philosophy of religion. If the gospel, to which Scripture and tradition attest, is the internal basis of theology, this engagement with culture represents, according to Gunton, its external basis.[38] He breaks theology's dialogue with philosophy into three general time periods. The first, the Greek period, evinces no independent place for a theology grounded in the gospel of Jesus. Philosophy itself is religious and in no need of content from a particular religious movement like Christianity, and vice versa. The second phase can be identified roughly as that of the medieval synthesis between theology and philosophy. In this era, the two modes of enquiry were fused together, since both were religious and were asking the same kinds of questions. 'On this view,' writes Gunton, 'Athens and Jerusalem are both the same kind of place, so that a treaty of alliance is concluded and worked out. The general religious intellectual quest and the Christian systematic task run at least in parallel, at most in symbiosis.'[39] During this period, theology and philosophy were positively related. The third phase – the modern – is somewhat a return to the first, wherein philosophy has pushed aside theology as a viable form of enquiry. Theology becomes problematic because it is primarily constituted and directed by particular historical claims that are resistant to some types of philosophizing and systematizing.

What is common to the three eras, and thus to the relation between the two disciplines, is their concern to give a picture of the whole, to answer the biggest questions of life, to reach into the realm of ontology. None of these three periods does justice, however, to the integral relation between these fields of study. Beyond sharing a common realm of interest, how are theology and philosophy to be related? First, we opened this section speaking briefly about intellectual culture or philosophy as the 'external basis' for theology, signalling that systematic theology arises when the church must defend its creed in the light of philosophies that oppose it. Philosophy is often the fuel and context for theology. Second, theology is dependent on philosophy for the conceptual tools to articulate a rational account of the faith. Gunton writes: 'What theology does on this account is to enable language to express, under the impact of the gospel, meaning beyond its former capacities.' Finally, while sceptical regarding the powers of reason, theology is pushed by philosophy to care about rational coherence and intelligibility. Thus, Gunton concludes, while the two fields have often been opponents, they are indispensable opponents and conversation partners.[40]

When speaking of intellectual culture more broadly, theology is seen as an indispensable contributor and not merely a passive recipient. In addressing the place of theology in the university, Gunton highlights four ways theology adds value to intellectual culture. First, theology provides one framework for addressing the many questions facing society. It provides some categories – not the only categories, mind you – that might aid one's attempt to understand why things are the way they are.[41] Second, in terms of content, theology aids culture by contributing to its plurality of perspectives and truth claims. A plurality of voices, which must include the theological, is necessary for preserving intellectual freedom and diversity within a community. In fact, theology is not inimical to plurality, but rather has, historically speaking, provided several rationales for intellectual and religious tolerance.[42] Third, because theology is concerned with the existence, nature and actions of God, it contributes to the concern for universality, that is, the meaning of the whole. Finally, and closely related to the last point, theology, with its concern for the nature of the triune God and his actions in the world, engenders the articulation of a particular vision of unity and plurality. The *one* God acts in a *variety* of ways through the Son and Spirit in a way that ennobles creatures and enables their freedom to be themselves, encouraging diversity rather than suppressing it in the world he has made. These various works of God surely illuminate the world with which an intellectual culture is concerned. For example, what it means to be human is elucidated by the incarnation and ministry of the Son.[43] These oft-neglected theological resources are indispensable for any intellectual community, like a university, concerned to articulate the whole truth about our world.

Gunton's practice of theology

Indeed, returning to Gunton's initial description, we are reminded that theology seeks after the truth, and not merely to restate what has been handed on from within whichever intellectual tradition one is found.[44] Therefore, theology must be shaped by its interaction with Scripture, tradition and culture, as all of these 'sources' bring the theologian into contact with truth that is gospel-shaped and only fully known eschatologically. These ideals are reflected, as we will see, in Gunton's many published works. In his published dissertation, *Becoming and Being*, for example, he is concerned with the truth concerning God and his relation to the world. In conversation with process theology, he argues that the fundamental issue is that truth must be rooted in what God has done in Jesus and not some *a priori* notions of what can and cannot be. He demonstrates an attentiveness to Scripture in several works including *Christ and Creation*, an apprenticeship to tradition in volumes like *Yesterday and Today*, *The Triune Creator* and *The Actuality of Atonement*, and an acuity concerning culture and its relation to theology in *Enlightenment and Alienation* and (especially) his magisterial *The One, the Three and the Many*.[45] On this last point, one author rightly avers that one cannot understand Gunton's theological project without seeing it as part of his struggle with modern culture.[46]

Gunton lived and worked consistent with his own principles, especially when we consider again his contention that theology is ultimately eschatological. It appears that much of his theological programme is shaped by this conviction. For him, theology is partial, provisional and, therefore, constructive. Because full knowledge lies in the future, all theological formulations are provisional. Yet, because theological formulations are provisional, theologians are free to be constructive, drawing from the past but remaining open to new truths and better answers to perennial problems. This openness to the future is demonstrated in the many subtitles of Gunton's work, for example: An Essay towards a Trinitarian Theology; Towards a Theology of the One and the Many; Towards a Theology of the Divine Attributes; Toward a Fully Trinitarian Theology.[47] His work demonstrates an awareness that the theologian is always approximating, ever attempting to give as truthful an account of the Truth as he or she is able. Theologians are always moving 'towards' a full understanding and articulation of all the implications of the gospel. This feature is the most fruitful and, for some, the most frustrating feature of Gunton's theology.

Conversation Partners

This open-ended dimension of his theology further highlights how Gunton sees theology as a conversation, one that takes place not solely between the theologian and Scripture, tradition or culture, but especially with particular theologians and thinkers. His constructive project was regularly fuelled and energized by his interaction with a particular set of thinkers, as will become clear in the chapters that follow. Thus, one way to introduce Gunton the theologian is to highlight briefly those who shaped his thought and the ways they did so. This is by no means an exhaustive list of writers, nor a complete exposition of the ways they shaped him. Each of the following chapters spells out their influence in more detail. But for the time being, I offer a snapshot of Gunton's interlocutors, under the headings of 'Fuel' or 'Foil', denoting respectively those from whom he (generally) drew positively and those to whom he reacted (generally) negatively.

Fuel

Barth

The Swiss theologian is arguably the most pervasive presence in Gunton's writing. From his early articles and doctoral thesis all the way to his last published book, Barth was a most significant conversation partner. From him Gunton would gain a nose for sniffing out theology that is not dictated by the gospel, theology governed by *a prioris* rather than the reality of the triune God and his work in the world. That instinct gained from Barth would govern much of Gunton's explorations of the Trinity, creation, revelation, Scripture and the nature of theology, among other things. Of course it is true that he regularly opposed or at least nuanced Barth's conclusions, so that he can never be accused of being a slavish follower. In fact, at the beginning of his lecture course on Barth, he would say:

> Not everyone buys into Barth. I don't, all the way along the line, as I get older *I get more and more dissatisfied with the details* of his working out of the faith . . . over the years I think I have developed a reasonable view of this great man who is thoroughly exciting and particularly, I can guarantee, if you do this course, that you will be a better theologian by the third year, whether or not you agree with him – *he is a great man to learn to think theologically with*.[48]

Note: Barth's conclusions, as we will see in subsequent chapters, were not always satisfying, but his approach to theology – his governing principles, if you will – was much valued by Gunton, so that throughout his own works he was compelled to repeatedly dialogue with the great writer of the *Church Dogmatics*.[49]

Coleridge

Almost as pervasive as Barth is Samuel Taylor Coleridge, who for Gunton is the exemplar of an English systematic theologian.

He was one who tried to think through the whole and bring seemingly disparate truths together. What was exemplary about Coleridge was his willingness to engage with the difficult questions of the modern age, especially those pertaining to the nature and freedom of human beings.[50] What emerges from this aspect of Coleridge's work is the insight that the being of the world, and of necessity humanity, is reflected or even derived from the being of the triune God. The doctrine of the Trinity is *the* resource for understanding human personhood and freedom. In fact, Gunton claims that Coleridge is the first theologian in the West to develop the connection between the Trinity and a relational view of the human person.[51] This is the insight to which Gunton would repeatedly return, the well from which he would regularly draw. He summarizes well the chief value of Coleridge's insights: '[His] proposals, with their tendency to be fragmentary and schematic, are in some ways more important for what they suggest and make conceptually possible than for what they actually deliver.'[52] While Coleridge's thoughts were not fully developed on these matters, and remained somewhat speculative, they provided for Gunton a starting place and the conceptual resources for much of his later work on the Trinity, creation and humanity.

Irenaeus

Another mainstay in Gunton's writing, especially in his mature thought, is the bishop of Lyons. Irenaeus was, for Gunton, the first true systematic theologian – and systematic in the best sense of the word.[53] He was also an exemplar in many matters theological: furnishing the church with an account of the goodness of creation, against gnostic portrayals; speaking of the eschatological perfection of the good creation; having a theology of mediation that preserved both the freedom of God and the freedom of the creature; and providing hints that the economy of creation and salvation should shape our account of the immanent being of God. All of these features of Irenaeus' thought were of great concern to Gunton, and in increasing measure throughout his career. You can, therefore, find appeals to Irenaeus in almost every monograph and collection of essays after the mid-1980s.

Other lights

While the above figures appeared most regularly in Gunton's writings, many other figures featured prominently. *Edward Irving* provided resources for thinking through the humanity of Jesus and particularly the work of the Holy Spirit in the formation and empowerment of his humanity. Paired with Irving would be *John Owen*, who would fund a picture of Christ's humanity, a humanity not swallowed up by his divinity. *Michael Polanyi*, the philosopher of science, looms large in Gunton's epistemology (religious and otherwise). He offers a view of knowledge that is personal and pre-propositional. We know things in the world even before we can articulate this knowledge because there is a real relation between knower and known. *John Zizioulas* was the vehicle through which Gunton encountered the Cappadocian Fathers and appropriated them in his later theology. What was of particular interest was Zizioulas' (or the Cappadocians') understanding of the mutually constitutive relations of the persons of the Godhead: God's being is a being in communion. This is a further development of the inchoate insights of Coleridge, and one with a rich theological heritage. Moreover, from the Cappadocians Gunton would derive probably his most characteristic depiction of the Spirit as the 'perfecting cause' of all creation. These thinkers, among others, provided creative fuel for Gunton's constructive theological project.

Foil

Contrary voices are, Gunton suggests, as valuable as confirming and complementary voices in the formation of a well-articulated theology. This is surely the case for Gunton. His early theology was shaped by a nuanced engagement and decisive rejection of process theology, especially as represented by Charles Hartshorne. His theology beginning around the mid-1980s was marked by an increasing discomfort with and eventual repudiation of much of Augustine's contribution to Western theology.

Hartshorne

Since the first part of the next chapter is devoted to Gunton's exposition of Hartshorne, I will simply highlight what he found most problematic. The process concept of God so immanentizes God that it is difficult to see how God and creature differ. One problem is the conception of freedom that derives from such a concept of God. If God is one with the world, neither has independent being and, therefore, neither has any real freedom. Since one of Gunton's major theological concerns is to give an account of divine and human freedom that refuses to see the two as competitive, doctrines of God that militate against such freedom were rightly a concern for him. In Hartshorne there was a correct (according to Gunton) rejection of classical theism (to be described in the next chapter), but in place of an utterly transcendent Other we get one who is essential passive and dependent on the creatures. Whatever Gunton's doctrine of God would become, it must preserve God's freedom, humanity's freedom, and be shaped by the economy of God's dealings with humanity in Jesus rather than *a priori*s.

Augustine

It is widely known that Gunton did not think highly of Augustine's contribution to Western thought. The two areas in which the bishop of Hippo fails most catastrophically are in the doctrines of the Trinity and creation – the two most important doctrines in Gunton's work. Possibly chief among Augustine's deficiencies in his doctrine of God is his inability to say anything substantial about the persons of the Godhead. In trying to solve the apparent problem of how one God could also be three somethings, he appeals to the concept of 'relations'.[54] The one God exists in three personal relations. However, Gunton notes, relations between persons is here treated as a logical category, rather than an ontological one. By this he means that the particular persons have no distinct character, but rather dissolve into the 'all-embracing oneness of God'. The danger is that if we cannot say anything about the persons, we cannot say much about the being of God. All we have is the being of God that underlies the persons, which smells of modalism. The distinctiveness of the persons was a difficulty for Augustine because he did not allow the economy of salvation to more decisively shape his doctrine of God. The same charge is levelled against his doctrine of creation, where philosophical assumptions provide the main lines rather than Scripture's testimony to God's work. Augustine's dualism, vision of an overly transcendent God, construal of creation as not inherently good, and radical separation of time and eternity are just some of the problems bequeathed to Western thought – with disastrous results. One could say with little exaggeration that the majority of Gunton's mature theology is a negative response to this Augustinian legacy.

A loose chronology of key decisions

Robert Jenson, Gunton's doctoral supervisor and friend, offers a helpful, though incomplete map of Gunton's theological development.[55] I will borrow from and modify his 'decision tree' as a way of providing a summary to this section on Gunton as a conversational theologian. The table presents a rough outline of key theological decisions throughout his career.

Time Period	Gunton's Theological Decisions
Mid 1970s	The first major decision is the rejection of classical theism, as represented by Aquinas, largely because of its philosophical commitment to divine simplicity and the results for a theology of God and his relation to the world. This decision takes place also through conversations with process theology.
	The beginning of an alternative approach is sought through the theology of Karl Barth, who emphasized a more gospel-shaped account of the being and act of God.
Mid 1980s	The rejection of Aquinas was gradually replaced by his polemic against Augustine's doctrines of God and creation.
	His engagement with Coleridge furnishes him with the basic ideas for building a more fully Trinitarian theology.
	A doctrine of the triune mediation of creation is developed through an engagement with Irenaeus.
Late 1980s	A new doctrine of God is sought through the Cappadocians' emphasis on the distinct personhood of Father, Son and Spirit and their mutually constitutive relations. The resulting ontology of personhood would fund discussions of creation, humanity, culture and church.
Late 1980s to early 1990s	Coinciding with these developments is an increased emphasis on the ministry of the Spirit, which would exercise decisive influence on his Christology (on this he borrows from Edward Irving) as well as eschatology (borrowing from Basil of Caesarea).

Again, these decisions are presented here only in broad strokes. The details of these moves, along with the contribution made by these various thinkers, will be taken up in the following chapters.

On Reading Gunton: Major Motifs

George Hunsinger, in his seminal outline of Barth's theology, provides several 'motifs' to aid in reading Barth, which have proven quite helpful. In a similar, though far briefer way, I offer three motifs in Gunton's thought that will help facilitate understanding. The first, *particularity*, relates to Gunton's focus on God's work in the economy of creation and redemption.[56] God does *these* things, and only these things determine an account of his act and being. Humanity, further, can only be understood in terms of particularity: we have this location, this vocation, this personality, and so on. He would develop his more mature account of particularity in conversation with the doctrines of the Trinity and Christ. Within the Godhead there is particularity and oneness; as for the Son, his human career is marked by particularity: born to this family, of Israel, at this time in history, for this ministry. Ultimately, particulars are neither incidental nor peripheral. They are the means by which we access and experience reality.

Second, *relationality* refers to Gunton's emphasis on relationships as the foundation of all reality. Once again, this begins with a certain understanding of God as Trinity whose being consists in the communion of three persons. Consequently, all of the reality created by this God corresponds in some way to this intra-Trinitarian relational dynamic. Human persons are constituted by relationships: with God, with each other, with the cosmos; atonement is about restoring all those relationships damaged by sin; the church is the harbinger of the redeemed relationship that will be in the *eschaton*; and the Spirit is the agent of such reconciliation. Reality is relational.

Finally, Gunton repeatedly emphasizes the concept of *mediation* as a central problem in much Western theology. This term refers to the ways God acts in the created order, particularly through the Son and

Spirit, but not exclusively so. Mediation is central in his doctrines of creation, revelation and Scripture, atonement, church and eschatology because he desires to underscore that all God does in this world is by the Son and Spirit. A failure to account for one or the other leads to deficiencies in any or all of the areas just mentioned. Throughout the book I will draw attention to these motifs. But being given advance notice of how Gunton sees reality can only help the reader navigate the various details to follow.

The Structure of the Book

Finally, a few comments on the structure of the book. I have arranged the material according to traditional loci, while still allowing Gunton's own emphases to shine forth. This was a difficult balance to strike. There is a benefit to both approaches: one brings together disparate and occasional writings into a common place; the other allows Gunton to dictate how his thoughts are read together. Additionally, in the full systematic theology Gunton had intended to write before his untimely passing, he proposed a unique ordering of the doctrines: the economy of the Spirit, then Father, then Son.[57] I begin with the Trinity and creation, and end with the Spirit – a complete subverting of his intention! – for material and heuristic reasons. Materially, the doctrine of the triune God and the doctrine of creation are two areas Gunton aims to rehabilitate. Thus they occupy centre stage in almost everything he writes. Heuristically, since many systematic theologies begin with God and creation, as I have done, arranging Gunton's material along similar lines will aid learning for those accustomed to such a configuration of doctrines.

Each chapter provides a synthesis and overview of Gunton's thought on a particular doctrine or set of doctrines. Where they are evident, I try to show any developments in his theology. In the concluding section of each chapter I offer some critiques of Gunton's work, usually framed in the form of questions. For these I draw primarily from authors who engage with his writings specifically and not just with his theological 'school' or orientation. Critiques are brief and usually limited to those that are most frequently put forward, those that are most provocative and potentially damaging, and those that address areas in which Gunton may appear especially idiosyncratic. With some I agree, while with others I do not. My aim, nevertheless, is to provide the reader with both a positive overview of Gunton's thought and *some* scholarly interaction with it, without getting bogged down in too many details. We begin our survey with the all-important doctrine of God, the theological and methodological centre of Gunton's project.

2

Persons in Communion: The Triune God and the Divine Attributes

Claims for the 'centre' of someone's theology are often controverted and less often accurate. In the case of Colin Gunton it would be difficult to dispute the centrality of the doctrine of God, generally, and Trinitarian theology, in particular, to his whole constructive project. A quick glance at his book titles makes this abundantly clear. Even when other doctrines come up for consideration – most notably the doctrine of creation – it is with a view to understanding how God's triune being illumines the doctrine under consideration. In this light, we begin with Gunton's doctrine of God, giving particular attention to its development from his earliest writings to his final full-length monograph, as well as to the conversation partners who shaped his thought – whether as foes or friends – so as to set the foundation for and orient the reader to Gunton's treatment of an array of Christian teaching.

Polemics against Process Theology

Much of Gunton's early work on the doctrine of God was developed amidst his engagement with and critique of process theology. He observes that process thought emerges out of a rejection of a 'classical concept of God', a rejection of which Gunton approves for at least the following reasons.[1] First, classical theism tends to define the supernatural in opposition to the natural, which makes the relationship between the two problematic. Second, the emphasis on God's timelessness makes much of Scripture unintelligible, since the Bible speaks often of the historical relation of God to the world. Third, if God is absolutely necessary and relates to the world in a timeless fashion, it is difficult to account for contingency and meaningful history. All that exists becomes necessary, and what results is a form of pantheism.[2] In short, the classical doctrine is internally inconsistent – seeking to maintain a wholly necessary God who is also the free creator of a contingent universe – and makes it 'impossible for Christian theology to ascribe to God characteristics that appear on other grounds to be essential to his being'. An immutable and impassible God is hard to reconcile with the reality of the crucified God-man.[3] Thus, another way must be sought beyond that of Aquinas, his predecessors and his successors. Process thought provides one such alternative and Gunton takes it up chiefly in his *Becoming and Being*, where he specifically assesses Charles Hartshorne's revisionist proposal.

Foundational to Hartshorne's account, according to Gunton, is the 'doctrine of relations', which can be summed up thus: (1) relations between entities are either *internal* or *external*; (2) if one entity is related to another externally, it is not affected by that relation; (3) knowing entities are internally related to other entities such that the act of knowing alters them. Therefore, for any being to know anything it has to be internally related to the other thing and thereby undergo change. Known things are static, absolute and unchanging, while the knowing subject is dynamic, relative and changing.[4] For example, events in the past are fixed and absolute. One's apprehension of the past, however, changes them, while the past itself remains unchanged. As this applies to God, if we are to say that God knows anything, we must accept that God undergoes some form of change and is in some sense dependent. This is something classical theism has been unwilling to concede. Gunton, however, believes Hartshorne makes a compelling case, at least on his own principles. God cannot be conceived as absolute since the absolute is the object rather than the subject. For God to be absolute would entail that he cannot know in any meaningful way. God as a knowing subject is in an internal relation to everything else, and must therefore be relative and mutable. As Hartshorne extends his critiques to the metaphysical and moral arenas, Gunton finds himself in (albeit cautious) agreement.[5] The issue is whether a process or neoclassical conception of God fares any better under scrutiny.

Classical theology depicts God as wholly other, without adequately attending to his immanence, his intimate involvement with the created order. Hartshorne seeks to correct this lopsidedness by positing a *dipolar view of God*. Within God there are two simultaneously existing poles. The first sees God as the absolute and abstract, the one traditionally known as the cause; the other represents God as the relative and concrete, or what we might call the effect. For example, in his concreteness God is relative, changeable and contingent. He knows and experiences the world and is affected by it. However, since he relates to *all* present and past reality he is, in the abstract, absolute in that he is absolutely related to everything. In this way, God can be both relative and absolute, concrete and abstract. 'A necessary inference from what has been said,' Gunton concludes, 'is that God is only absolute *because he is relative* to the whole of reality; in other words, his absoluteness *consists in* his all-embracing relativity. The most real thing about God is his relativity.'[6] God is complete immanence and, as such, is completely transcendent. The classical categories of absoluteness, immutability or impassibility are preserved, but relegated to God's abstract pole. For God, as the sum of all past experiences, is fixed and unchangeable – absolute. Nevertheless, God is ultimately a being in becoming. In this light, he performs two functions. First, he unifies reality by being that which experiences and remembers the whole of it. Second, by experiencing and remembering all past reality, God is the receptacle or repository of the universe's experiences and thus provides the material from which future progress will be built.[7] God, in essence, provides the possibilities for and the certainty of a better future.

Gunton's chief criticisms arise in response to this conceptuality. He asks, 'Does God actually *do* anything other than act as the recipient of the cosmic activity, and so exercise causality indirectly in this way?'[8] It does not appear to be enough to say that God influences the actions of finite beings by giving them past material from which they build. The Bible presents a God who takes the initiative to create, enter into covenant, and redeem in Jesus.[9] This picture is far different from the essentially passive deity of process thought. If God, in his concreteness, is the supreme effect, he can only be a cause in the abstract. Gunton writes: 'It is difficult to see how a cause can be abstract, in any recognizable meaning of the word.'[10] In other words, abstractions do not act. Thus, divine initiative loses all meaning: creation, covenant and consummation are attributed to the cosmic process of which God is chiefly a passive experiencer. This necessitarian account robs God of his freedom and diminishes the character of the gospel as a gift of free grace. In the end, process theology does not make much sense out of the Christian message, a message about the breaking in of the kingdom or the God who seeks and saves the lost. Surely this is a picture of a more active God than is on offer in the process vision.[11] Moreover, on this account, it is difficult to conceive of God as loving. Hartshorne defines love as 'social awareness' and argues that God's supreme awareness of the world implies love for it, since God's relation to the world is always positive (in terms of providing for future progress). Gunton retorts that love can hardly be defined so passively and that awareness does not logically entail personal love, for a computer could have supreme awareness and relativity within a particular system, yet not love anything. The problem remains: a God that is primarily passive and receptive cannot also be primarily active, nor personal, and therefore cannot love in any recognizable sense of the word.[12] Finally, the notion of divine control is rendered relatively meaningless. For while a human can take action to remove and reduce pain, God cannot do likewise. Gunton writes:

> This would seem to be impossible for God, who can but wait upon the next instalment of experience brought to him by the autonomous process. The whole implication of the difference between the finite experience and the divine is that I can take action about the pain by cutting

myself off from that part of the cosmic process that I find unbearable. God cannot do this, for he is logically bound to experience as his internal environment the totality of the process.[13]

If God is simply one who experiences, divine providence and sovereignty must be redefined significantly or jettisoned altogether. In fact, the distinction between God and creation is minimal, and neither has the freedom intrinsic to being a true other.[14]

Gunton is able, however, to identify the potential contribution of process thought to a concept of God. First, it has rightly called into question the classical notion of divine impassibility, which renders a God who is impervious to the lives and suffering of the created order. In a criticism that will be echoed throughout his career, he charges that such an idea 'owes more to a priori Greek metaphysics than to a Christian understanding of God'. Second, process theologians have made clear that the classical concept of God need not exercise hegemony over other potential Christian understandings of God.[15] Other candidates may more seriously be entertained. One such candidate is the theology of Karl Barth, who himself calls into question the doctrine of a timeless deity and calls for a more gospel-shaped understanding of God.

Early Soundings in Barth's Theology

Gunton's exposition of Barth's doctrine of God in *Becoming and Being* sets out to make plain the similarities and especially key differences between Barth and Hartshorne. Although he puts Barth forward as a way beyond Hartshorne, he highlights throughout the overlap between the two conceptions of God. To begin, they both hold to a dynamic understanding of God's being, that is, that God's being is tied to his becoming in some fashion. For Barth, the becoming of God is demonstrated in the event of Jesus Christ, which reveals that God is One who moves outward towards what is other and becomes that which he is not. This outward movement is grounded in who

God is. There is no other God than the One who moves towards others – whether *ad intra* or *ad extra*.[16] Gunton summarizes:

> The incarnation is the movement of God into relation with the world he has created. Because this movement is God, there is no unmoved God behind or underlying it; rather it entails that God's being consists in a movement 'outwards' to what is not God. But because this movement is triune, and so not necessitated, it is a movement with a double aspect. God is movement towards the other, and this movement is expressed conceptually by the eternal relation of the Son to the Father in the Spirit. In its turn, this inner movement provides the ontological grounding for the outward movement we see to have happened in the life of Jesus.[17]

Therefore, his being is active; it is a becoming, an event. Closely related to this, both Barth and Hartshorne want to preserve God's true relatedness to the world, and they do this through a dipolar conception of God. The first pole represents the immanent, relative and concrete, and for Barth is summed up in God's becoming in Jesus Christ. The second pole represents the triune God as Lord even in his outward movement, thus emphasizing freedom and non-necessity. Finally, both theologians stress the subjectivity of God over against the classical view that makes the absolute or God an object before he is a subject. This emphasis can be seen, for instance, in Barth's treatment of the Godhead as the ultimate person.[18] In the end, for Gunton, these are by and large but 'surface' similarities. When we dig a little deeper, we find significant differences between the two conceptions of God.

The key differences Gunton observes can be placed into two broad categories: methodological and material. Concerning the first, Gunton charges that Hartshorne's account derives from *a priori* notions of what reality is or what is possible and tries to fit God therein. Barth, however, takes his starting point in God's giving of himself in revelation, so that his reasoning about God is *a posteriori*. According to Barth, we cannot decide in advance what God can and cannot do or be, but must take our cues from God's self-revelation.

The failure of neoclassical theology to do just this is evidenced in one important way: it makes both the Trinity and incarnation appear superfluous in an account of God's being. The very realities that make known the being of God in Barth's account are ancillary in Hartshorne's.[19]

From this fundamental methodological divide flow a number of critical material differences. While both writers hold a dipolar view of God, Hartshorne's God has no freedom to act. Barth's God, though intimately involved in the created order, is free in his movement towards it.[20] Although God gives himself entirely in his revelation, he is not bound to do so. In his freedom he chooses to give, so that his self-giving may truly be called gracious. Gunton calls this an 'asymmetry of understanding' and its primary function is to safeguard the freedom of God. For it denotes that 'while act is indeed a true guide to essence, knowledge of essence does not entail knowledge of the particular acts that God is going to perform'.[21] Put differently, God's acts do not exhaust his being, nor are they predictive of God's future acts. Hartshorne also held to an 'asymmetry', but with respect to time, holding that the future remains unknown and undetermined. The future of God (or one could simply say the world) is not predictable on the basis of past events. It is open-ended. By asserting this asymmetry Hartshorne sought to protect freedom, but his aim was fundamentally different from Barth's. Gunton observes:

> Hartshorne is not interested in the freedom of God to act graciously but in a general metaphysical freedom – a kind of indeterminacy – in the world process. Because the past alone and not the future is fixed and definite, there is room for each personal event to possess some freedom of its own. Indeed, this creaturely freedom is won at the expense of the freedom of God.[22]

According to Hartshorne, future acts are unknown to everyone, God included. God is not free to act in the future, but awaits the free actions of creatures. Barth's version of asymmetry aims to preserve the freedom of God over the created order.

Divine freedom, or the lack thereof, is the fundamental difference between these two theologians, and it is expressed in how both construe God's relatedness to the world. In Hartshorne's treatment, God relates to the world monistically; that is, everything is related to God in precisely the same way. For Barth, God's relatedness varies depending on that to which he relates. Within the Godhead, there is a necessary relation between Father, Son and Spirit. Towards creatures, however, God's relatedness is selective; it is freely determined by God where and when he will become fully related to the world. In this way, again, God's freedom and ontological distinction is preserved.[23] It follows from this that traditional divine perfections such as aseity, immutability (or constancy), omnipotence and omniscience will be configured rather differently in both accounts. Regarding aseity, Barth's God determines himself and Hartshorne's is determined by everything but himself.[24] Moreover, Barth views divine immutability as the constancy of freely given divine love, while Hartshorne views it abstractly in terms of the unchangeableness of God's past experience and knowledge and his universal relatedness to all reality.[25] Finally, in Hartshorne God's knowledge stands over his omnipotence, in that God can only influence the future by fully knowing and containing the past. For Barth, omniscience and omnipotence are held closely together, and neither is determined by anything outside of the God who freely knows and freely wills.[26]

It should be clear that Gunton, in the end, favours Barth's treatment over that of Hartshorne. What Barth achieves is at least twofold: (1) he maintains the close relation between God and creation without compromising divine freedom; (2) by safeguarding God's freedom, he also safeguards our ability to speak of God as loving and gracious, for there is no grace that is not freely given.[27] Nevertheless, Barth's account is not without its own problems, the chief being its 'orientation to the past' and, related, an underdeveloped doctrine of the Holy Spirit.[28] His orientation to the past is most conspicuous in his doctrine of election and the related understanding of the future as a repetition of a timeless eternity.[29] Moreover, Barth is ambiguous concerning the eschatological dimension of the Spirit's work and being, sometimes even saying we need to speak *non*-eschatologically about the Spirit. The future is only future in terms of our experience, not God's. 'The corollary would be,' Gunton asserts, 'that *objectively*, so far as God is concerned, there is no divine futurity, and all has been already decided in a timeless past.'[30] While Barth takes seriously the temporality of Jesus as a past event that reveals the being of God, he does not do so with the Spirit, thus making the Spirit less determinative in our understanding of the essence of God. The Spirit ends up taking on a passive role within the Trinity, and his eschatologically oriented agency is diminished. Barth's effort to more closely relate time and eternity, God and the world, falls short because it is ambiguous concerning God's involvement in the future through the Spirit. In fact, Gunton concludes, 'If the meaningful activity of God is already completed in past – or timeless – eternity, the outworking of the divine decision has all the necessity of a timeless concept, and our theology becomes the quest . . . for timeless truths.'[31] Taking seriously God's action requires giving attention to his future, which means taking seriously the Holy Spirit, something Barth has not done. In the end, Barth's Trinitarian doctrine is the way forward even though Barth himself was not 'Trinitarian enough'.[32]

Augustine as Foil, or The Woes of the West

Throughout his polemic against the classical and neoclassical doctrines of God, Gunton primarily directed his critiques towards Aquinas as the source of many ills.[33] The failure to rightly construe the God–world relation, the inadequate account of the Trinity, and an overemphasis on the oneness of God were by and large bequeathed by Thomas and his heirs. In time Gunton would sharpen his critique of Western doctrines of God – now focusing explicitly on the doctrine of the Trinity – and shift the focus of his criticisms to Augustine, the father of Western Trinitarianism.[34] In his 1985 inaugural lecture as Chair of Christian Doctrine at King's College, he gives early indication of the problems in Augustine's doctrine of the Trinity, chiefly, his inability to account for the divine persons and their distinctiveness.[35] However, Gunton's boldest and programmatic early explication of the critique is found in the 1988 lecture entitled, 'Augustine, the Trinity and the Theological Crisis of the West', which aims to 'bring together the two questions – of the problem about the knowledge of God and of the relegation to secondary status of the doctrine of the Trinity – by enquiring how far responsibility for the state of affairs is to be laid at the door of St Augustine'.[36] A careful exposition of this lecture is critical for understanding his developing problems with the Western tradition and his own positive proposal.

Speaking broadly, what Augustine bestowed upon Western theology, according to Gunton, is an overemphasis on the oneness of God. What Gunton investigates is the effect of Augustine's underlying neoplatonic presuppositions on his doctrine of God. The first notable effect is the latter's suspicion of the material world, and this is expressed in his inadequate treatment of the incarnation of Christ. In the formulation of Trinitarian doctrine, it is crucial to emphasize the humanity as well as the divinity of Christ, lest the doctrine of the Trinity be divorced from the economy of salvation. Augustine stressed the deity of Christ, not only because he was engaged in an anti-Arian polemic, but because of his 'neoplatonic assumptions of the material order's incapacity to be really and truly the bearer of divinity'.[37] This charge is confirmed in at least three ways. First, when Augustine treats Old Testament theophanies and prefigurations of Christ, he asserts that they are mediated not by the Word, but rather by angels. Angels take the place of the Word as the mediators of God's relation to the world, and this results in distancing God from the created order and flattening out the distinctions between the persons of the Trinity, rendering the distinctions irrelevant. 'In place of the tradition, going back to Irenaeus, of the Father relating himself to the world by means of the Son and Spirit,' Gunton writes, 'we are in danger of supposing an unknown God working through angels.'[38] Rather, since divine action is mediated by the incarnate Word, it is conceivable that other forms of divine action throughout salvation history are carried out by the same Word.[39] Augustine shies away from allowing the economy of salvation to inform his doctrine of the Trinity. Second, when he discusses the humanity of Christ, he is unwilling to concede that Jesus received, or came into a new relationship with, the Holy Spirit at his baptism. The result is that the full humanity of Christ is not given due regard, and Jesus' life appears 'preprogrammed' from the womb by the Spirit and not as coming to full flower through the same Spirit.[40] Third, since ultimate meaning is not to be found in the material world, it is not an adequate source of analogies for the Trinity. Rather, Augustine primarily seeks Trinitarian analogies within the rational, immaterial realm, as this is most fitting with respect to God. Augustine's Platonic suspicion of the material world is thus confirmed in at least the three above ways.[41] Yet these are only the beginning of sorrows.

A whole complex of issues surrounds Augustine's misunderstanding of classical Trinitarian language as handed down by the Cappadocian Fathers. The terms *ousia* and *hypostasis* were traditionally adopted to distinguish between the oneness and threeness of God – God is one *ousia* and three *hypostaseis*. What is important for Gunton is that this conceptuality implies that the being of God cannot be thought of apart from the communion of persons. Augustine has difficulty grasping the importance of the distinction, writing: 'I do not know what distinction they [the Fathers] wish to make.'[42] In fact, he treated the distinction as a linguistic convention concocted to answer the question of why there are three persons in God. In other words, since something has to be said about the three, we use the words *ousia* and *hypostasis*, though there is no real difference.[43] Augustine's failure to adequately understand this distinction is further evidenced in his near equation of persons with *relations*. The problem flows from his dualistic ontology, in which accidents cannot be predicated of the being of the one God. When we speak of persons in God, we dare not conceive of them as accidents since there was never a time when there was not Father, Son and Spirit. Thus another term must be employed, namely, *relation*. However, according to Augustine, when relations, and the particular features of them, are predicated of God, we are not referring to God in his essence, but rather speaking 'relatively'.

Gunton concludes: 'Because Augustine continues to use relation as a logical rather than an ontological predicate, he is precluded from being able to make claims about the being of the *particular* persons, who, because they lack distinguishable identity tend to disappear into the all-embracing oneness of God.'[44] Distinct persons in relation do not constitute the divine *ousia*; rather the divine substance or being underlies the three relations, however conceived.[45] Two potential dangers emerge: (1) God's being will be unknown, since it is other than that disclosed in the particularity of the Trinitarian persons, or (2) God's being will be made known through something other than the persons and, thus, divorced from the economy of salvation.[46]

This leads to a third set of concerns with Augustine's conception of the Trinity – those related to Trinitarian analogies. Gunton contends that Augustine's use of analogies, particularly that of the threefold mind, imposes a neoplatonic notion of threeness upon the doctrine of the Trinity and ignores how the economy of salvation might shape his conceptuality. This depiction of God as an individual mind with three components – memory, understanding and will – is fraught with difficulties. First, it suggests that there is a reality underlying the three persons (the mind), rather than seeing the three persons in relation as constituting the overall reality of God. Correspondingly, the emphasis falls on the oneness of an unknown God and is reminiscent of the problem we encountered earlier.[47] Second, his analogy, funded by his suspicion of materiality, compels him to conceive of the Word of God in primarily intellectualistic terms, as existing in the eternal mind, rather than as the concrete Son of the Father. The mind, and not material, is the most appropriate image for the being of God. Gunton summarizes: 'The crucial analogy for Augustine is between the inner structure of the human mind and the inner being of God, because it is in the former that the latter is made known, this side of eternity at any rate, more really than in the "outer" economy of grace.'[48] Finally, the Platonic triad imposes artificial constraints on how one understands the Spirit. Quite apart from attention to the economy of salvation, the Spirit is conceived as the logical correlate of the relationship between memory and understanding, or Father and Son. Augustine writes: 'These two, begetter and begotten [memory and understanding], are coupled together by love as the third, and this is nothing but the will seeking or holding something to be enjoyed.'[49] The Spirit is conceived as will, when, according to the history of salvation, it might be more fitting to see the Father as such. Thus, in what Gunton refers to as Augustine's 'Achilles' heel', we have a doctrine of the Spirit too strongly determined by philosophical assumptions.[50] To close his lecture, Gunton expands on this critique.

While acknowledging that Augustine has some biblical grounds for describing the Spirit as love or gift, Gunton asks why the Son could not be conceived similarly, since the New Testament presents him as the gift God gave for the sins of the world. Augustine concedes that all three persons of the Godhead could be referred to as love, but ultimately asserts that it is most fitting to give this attribution to the Spirit. Gunton simply concludes that there are no adequate grounds for limiting love to the Holy Spirit other than those imposed by the schema of the threefold mind. If God's work in the created order were taken into account, a different, more substantial picture of the Spirit would undoubtedly emerge.[51] However, as it stands, Augustine's pneumatology is lacking on at least three fronts. First, it neglects the New Testament's emphasis on the eschatological dimension of the Spirit's work in bringing future realities proleptically into the present. Second, his neglect of the communal dimensions of the triune life leads him to ignore the work of the Spirit in forming a community comprised of mutually consenting individuals. Finally, his notion of love is not informed by the incarnation, resulting in a view of love as unitive rather than outgoing and other-oriented. Thus, the Spirit as love merely unites Father and Son, but his unique and concrete personhood is overshadowed. Since the doctrine of the Spirit will be taken up in a later chapter, this brief outline of criticisms must suffice.

To sum up, all the above issues conspire to render a God who is markedly different from that revealed by the Son and Spirit. Instead of a God whose being derives from the Father and who is made known in the history of salvation – and is therefore personal – we are left with an unknown and impersonal substance underlying not only the Godhead but all of reality.⁵² From this poisoned fount flow many of the woes of Western thought and life.⁵³

Towards a Fully Trinitarian Theology

So much for the ground clearing. We turn now to consider the features of Gunton's mature doctrine of God. It might be that 'ground clearing' is not an entirely accurate description of Gunton's work thus far, since he did pick up key ingredients of his theology along the way, such as (1) the need to preserve divine freedom, particularly the freedom to love; (2) the importance of articulating a satisfying account of God's close relation to the world; (3) the guiding and guarding function of the economy of salvation for constructing a doctrine of God; and (4) attention to the Holy Spirit as essential to understanding the being of God. The solution to all these concerns and the ultimate key to a properly Christian doctrine of God is a robust doctrine of the Trinity. Trinitarian theology is a rough and tumble road fraught with pitfalls, especially in modern thought, but it is the way we must traverse if we are to give an adequate account of the God revealed in Scripture.

The demise of Trinitarian theology in the West during the modern period can be traced to at least two factors, according to Gunton. First, the Enlightenment attacks on the divinity of Jesus made the Trinity appear untenable. If Christ was not true God in human flesh, then the real God is something other than him. There is no plurality in the Godhead. Second, and related, there was an emphasis on the oneness of God, which made the assertion of three divine persons seem problematic. If God is truly one, then it merely complicates things to have to demonstrate that the doctrine of the Trinity is logical. Thus arose an approach to Trinitarian theology that was more epistemological than doxological, more about rational justifications and analogies than about worship and life.⁵⁴

The tide of the neglect of the Trinity turned significantly in the late twentieth century, and Gunton is among the purveyors of the

Trinitarian revival in modern theology. By way of summary, the key emphases of Gunton's Trinitarian theology (and *any* doctrine of the Trinity, according to Gunton) are as follows. First, the Son and the Holy Spirit are equally God along with the Father since it is through them – his 'two hands', to borrow from Irenaeus – that he reveals himself to the world. Gunton writes: 'If God is like this in his action and presence with us; if it is through Jesus and the Spirit that he makes himself known; if they truly are his hands, God in personal action; then that is what he is always like. God does not tell lies. What you see is what you get.'[55] The point here is straightforward: if God works through *his* two hands, then they must be intrinsic to the being of God; God *is* Father, Son and Spirit.[56] Second, the central concept for understanding the relationship of the one and the three in God is that of *person*: God is one being in three persons. A proper grasp of personhood then becomes vital for an accurate conception of God.[57] More need not be said here, since this point will be elaborated in the next section. Third, while God consists in three persons, the unity of God cannot be compromised. The oneness of God must be conceived along Trinitarian lines, allowing Father, Son and Spirit to comprise all there is of the being of God. Therefore, there is no prime substance revealed as Father, then as Son, and finally as Holy Spirit; nor are there three beings in a family of sorts. God is one in this particular threefold way.[58] At the same time, fourth, there cannot be excessive stress on the patristic dictum regarding the undivided works of the Trinity in the economy. If God is known through his acts in the economy, but his acts are undivided, there will be a tendency to not draw enough distinction between the persons.[59] More will be said about this towards the end of the chapter. Finally, the relations of the three persons, and thus the being of God, are best described as love. This drives all that is entailed in love – freedom, communion, otherness, mutuality – to the very heart of the being of God.[60] 'God is love' means God is a being in loving relation within himself.

These are the rough contours of a doctrine of the Trinity. Many of the shortcomings of contemporary Trinitarian theology derive from transgressing these parameters or stretching them beyond recognition.

A prevalent tendency is to draw economic and immanent Trinity so close together that the latter collapses into the former. God's triune being becomes identified with an aspect of the economy of creation and salvation, so that the concept and reality of an immanent Trinity is called into question. Gunton appeals to two representative figures that illustrate this approach. Jürgen Moltmann strictly identifies the Trinity with the suffering Son on the cross, turning the cross into a principle regarding a suffering God; Catherine Mowry LaCugna explicitly rejects the immanent Trinity, claiming we can only speak of the triune God in relation to the economy of salvation. On the one hand, these views rightly hold that God's action in the economy of creation and salvation reveal the being of God.[61] On the other hand, they fail to account adequately for divine freedom in their attempts to demonstrate God's love. Moltmann's God is a victim subject to external necessity and, therefore, is no longer God in any meaningful sense. LaCugna's God destroys creaturely freedom by undermining divine freedom. 'It is because God is a communion of love prior to and in independence of the creation,' Gunton asserts, 'that God can enable the creation to be itself.' The doctrine of the immanent Trinity, Gunton writes, 'serves as a foundation for the relative independence and so integrity of worldly reality also, and thus for human freedom'.[62] It is not difficult to detect the lurking spectre of pantheism. These are projectionist theologies, seeking to answer one contemporary socio-ethical matter or another, rather than rich reflection on the works of God and its meaning for the being of God. In these accounts the immanent Trinity, and much that derives from it, vanishes. One remedy for this type of anaemic Trinitarianism is to give ear to Eastern Orthodoxy, and particularly the so-called 'conceptual revolution' devised by the Cappadocians.[63] If God is an eternally free communion of persons, then, as we saw earlier, this provides the ontological basis for freedom, love and community – the very things modern theology has sought to uphold – since God is the one who loves in freedom apart from the creation. As mentioned earlier, at the heart of the doctrine of the immanent Trinity is the concept of persons, a concept critical to Gunton's Trinitarian theology.

On Persons and Particularity

Two related (and chief) concerns arising from Gunton's criticisms of Augustine are the need to (1) better define the concept of person and (2) more clearly delineate the specific actions (and thus characteristics) of each person of the Trinity. While these concerns were evident in the two aforementioned early lectures, they became prominent features of Gunton's mature doctrine of God.[64] We begin with his concept of the person.

According to Gunton there are broadly two ways to think of persons. First, there is the individualistic understanding, in which persons are individuals, 'beings with certain shared characteristics, whose chief defining character is their distinction from other such beings'. On an individualistic account, persons enter into relation only by volition.[65] Second, there is the relational conception, in which persons are somehow constituted by their relations with other persons. On this account, personhood and individuality are not identical. Rather than being threatened by others, persons are 'established in their particularity by their relations with one another'.[66] Gunton clearly favours the latter view. Persons are not primarily defined by attributes, inherent characteristics, or even agency, but by their relatedness in terms of love and freedom. 'According to the first,' Gunton writes, 'persons are what they are by virtue of their positive and mutually constitutive relatedness to one another. According to the second, such relatedness is personal only if it is in some way unnecessitated.'[67] This concept of personhood derives from a particular understanding of the triune being of God. Specifically, Gunton attributes the development of this relational view of persons to the fourth-century Cappadocians, who, as we saw earlier, carefully distinguished between *ousia* and *hypostasis*, being and persons. Their work of 'desynonymization' – as Gunton calls it, borrowing from Coleridge – allowed them to draw out the true distinctness of each person of the Trinity, affirming their oneness of being as well as uniqueness of personhood in terms of their relatedness.[68] In what Gunton will refer to as *perichoresis*, the Trinitarian persons are not individuals who then enter into relations, nor are they – contrary to Augustine – relations themselves, but rather they are constituted by their relations.[69] Personhood-in-relation (or being in communion) is thus ontologically basic since it is the very being of God.

While personhood is not synonymous with individuality, it does imply particularity – a correlate of perichoresis, at least as Gunton conceives it. He deploys the notion of 'personal space' as a way to describe how the three in the Godhead are not blurred into the one, writing: '[It is] the space in which three persons are for and from each other in their otherness. They thus confer particularity upon and receive it from one another. That giving of particularity is very important: it is a matter of space to be. Father, Son and Spirit through the shape – the *taxis* – of their inseparable relatedness confer particularity and freedom on each other.'[70] What is crucial for the concept of person is not simply relationality but also true otherness, the freedom to be a concrete other. This emphasis on otherness-in-relation is important if we want to avoid collectivism, that is, the engulfing of the many by the one. Gunton writes:

> The Son is not the Father, but receives his being from him; the Father cannot be the Father without the Son; and so on. Being in communion is being that belongs together, but not at the expense of the particular existence of the members. The Father, Son and Spirit are persons because they enable each other to be truly what the other is: they neither assert at the expense of, nor lose themselves in the being of, the others. Being in communion is being that realizes the reality of the particular person within a structure of being together.[71]

He is, however, not content with merely affirming particularity rooted in relations. Rather, he wants to identify more precisely what makes each person of the Godhead unique, or rather, what modes of action are peculiar to each person. If attention is paid to the economy of creation and salvation, it becomes evident that more can be said of the Son and Spirit than that they are one with the Father and related to him as begotten and spirated respectively.[72] Therefore, Gunton readily affirms Calvin's distinctions: 'To the Father is attributed the beginning of activity, and the fountain and well-spring of all things; to the Son, wisdom, counsel and the ordered disposition of all things; but to the Spirit is assigned the power and efficacy of that activity.'[73] More often Gunton borrows from Basil, who speaks of the Father as the 'original cause', the Son as the 'creative cause' and the Holy Spirit as the 'perfecting cause'.[74] It is the Father's distinct action to initiate; the Son mediates between the Father and creation, unifies all things and holds all things together; the Spirit particularizes each life and brings all things to their eschatological perfection. These economic actions of the persons speak to who they are *ad intra*. For example, the Spirit not only brings creatures to perfection, but can be said to be the agent of perfection within the Godhead, perfecting communion between the persons by enabling each person to fully be themselves and, thus, particularizing each person.[75] It is not enough to identify the Spirit as he who proceeds from the Father; we are, on scriptural grounds, authorized to say more about the distinct personhood of the Holy Spirit. Similar things can of course be said of the Father and Son. In the end, then, personhood and particularity are primal concepts – transcendentals even – basic to understanding the triune God (and all reality, for that matter) [76] According to Christoph Schwobel, it is the deployment of these concepts, coupled with an emphasis on the Holy Spirit, that makes Gunton's Trinitarianism unique.[77] If given due weight they move us well beyond a classical idea of God and ultimately transform our grasp of even the divine attributes, which are the focus of our final section.

'The Difference the Trinity Makes'

Gunton engages in one more act of ground clearing as he essays a reconfiguration of the doctrine of divine attributes in his final book, *Act and Being*. The fundamental question he seeks to answer is: how does the doctrine of the Trinity affect our understanding of the divine attributes?[78] Underlying that question is a claim regarding the tradition's inadequate treatment of the topic, namely, that it accepted a 'hybrid deity', derived partially from Scripture, partially from Greek philosophy. In fact, Gunton laments, 'It is one of the tragedies – one could almost say crimes – of Christian theological history that the Old Testament was effectively displaced by Greek philosophy as the theological basis of the doctrine of God, certainly so far as the doctrine of the divine attributes is concerned.'[79] A chief example of this tradition is Pseudo-Dionysius, whose concept of the divine names was governed largely by *a priori* notions of deity and, particularly, of the natural opposition of the divine to the creaturely. God, in this schema, is the unitary Uncaused Cause who created a world utterly distinct from himself. Creation, for example, consists in multiplicity, but God in unity. Materiality and spirituality (or intellect), time and eternity are opposed. The relationship between God and the world is construed negatively: God is what the world is not and vice versa. Thus, if we are to deploy creaturely language (for all language is creaturely) to predicate anything of God, it is to be done analogically and by way of negation. In Pseudo-Dionysius, for example, we find:

> The God who is transcends everything by virtue of his power. He is the substantive Cause and maker of being, subsistence, of existence, of substance, and of nature . . . He is the reality beneath time and the eternity behind being . . . He was not. He will not be. He did not come to be. He is not in the midst of becoming. He will not come to be. No. He is not. Rather, he is the essence of being for the things which have being.[80]

According to Gunton, it is not that most of these statements are untrue. Rather, a chief problem is 'a relentless concentration on what God is not, on the analogically reached doctrine that God is essentially what the world is not'.[81] At least three complaints emerge from this account and are tackled at length in Gunton's volume. First, God's particular actions in the economy of creation and salvation are effectively ignored so that positive knowledge of God is difficult to attain, or is at least distorted. Second, the divine attributes are conceived in terms of God's timeless causal relation to the world, so that time and eternity are opposed. The result is that those attributes implied by God's action in time are excluded. Finally, this account fails to acknowledge the positive relation God has to the world, even in their otherness. A Trinitarian account of God would observe that God's otherness from the world is only grasped through his relation to it.[82] With these issues in view, Gunton continues his questioning of the tradition, beginning chiefly with the problem of negative theology.

The *via negativa* is rooted in the assumption that God cannot be known in his essence. It holds that if we are to speak of God, we must do our best to eliminate the limitations inherent in our words and concepts. Gunton cites John of Damascus as a prime example of this way:

> God is without beginning, without end, eternal and everlasting, uncreate, unchangeable, invariable, simple, uncompound, incorporeal, invisible, impalpable, uncircumcised, infinite, incognisable, indefinable, incomprehensible, good, just, maker of all things created, almighty, all-ruling, all-surveying, of all overseer, sovereign, judge; and . . . God is One . . . and [rather as an afterthought, it must be said] has his being in three hypostases.[83]

What is noteworthy in the Damascene's account (as well as those who follow him) is that although we can say God is good or just, these do not speak properly of his essence; they are qualities we (doing our best) ascribe to a God whose nature is unknowable. Gunton opposes this orientation, simply asserting that the gospel makes clear that we can truly know who God is.[84] Aquinas follows closely in John's train, claiming that God is known primarily in terms of how he is unlike creatures. Moreover, in Thomas the emphasis on the metaphysical and impersonal attributes – simplicity, immutability, oneness – overwhelms and marginalizes the discussion of personal attributes like mercy, justice, and even love. Again, this treatment owes more to natural theology than the gospel, especially when one observes that Aquinas' treatment of divine love is carried out largely devoid of mention of the Trinity.[85] The chief weakness here, then, is that this apophatic tradition is determined not by God's revelation, but by an *a priori* negation of congruity between God and the world. Not only are Creator and creature distinct, but they are also opposed as Cause and caused, the spiritual One and the material many. A related weakness is its valuing of the intellectual over the material, which makes it difficult to see how God's action in Israel and Jesus might contribute to a doctrine of divine attributes.[86]

Gunton then tackles the issue of predication more directly, beginning with two 'rival' options. The first is that of analogy: predicating certain things of God, but qualifying them by negation or exaltation. However, this option, Gunton argues, is rooted in the assumption of a neoplatonic hierarchy of being – a foreign cosmology – rather than revelation. We determine what aspects of creaturely reality are fit to be applied to God and we qualify them as we deem appropriate. In the end, our picture of God is to a large degree a human projection. The second option is offered by Duns Scotus and his doctrine of univocity, that is, that words and concepts may be used in the same way for Creator and creature. Every attempt to describe God presupposes a univocal concept obtained from the creaturely realm. For example, Gunton writes, 'It would perhaps not be too crude to say that unless, let us say, the concept of good meant in some way the same in respect to God and to the creatures, there is no way of knowing how it is to be predicated of either.'[87] Similar things may be said about the concept of love or any of the other 'communicable' attributes. The theological basis for univocity is Trinitarian. Citing 1 John 4:11 ('since God so loved us, we also ought to love one another'), Gunton argues that divine love is the pattern for human love, and even becomes human love by the work of the Spirit. This is paradigmatically the case with Jesus Christ: by the power of the Spirit, he is God's love in action as human love. According to Gunton, all words are creaturely realities that the Spirit may enable to speak rightly about God and creation. Even fallen creatures can be redeemed in such a way that their language becomes an accurate articulation of God's being, but only by the work of Christ and the Spirit. Once it is no longer assumed that language, being creaturely and tied to the world, is unable to depict

God since it is fundamentally opposed to God, then we are able to speak more positively about the being of God; negation and excessive qualification are no longer the only way to speak of the divine being.[88]

Where this has all been leading is to the fundamental question of what difference the Trinity makes to a doctrine of the attributes. Gunton's contention is that if we first heeded God's Trinitarian action in the economy of creation and redemption, our account of the attributes would be quite different from the tradition. The key concept here is *mediation*: all the Father's actions in the world are carried out by the Son and the Spirit, and these actions reveal the being of God. Both the Son and Spirit work to redeem not just the spiritual world, but the material as well – the Son as the immanent one, the Spirit as the transcendent one.[89] The point is that the 'two hands' that reveal God do so in the creaturely realm and through creaturely mediums. Irenaeus, Gregory of Nazianzus and Duns Scotus are examples of those who refused to define the attributes *a priori*. Rather, they reconfigured attributes like divine unknowability or infinity in the light of God's action in the world. For example, Irenaeus writes: 'God cannot be known without God: but this is the express will of God, that God should be known.'[90] Indeed, God is unknowable, yet because of Christ we must qualify what we mean by God's unknowability. As Irenaeus continues: 'All saw the Father in the Son: for the Father is the invisible of the Son, but the Son is the visible of the Father.'[91] It is of great consequence that the Son, as a human being, made the unknowable Father known. For these three theologians – Irenaeus, Gregory and Scotus – as for Gunton, knowledge of the attributes is always *a posteriori* and mediated. Thus priority is given to the personal attributes and not the so-called metaphysical ones, not meaning we ignore the latter altogether, but we must qualify them by the former.

How might the Trinity, then, shape our understanding of these more abstract and metaphysical attributes? To begin, we must take seriously (1) that God's being is constituted by three persons in loving relation to one another and (2) that there is an outward orientation intrinsic to the Godhead, so that the perfected love within God is turned to that which is not God by the Spirit.[92] Therefore, something like divine aseity can be described as the fullness and integrity of God's intra-Trinitarian love, but must be qualified by God's movement outward in love and grace in Christ. God is from himself so that he can be for the other. Creation has its own freedom and integrity because God has his.[93] This might suggest that the so-called incommunicable attributes form the ontological basis for the communicable. To be sure, God is *a se*, but a function of his aseity is to give the world its own kind of (albeit dependent) free existence. In the end, then, Gunton contends that there really is no strict divide between incommunicable and communicable attributes, since they exist for and from the other. 'In the order of knowing,' he concludes, 'we move from the communicable to the incommunicable – rather than from some a priori considerations about what "God" means; while in the order of being, things move in the reverse direction, because God's action flows from what he truly is in eternity.'[94] We truly know God's attributes from his self-revelation in time, as his revelation is merely a disclosure of his immanent being-in-communion.

The final issue is a concern of Gunton's mentioned earlier in this chapter, namely, the distinguishing attributes of each person of the Trinity. At the heart of the matter is the question of whether we can speak of the Trinitarian persons as persons univocally. Much of the tradition has resorted to limiting the distinctions to relations of origin, but Gunton, among others, recognizes the need to move beyond that if we are going to speak of Father, Son and Spirit as persons in a meaningful way. How does one differentiate the persons in the light of the fundamental Trinitarian principle of *opera trinitatis ad extra indivisa sunt* (the external works of the Trinity are undivided)? Many attempt to appropriate specific works to the persons: the Father creates, the Son redeems and the Holy Spirit sanctifies. However, all these actions, biblically speaking, are attributable to all three persons – the Father initiating and the Son and Spirit mediating. What is needed, then, is an account of the kind of person the Father is in initiating, and the Son and Spirit are in mediating the Father's action. 'We need, that is to say, a distinction in terms of initiation and mediation rather than of actions in the economy, which are indeed the work of the whole Trinity, undivided certainly, but not homogeneous or monotonous.'[95] Taking our cue from 1 John 4, we may describe the Father as love – in creating, sustaining, redeeming and perfecting the world. These acts – God's love in action – are carried out by the Son, who brings the grace and mercy of God to his enemies, and the Spirit who perfects loving communion between God and humanity, and among humanity. If we are to define personhood by agency, or the kinds of actions performed (as Gunton does), then the Father is to be known in terms of loving action, the Son in terms of self-giving, and the Spirit in terms of the eschatological perfecting of communion. The particular hypostatic attributes are intrinsic to the form of action taken by each person in the economy of creation and salvation. What is critical are the particular ways the Father's actions are mediated. The Son mediates the Father's saving love as *incarnandus* and *incarnatus*, the one who will and does become incarnate, enters the world and liberates it from its bondage. The Spirit mediates the Father's salvation by giving life, sanctifying and perfecting through the Son.[96] These distinctive modes of mediation are not mere 'appropriations' but rather real, distinct attributes of each person.[97] Finally (and this brings us back to the issue of predication), if God's love takes the form of Jesus' human love, then the attribute of love can be used univocally with respect to God and humanity. Similarly, since Jesus Christ is the 'exact representation' of God's being as a human (Heb. 1:3), what it means to be a human person is at some level identical with what it means to be a divine person. Thus the term 'person' may be applied univocally to God and human beings.[98]

This reassessment of the attributes began with a critique of the negative theology inherited from Greek philosophy rather than Scripture, which resulted in what Gunton called the 'hybrid deity'. Gunton's main line of argument is that if we attend to God as he has revealed himself in the economy we can have a more kataphatic, positive knowledge of God's being and attributes. Knowledge of God is not attained *a priori*; it comes to us only as we behold the Father's work through his two hands, the Son and the Spirit.

Conclusion

Gunton's doctrine of God developed through extensive engagement with some major figures: Hartshorne, Barth, Augustine, Irenaeus, Basil, Gregory, and even Aquinas. While there were some that he rejected almost in their entirety, from others he gained the valuable insights and ingredients for his constructive doctrine of God. At the heart of his treatment were two questions: what does it mean that God is personal and what is the nature of God's engagement with the world? A thoroughly Christian response requires a tenacious and unflinching commitment to the truth that God is triune. This triunity is God's being and is the basis of all God's actions *ad extra*. Not too much controversial there. The potential problems arise from the centrality of the concepts of 'person' or 'relationality' in Gunton's account of the Godhead. It can be wondered if his concept of person is too much derived from human experience rather than God's self-revelation and then read back into the being of God. Persons, according to Gunton, must have a 'particular being' – indeed constituted in relation to others – but a distinct being nonetheless; they are 'centres of distinctive kinds of action to which reference can be made'.[99] But does this not somewhat tend towards tritheism?[100] One of Gunton's concerns is the problem of the one and the many: how can God be genuinely three yet one? This is a driving concern and, according to some, pushes him to overly individuate the divine persons. Whatever it means for God to be 'personal' must be derived from his revelation. Human personhood cannot be assumed to illuminate anything about God's personhood. In an important critique, Richard Fermer argues that Gunton too quickly equates *hypostasis* with modern conceptions of personhood. Fermer contends that if Gunton paid closer attention to how the Cappadocians actually explicated the term *hypostasis*, he would see that the three 'persons' are distinguished by their mode of origin, which is 'not usually the way we distinguish persons'. The point is that there is probably a greater difference between *hypostasis* and modern understandings of personhood.[101] Lewis Ayres charges that Gunton's conceptions of persons and relations 'owe far more to modern social preoccupations than to actual strands in the complex history of theological metaphors', and faults his lack of careful engagement with this history for his conceptual haziness.[102]

An example of Ayres' concern might be found in Gunton's use of the concept of *perichoresis* – an ancient term used to describe how God, unlike all creatures, could be three and yet one. The concept draws attention to how this mathematical difficulty was problematic only for creatures but not for God. It was meant to stress the oneness of *God*.[103] However, Bruce McCormack observes, Gunton wields the concept to stress the similarities between divine and human personhood, rather than the dissimilarities. This leads McCormack to conclude: 'The price he pays for this is a conceptual fuzziness in his doctrine of the Trinity . . . He so erodes the distinction between divine persons and human persons with his use of the concept of perichoresis that the recollection that humans are individuated by their bodily existence is not allowed to play the role it should.'[104] Karen Kilby, in an important essay, captures the logic of models like Gunton's. First, she observes, they begin with a picture of God that more resembles three humans with distinct centres of will and self-consciousness.[105] In order to resist tritheism they must find a way to show that these three are one God. They, therefore, appeal to something beyond our experience that binds the three together as one, namely, divine perichoresis. Next, perichoresis is explained by those things which bind human persons together – mutual giving, love, interrelatedness, and so on – and used to show what binds the three persons of the Godhead as one.[106] What unites the Godhead is like the best we know of these things, but at an unimaginably greater level, lest we posit three gods in a family and not three persons in God. Is it possible that Gunton comes close to the projectionism that he himself vehemently opposed?

The issue here has much to do with the nature of theological language. Can the terms 'person', 'relation' and 'perichoresis' be applied univocally to God and to creatures without obscuring the true nature of God?[107] Gunton answers this question in the affirmative. While Gunton does note that this univocity is bound up with the work of the Son and Spirit, he may have been aided by more tightly rooting it in Christology, as Barth did. Katherine Sonderegger makes this point. Comparing Barth and Gunton, she writes: 'All our terms are most properly his and through him and in him, they mediate what they have no merit or power or righteousness to bear, the truth and perfection of God.' So might we speak univocally of God, as Gunton desires? She responds (and this is worth quoting at length):

> We may so, yes: when we describe Christ in his personal work, we speak directly, univocally of this God with us, the Victorious Redeemer; but no, we cannot 'say' Jesus Christ directly . . . for we cannot ourselves enter into the mystery, the hiddenness which is the incarnate union of God and humanity. So our creaturely terms, righteousness and justice, do indeed mean what we mean when we speak them, but that is so only because God has come among us to simply be our righteousness and to work for us divine mercy.[108]

Only in Jesus, and only as God graciously commandeers human language, do we speak directly about God.

Finally, another form of 'projecting' – one deriving from sound principles – occurs when Gunton (rightly) moves from the economy of God's works to God's inner being. For example, when speaking of the Spirit's operation, he follows Basil in attributing to the Spirit the perfecting of the created order. However, Gunton makes the move of taking this economic work all the way up into the life of God, so that the Spirit not only perfects creation but also somehow perfects the being of God. A question to be raised to this notion is simple: does the divine communion of persons really need to be perfected? Is it not already perfect by virtue of what it is: the communion that is the God who loves in freedom? We seem to be trying to penetrate into the mystery of how God could be thus, rather than accepting that he is thus as something grasped by faith.[109] Along similar lines, Fermer is concerned that to claim that God's being *is* the communion of persons is to claim to know too much about the divine being, such that 'the mystery of God's being is impaired'.[110] While Gunton is adamant about not collapsing together the immanent and economic Trinity, it may be wondered whether the attempt to explicate the particularities of the persons and their true eternal personhood sometimes works against that desire.

Conceptual questions aside, Gunton's doctrine of the Trinity was driven by the conviction that we know God only as a gift, as he reveals himself to us. Although not always successful in practice, he believed that if the Trinity, as revealed by God's works, does not drive our doctrine of God, something else will and with negative ramifications beyond theology proper. It is to that 'beyond' that the next chapter ventures with an exploration of Gunton's doctrine of creation. As we have seen, he was not merely concerned to understand God in isolation, but also to grasp the way God intersects with the world he created. If, as Gunton said, 'everything looks different in the light of the Trinity',[111] then there will no doubt be some required remediation of our view of the created order generally and humanity in particular.

3

'It Is Very Good': Creation, Providence and Human Personhood

The doctrine of God is always accompanied by the doctrine of creation in Gunton's theology. Our construal of God, on the one hand, has everything to do with how we understand his relation to that which is not himself. On the other hand, our grasp of creation is fully dependent on what we make of its Creator. Many of the themes that would become central to Gunton's doctrine of creation took nascent form in his dissertation, such as the need for true otherness in creation, freedom as essential to being a creature, and the distinction, but relatedness, of God and creation. These themes are developed further on in his career and become characteristic features of his theological project. Gunton often lamented the current state of the doctrine of creation, feeling it had been reduced to unproductive debates between science and religion, evolution and the Bible.[1] His project is one of rehabilitation and this through a dogmatic engagement that finds its roots in the doctrine of the Trinity.

Platonizing Creation: A Historical Sketch

As is the case with much of his work, Gunton's views on creation are forged through a critical conversation with the tradition. This is best exemplified in his most developed treatment of the doctrine found in his monograph, *The Triune Creator*. In this first section, I will begin to outline his account of creation through an exposition of some of the key historical arguments in this important volume.

Greek cosmologies

The early Christian doctrine of creation, according to Gunton, arose out of the faith's complex interaction with Greek cosmology. One strand of early Greek cosmology, as reflected in Heraclitus, saw the world as a cosmic flux, as a perpetual conflict between opposing principles. In this vision, the 'creation' is exemplified by change, not stability – many different elements constantly in violent conflict – so that the fundamental reality is the 'many', not the 'one'. The opposite early vision comes from Parmenides, who sees reality as fundamentally unchanging. What he posits is a metaphysical dualism: what is immutable is eternally real, while ordinary, material things, being changeable, are not 'real'. Along these lines, there is a dualism of reason and sense: the world of sense – consisting of change and movement – is unreliable; only reason gives us access to what is ultimately and eternally real. Reality, then, is one, unmoving, unchanging and eternal.[2] Parmenides thus diminishes the value of the material world, and this certainly puts him at odds with the Christian doctrine of creation, as we will see later.

This basic configuration is adopted by Plato, who argues that matter, being subject to change and characterized by particularity, cannot be understood rationally. True reality, for Plato, is in the realm of forms. All earthly realities are simply representations – more or less accurate – of the forms. Reality is hierarchical: at the apex are the eternal and immaterial forms, and lower down are their material representations.[3] It might be said that material objects are only half real, existing between being and non-being. Material reality is not the whole of reality, but merely the shadow; the forms are true reality.[4] Moreover, Plato moves beyond Parmenides by providing a cosmogony, as well as a cosmology. There is, first, the creation of a single spherical universe, comprised of fire, water, air and earth, which moves in perfect circular motion. This timeless realm supplies the pattern for our world, the world of time, which is created subsequently. In addition, there are three eternal realities in Plato: the forms, the receptacle (or unformed, chaotic matter), and the demiurge who fashions the eternal, shapeless matter into a copy of the form.[5] While there is here some overlap with the biblical doctrine of creation, the relative non-being of creation, the eternality of matter, and the shaping rather than creating of the world puts the views at odds. Aristotle, while rejecting the doctrine of the forms, retains and develops aspects of Plato's view regarding the eternality and divinity of the universe.[6]

Arguably the most important philosopher for the development of the early Christian doctrine of creation is Plotinus, the third-century disciple of Plato. Plotinus adopts and modifies his predecessor's hierarchy of being. At the top of the hierarchy is the One, who is the absolutely transcendent and changeless source of all being. At the bottom is formless matter, which can be described as 'nothingness' since it has the least being in the hierarchy. Matter is but a shadow of real being and thus is 'evil', and not good by definition. Between the One and matter are a series of mediating realities: first is the Mind (corresponding roughly to Plato's demiurge) and then the Soul (which mediates between immaterial and material reality). The One 'creates' by emanation: the creation flows from the One like a stream from its self-sufficient source. That which is furthest down the chain of emanation is least real, like light dimming the further away it is from its source. Gunton argues that even if the material world is less real, it is (in some way) indistinguishable from the One. 'A stream and its source,' Gunton concludes, 'are ontologically continuous, whereas the heartbeat of the doctrine of creation is that God and the world are ontologically distinct.'[7] So, to a certain degree, the material order is both insignificant and maximally significant: insignificant because it resides at the lowest level of being; significant because its being is somewhat continuous with the One. It is primarily to something resembling this perspective that early Christian theologians would respond – whether by accommodation or rejection.

Patristic appropriations

Within a Platonic milieu, Irenaeus offers, according to Gunton, an exemplary response to Greek cosmology. Responding specifically to Gnosticism, an extreme form of Platonic dualism, he argues that everything created by God – including matter – is good. Material reality is confirmed in its goodness by virtue of the Son taking to himself human flesh. If God himself deigned to adorn himself in materiality, then matter cannot be treated as unreal, half real or intrinsically evil. Another feature of Irenaeus' doctrine of creation is his emphasis on creation out of nothing. Contrary to a Platonic view, God did not create from pre-existing matter. God's freedom and omnipotence dictate that there be no material co-eternal with or prior to God constraining him to create in this or that way. Corresponding to these insights is Irenaeus' emphasis on the Trinitarian shape of the doctrine of creation. God creates by his 'two hands', the Son and the Spirit. In this way, God creates and relates to his creation in a mediated fashion, not through created mediators, but by means of his own 'hands'. It is God himself freely and lovingly interacting with the created order. Arising from these insights is a different ontology altogether. Instead of degrees of being, we have only two orders of being: God and creation. The latter is real and good, even though it is ontologically distinct from its Creator. Finally, Irenaeus meaningfully relates creation to eschatology. That which God created out of nothing is destined for perfection, and this through the redemption wrought by Christ and the renewal by the Spirit.[8]

Most of those who followed Irenaeus failed to negotiate well between biblical revelation and Greek philosophy.[9] One stark example is Origen of Alexandria, who, like many Platonists, argued for a two-stage creation. The first stage consists of the eternal creation of a world of spirits, or *logika*. This world is intermediate between God and the world we inhabit. The *logika* are essentially good, but misused their freedom and were torn from unity with the divine, descending into plurality. The second stage involved the creation of the material world, which would function as the place where these spirits will be reformed and returned to unity with God. This cosmology is funded by a spiritualized reading of Genesis 1 – 3, where the creation and fall of humanity is viewed by Origen as taking place in a pre-historical realm.[10] The chief negative results of this view are that it denigrates the material creation by (1) positing an intermediate created world, (2) conceiving of the material world as negative, and (3) seeing this world as merely instrumental, that is, as the fragmented place that spirits pass through on their way back to unity with the divine.[11] Origen's doctrine of creation is an unsuccessful wedding of biblical teaching and Greek cosmology.

As unsatisfactory as Origen's treatment is, it pales in comparison in terms of the problems and influence of Gunton's chief interlocutor, Augustine of Hippo. According to Gunton, the neoplatonic influence on Augustine's thought is pronounced. What is commendable is that he argues christologically for creation *ex nihilo*, against the emanationist view. If creation flows from God's own substance – it is *homoousios* with the Father – then it is equal with the eternal Son, whom we confess as of one substance with the Father. Since the Son is *homoousios* with the Father, creation cannot be. The problem here, however, is that Augustine fails to make any appeals to the economy of salvation, the incarnate Son's life and work therein, and how the Son's materiality affects the status of the material world.[12] The problems are manifold in Augustine, especially as he wrestles with how to interpret Genesis 1 – 3. For example, he interprets the command to 'be fruitful and multiply' spiritually because it is inconceivable that it could only be referring to physical, sexual reproduction. Rather, it is a sinful tendency that makes one read the text as ultimately referring to anything other than spiritual fecundity. Augustine has a difficult time affirming the bodily aspect of our existence.[13] Furthermore, the account of God's creation in six days presents a problem for him because it depicts God's actions as taking place in time. However, since God is timelessly eternal, all that he does is instantaneous; there can be no taking of time. Therefore, the language of six days is God's way of accommodating to our weakness, and must be interpreted allegorically – referring to six as the number of perfection, the ages of the world, or the stages of spiritual life.[14] Augustine also posits a two-stage creation. The first stage, taking place in Genesis 1:1–2, consists of the creation of a heavenly world that somehow partakes in God's eternity. It is the realm of the intellectual creature and of the ideas that form the basis of the next stage. In the second creation, God creates formless matter out of nothing and then shapes it into forms corresponding in some way to the first stage of creation. There is a resemblance to Plotinus' hierarchical cosmology: first, God, then the heavenly realm, which is closer to God, and finally the world of matter, which is furthest away from God. Augustine even says the material world is 'close to being nothing'.[15] Gunton acknowledges that there are features of Augustine's doctrine of creation that are commendable, such as the latter's emphasis on God's freedom from time. God is timeless and does not create the world *in* time, but rather *with* time. This emphasis, however, is also the besetting weakness of Augustine's treatment. Since God is timeless by definition, it proves difficult for him to imagine the shape or possibility of God's involvement in time. Moreover, when taking time is conceived by Augustine as a sign of fallenness, it becomes doubly difficult to tie the eternal God to the created order of time and succession.[16] In the end, Augustine fails because he pays inadequate attention to the economy of God's work in time, especially the history of the incarnate Son, as we find in Irenaeus. The life of Jesus Christ is an act of the eternal, timeless God 'stretched out in time'. Gunton concludes:

> In the light of this, we can interpret Genesis 1 as relating a series of creative acts which set the stage, so to speak, for God's continuing interaction with his world. That is also why we may, without being naïve creationists, take with complete seriousness the narrative form of Genesis 1 and 2. God's action both in the creation of time and towards and in that time once created, is action that 'takes time,' just as his inaugurated completion of that creation in Christ's recapitulation of it also takes time.[17]

Although creation is the act of the eternal God, 'before' time even, it also takes shape in time. That this is the case is an affirmation of the goodness of time, specifically, and the created order, generally.

Whatever problems existed in the early Christian doctrine of creation are, for Gunton, the result of its accommodation to Greek thought. Two-stage views of creation, the elevation of the intellectual realm and consequent diminishing of the material, the relative non-being of matter, and the sometimes lack of distinction between or effective separation of Creator and creature are among the errors imbibed by Christian thinkers like Origen and Augustine. The insights of Irenaeus, though obscured largely in these later theologians, are the way forward, particularly because they derive from his attention to God's particular activity in the economy of creation and redemption carried out by the Son and the Spirit.

Medieval emphases

While much of Augustine's perspectives were carried into the Middle Ages, this period also saw some important shifts and emphases that must be highlighted briefly before speaking of the Reformation's contribution to the doctrine of creation. According to Gunton, the chief problem in the medieval period is its 'reliance on the concept of cause *along with* the almost total absence from their conceptions of the mediation of creation of any trinitarian reference', something we saw in Irenaeus.[18] When Gunton refers to 'cause', especially in the negative sense, he is speaking of cause as logical entailment devoid of personal, divine agency.[19] In Aquinas' Five Ways, for example, causality is conceived in terms of a hierarchy of being: one thing is caused by something higher in the order of being. The neoplatonic influence is obvious. Although this causation is an act of the personal willing of God, it is a willing conceived monistically rather than Trinitarianly. The Trinity, and specifically the mediating roles of the Son and Spirit, plays little role in his doctrine of creation and his understanding of divine action. Moreover, by denying that in creating God acts to accomplish a purpose – except to communicate his own completeness – and by viewing creation merely as a relation, he deprives the creation of its true otherness by tying it too closely to God. Finally, Aquinas speaks of eternal ideas in the mind of God, which are the pattern for the actualized material creation. What this suggests is that creation is eternal and necessary, and that the material world is relatively insignificant, a weakness we saw in Origen and Augustine.[20]

Duns Scotus moves in a slightly different direction from Thomas. First, he de-emphasizes causality and its attendant hierarchical conception of being, and lays the stress on divine willing. What results is a view of God as the creator of all things, including forms, so that the forms are not an eternal reality in the divine mind, but rather part of the ordinary created order. Thus the material world has its significance in itself, not in being the outworking of an eternal idea; its particularity has true value. Related to this is Scotus' doctrine of univocity and its connection to the concept of 'being'. The term 'being' (or existence) means the same thing when attributed to one created thing as when it is attributed to another. Therefore, there is no hierarchy of being. To ascribe being to all created things is to assert their ontological equality or homogeneity (to use the term adopted from Basil earlier). Finally, he appeals to the authority of Christ in creation, which at least allows his account of creation to be somewhat shaped by the incarnate, and not only the eternal, Son.[21] For Gunton, Scotus is something of a bright spot in the bleak medieval period.

William of Ockham extends to a further extreme Scotus' emphasis on divine willing in his effort to affirm the doctrine of creation *ex nihilo*. What results, according to Gunton, is a picture of arbitrariness and immediacy in God's work of creation: God simply wills the world to be for no reason or purpose and he does this without mediation. The world that is made is merely a function of the divine will, which entails that the world has no real freedom to be itself. On the other hand, Ockham's denial of universals and concomitant stress on particulars enabled him to sever the logically causal ties between God and the world. No thing participates in the nature of another thing, so that connections between them are largely functions of our minds. For example, one thing may cause another thing, but that causal relationship is neither objective nor necessary. Rather, it is simply a regularly observed fact or state of affairs. The concept of cause is replaced by that of the will with respect to God's relationship to the world. The world is fully contingent; it does not have to be, but exists by the free willing of God. There is no logical connection between God and creation. As a consequence, creation has its own being, its distinct reality, unlike some of the previous views on offer. The chief problem in this view, according to Gunton, is that creation is the result of sheer will; love plays no determinative role in God's act. A different conception would no doubt emerge if attention were paid to God's actual economic acts through the Son and Holy Spirit.[22]

Reformation retrievals

Luther and Calvin spark what Gunton calls a 'return to the Trinity' in the Reformation age. The German Reformer, for example, read the first chapter of Genesis Trinitarianly, affirming a creation out of nothing alongside a respect for a form of mediation in which the Son 'adorns and separates the crude mass' and the Spirit vivifies. Since creation is mediated in this way, it is evident that the material world is not devoid of value, as in neoplatonism. Luther rejects the allegorizing of Genesis 1, holding that the text speaks of real creatures and the material world that is experienced by our senses. God's relation to this world is personal; he shapes and cares for it with his own two hands, so to speak, and orders it for the benefit of humanity. The notion of love, rather than sheer will, is made central to the theology of creation, something largely absent in Luther's predecessors.[23] Calvin shows similar strengths, while augmenting them with a highly personal account of God's providential care of every aspect of creation. He and Luther are successful in conceiving of creation less in terms of causality and more in terms of personal action. Gunton remarks: 'The result is that the doctrine of creation is taken out of the largely philosophical context in which it had tended to be located, where it had become a semi-independent propaedeutic for faith, and returned to the confessed creed.'[24] Undoubtedly this shift is connected with the radically biblical orientation adopted by the Reformers. Scripture depicts God as personally – indeed Trinitarianly – engaged with the world he created. Moreover, they (especially Calvin) continued

Ockham's programme of conceiving of creation as a free act of the divine will. In that light, they were responsible for reasserting the contingency (i.e. relative autonomy) of the world, the ontological distinction between Creator and creature, and the corresponding ontological homogeneity of the created order.[25] These two Reformers represent a renaissance in the doctrine of creation. Taken together with the best achievements of the patristic and medieval eras, we have the raw materials for an outline of the basic shape of a doctrine of creation conceived Trinitarianly.

Triune Creation: Its Basic Shape

The doctrine of creation was (and is to be) distinguished within its cultural context(s) by at least three features: (1) its form as creedal response to divine revelation; (2) the notion of creation *ex nihilo*; and (3) its Trinitarian shape.[26] These features – and particularly the last – give rise to a distinctively Christian view of creation, which may be outlined as follows. First, creation out of nothing is an affirmation that God did not need anything outside of himself to create, so that creation is a free, sovereign, personal act of God. As such, creation does not have being of itself, but is contingent, limited and dependent in its being. 'It has a beginning in time and a limit in space. "Once" there was nothing; then there was a universe, because and only because God willed it.'[27] Creation *ex nihilo* also implies that the world did not come from the being of God, but is created distinct from God by an act of his will.[28] Thus, the only ontological distinction that matters, as we saw in our previous discussion, is that between Creator and creation. There are no intermediate forms of being, no semi-divine realities.[29] Everything that is not God is a creature – equally.

Second, the creation that proceeds from God's sovereign will is the result of God's loving, purposeful intention; it is not arbitrary. The love out of which creation is birthed is that loving communion of three persons that eternally is the being of God. An implication of this is that God does not need the world in order to love; yet, he creates a world and confers on it its own value and dignity – its own being and existence. This is what Gunton refers to as the *contingency* (not contingence) of the created order: the world's freedom to be itself and its 'value as a realm of being in its own right', as conferred by God.[30]

Third, God maintains close relations with the created order, not by being bound to it (as in process thought), but through his free and mediated action within it. Here lies the centre of Gunton's doctrine of creation: the concept of *mediation*. God indeed creates by fiat, by a word, but Scripture also depicts his work through varied modes of mediation. For example, God is portrayed as a craftsman, forming things out of already existing material (e.g. Gen. 2). He also creates through already created beings, empowering parts of the world to be mediators of the creation of other parts. 'Worldly agencies,' Gunton writes, 'are enabled by divine action to achieve their own "subcreating", not in the absolute way that God creates, but relatively, as creation from what already is.'[31] Chief among mediators of creation, as we have already encountered, are the Son and the Spirit. The Son, the Word through whom all things were created, became incarnate and thus a part of the creation. The incarnation speaks to God's freedom to act within the material world. God acts freely in creating by his Word, but also freely identifies with the world through that same Word. The Spirit's work is characterized by its freedom and transcendence over against the world, while maintaining close relation to it. The Spirit never identifies with the world (like the Son), but acts from 'outside', transforming the created order.[32] This theology of mediation, in all its aspects, affirms that the creation is good because not only does God give it space to be itself, but he also continues in close, intimate relation to it.

Fourth, creation has a goal, an eschatological orientation. 'Creation was not simply the making of the world out of nothing,' Gunton writes, 'not even that world continually upheld by the providence of God, but the making of the world destined for perfection, completedness.'[33] The emphasis on completion directs us predictably to the work of the Spirit: as the 'perfecting cause' of creation, he establishes the particularity of each element of creation and directs everything to its appointed end. God is present with the world through the Spirit, moving creation to a real destiny. Creation is what Gunton calls a 'project': something 'God creates not as a timelessly perfect whole, but as an order of things that is planned to go somewhere, to be completed or perfected, and so *projected* into time'.[34] The world was created 'very good', perfect even, but this perfection is a 'relative' perfection. It is only in the light of creation's completion that its perfection may be comprehended properly.[35] What is the *telos* of creation? Gunton describes it thus: 'To make something that is valuable in itself, and to make something that is valuable in itself because it is created to serve God's glory.'[36] God created the world in order that it would be offered back to him perfected through the proper dominion exercised by humanity.[37]

These points summarize the fundamental features of a Trinity-shaped account of creation. Before leaving his broad treatment of creation, we will attempt to trace a further effect of Trinitarian theology on the doctrine of creation as Gunton essays an ontology of the created order.

The Being of the World

Another critical entry point for understanding Gunton's ontology of creation is his presentation of what he calls 'open transcendentals', as found in his seminal *The One, the Three and the Many*. In considering the nature of transcendentals, Gunton asks: 'Can we find a place for both the unity and plurality of being; for both the unity and plurality of the human cultural enterprises that would be true to the world of our experience?'[38] At issue here is the classical philosophical quest for the unity of all things. Transcendentals – truth, goodness and beauty, traditionally – are ways to grasp the unity in diversity, or the coherence of the one and the many, within the created order. Gunton describes an 'open' transcendental as:

> a notion, in some way basic to the human thinking process, which empowers a continuing and in principle unfinished exploration of the

universal marks of being. The quest is indeed a universal one, to find concepts which do succeed in some way or other in representing or echoing the universal marks of being. But it is also to find concepts whose value will be found not primarily in their clarity and certainty, but in their suggestiveness and potentiality for being deepened and enriched, during the continuing process of thought, from a wide range of sources in human life and culture.[39]

These suggestive and open-ended notions ultimately arise from the doctrine of the Trinity. Borrowing this line of thinking from Coleridge, Gunton's basic contention is that if the triune God is the source of all being, then all things will reflect, in some way, the being of their Maker.[40] The open transcendentals are thus Trinitarian in shape. Rather than an *analogia entis*, we have what one theologian calls Gunton's *analogia trinitatis*.[41] One basic result of the doctrine of the Trinity is that it prevents our minds from resting on either the one or the many with respect to God *and* creation; it writes a unified plurality into the very fabric of the world. What emerges from the doctrine of the Trinity, or specifically God's triune action in the world, are three transcendentals: perichoresis, substantiality and relationality.[42]

First, *perichoresis* refers to the unity and plurality of the being and act of God. Specifically, what it implies is that God only exists as the relation of three persons in 'reciprocal eternal relatedness' and that the three persons mutually constitute each other in that eternal relationship. Gunton adds: 'Perichoresis implies an ordered but free interrelational self-formation: God is not simply shapeless, a negatively conceived monad, but eternal interpersonal life. There is thus a richness and space in the divine life, in itself and as turning outwards in the creation of the dynamic universe that is relational order in space and time.'[43] It is that last clause that is critical for our purposes. Gunton proposes that the concept of perichoresis does not only illuminate our understanding of God, but also enables us to see the world as fundamentally perichoretic, that is, displaying a dynamism of relatedness. Everything in the world contributes to and constitutes the being of everything else.[44] This is true of the personal world as well as the impersonal world and our interaction with it. A relational doctrine of the *imago Dei* confirms that humans do not merely exist with others, but rather are bound up with each other, mutually constituting one another. The impersonal realm also displays the marks of perichoresis. Modern physics, for example, has demonstrated that the nature of things is derived from their relations to other things, and vice versa. All things affect everything else – whether directly or indirectly – and make each thing what it is.[45] However, this is never done to the detriment of the particularity of each person or thing.

This concern to preserve particularity brings us back to the ministry of the Spirit and eventually to the second transcendental, *substantiality*. It is the work of the Spirit to bring everything to its eschatological perfection; it is his unique function to 'realize the true being of each created thing by bringing it, through Christ, into saving relation with God the Father'.[46] Put another way, the Spirit grants to and sustains in each being its particularity. If this is the Spirit's business in the economy of creation and redemption, can something comparable be said to take place in the inner life of the Trinity? Gunton contends that not only does the Spirit bring unity between the Father and Son, but he also grants to each their particularity; he liberates them to be the particular persons they are in communion with one another. He concludes: 'The Spirit's distinctive mode of action in both time and eternity, economy and essence, consists in the constituting and realization of particularity. There is, then . . . a form of particularity at the very heart of the being of God.'[47] In making such an assertion, Gunton calls into question traditional Western notions of divine substance. As we saw in the previous chapter, rather than seeing substance as something underlying the particular persons, he argues that God's *ousia* is constituted entirely by the perichoretic and particularizing relations between the three persons. Substantiality, then, refers to concrete particularity, a particularity at the centre of God's life, which is reflected in creaturely life.[48] As each person in the Trinity derives their particular character by their mutual relation, so people and things are constituted as substantial particulars through the pattern of their relations with all reality. Thus, the created order is to be characterized as a web of mutually indwelling relationships that establish, rather than subsume, the particularity of each being.

The final transcendental, *relationality*, flows naturally from the other two. That beings indwell one another and constitute the particularity of each points to the ultimate fact that all things have their being in relation – to God, primarily, and to all other creatures. All this finds its source in the being of God, who is a 'dynamic order of giving and receiving'.[49] This giving and receiving is asymmetrical, both in God and in his action in the world, and thus sets the basis for the kind of variety present in creaturely relations. 'All things are what they are by being particulars constituted by many and various forms of relations,' Gunton concludes. 'Relationality is thus the transcendental which allows us to learn something of what it is to say that all created people and things are marked by their coming from and returning to the God who is himself, in his essential and inmost being, a being in relation.'[50] Thus, the three mutually informing transcendentals – perichoresis, substantiality and relationality – provide another entry point for a theological understanding of creation.[51]

On Providence

We have already highlighted that the world came to be with a *telos*, an eschatological orientation, and this is immediately to evoke notions of providence. If creation is about establishing the world, providence is concerned with its upholding and purposeful movement towards completion. While Gunton indeed views providence as preservation, he views preservation as too reductive a description, particularly because it has too little view to the future. Teleology, or better eschatology, is a main operative principle for Gunton, and enables him to make sense of God's providential design both before and after the fall of humanity. Concerning creation pre-fall, Adam, for example, is provided with a companion with whom he would fulfil God's intention of subduing and cultivating the uninhabitable world, to the praise of the Creator.[52] Providence has to do with making provision for the fulfilment of God's ends for the created order.[53] Now, the world with which we are primarily concerned in an account of providence is a fallen one, which of necessity brings the idea of redemption into our purview. Gunton writes: 'We must take account of the fact that providence can be understood in our world only in respect of the fact that its present shape is now distorted, so that within God's providing are embraced acts devoted at once to *maintaining* the direction of the universe to its perfecting; and to *redirecting* its movement away from dissolution to its proper destiny.'[54] Not surprisingly, then, his treatment of providence centres on an account of the triune mediation of redemption through God's 'two hands'.

In the course of setting out the relationship between 'general' and 'special' providence – that is, God's upholding and directing of creation generally and his saving acts, respectively – he describes the centrality of Christology for an understanding of providence:

> The incarnation of the Son of God in Jesus of Nazareth provides a way of showing that the distinction of forms of providence is yet embraced within a unity of activity. God's historical action in Christ is, as we have seen, the means by which the order of creation is redirected to its original end. 'General' providence is maintained by a new and unique – special – form of divine interaction with the world, effecting the eschatological destiny of things as a whole by means of particular outcomes involved with and anticipating it . . . Eschatologically conceived, those activities that are sometimes called 'general' as distinct from 'special' or 'particular' providence are both aspects of the same divine activity bringing the world to its intended destiny.[55]

The present and future shape of the world is bound up with the present shame and future glory of humanity. Therefore, the work of Christ – atonement and resurrection – which is directed primarily at humanity, is at once an act of special and general providence; it brings the redemption of human beings, but is also the key to the renewal of creation. It is by the ministry of Jesus that we fully understand that creation is in 'crisis' and that its liberation to perfection has been inaugurated, indeed guaranteed.[56] In addition, the life and ministry of Jesus sets the parameters for our understanding of freedom, that perennial issue in discussions of providence. While the Reformers aided in the recovery of a Trinitarian model of mediation in creation, they failed to allow those insights to spill over into the doctrine of providence. The result was a deterministic tendency, a compromising of the freedom of the creature (which we will address more fully later). However, Gunton argues, 'if Jesus Christ is a model of God's determination of the creature, then clearly it is a determination that realises rather than stunts freedom'.[57] The concern is less about what God *knows* in advance, but rather how God *acts* in time. In this case, divine providential action takes place in and through the free action of the man Jesus Christ, who is the pattern for all humanity.

This insight leads naturally to an account of the Spirit's role in the mediation of providence, which might be said to consist of at least two aspects. First, the Spirit forms, liberates and enables Jesus to be who he is and to carry out his work. He further mediates the Father's action by raising Christ from the dead, transforming his body into the firstfruits of the age to come. The focus on the Spirit's action rather than the Father's foreknowledge makes providence less about determining outcomes and more about enabling perfection.[58] This operation of the Spirit towards the human Christ is paradigmatic of all works of providence. Therefore, second, the Spirit enables all things to be themselves and become what they are destined to be by relating them to the Father through the incarnate Lord. This is what was referred to earlier as the particularizing and perfecting function of the Spirit. The Spirit enables eschatological perfection by liberating people and creation generally to fully realize what they were created to be.[59] In summary, providence, as seen through the lens of the mediating action of Son and Spirit, may be defined as the activity wherein God 'upholds the creation against its utter dissolution and provides for its redemption by the election of Israel and the incarnation of the one through whom all things were made and are upheld, and to whom, as the head of the church (Colossians 1:18), in the Spirit all things move'.[60] Providence is particular, liberating and redemptive provision of that which enables the completion of every particular aspect of God's creation.

On Human Being

The final section of this chapter will take up Gunton's doctrine of humanity, focusing on the four interrelated issues of human personhood, the image of God, freedom and sin.

Human personhood

Contrary to the Feuerbachian dogma that our view of God derives from our view of humanity – a theology from below – Gunton unsurprisingly argues that our view of human personhood derives from what we understand God's personhood to be.[61] Recall from our earlier discussions that the persons comprising the Godhead are who they are only by virtue of their mutual relations. These relations constitute the particularity and otherness of each person rather than undermine them. In this way, individualism and collectivism – the dominance of the 'one' and the dominance of the 'many' – are avoided, not only in God, but also among human persons.[62] Human personhood mirrors divine personhood – excepting the presence of limits absent in God – and is also to be conceived in terms of relationships: first, with God; second, with other humans; third, with the rest of the created order.[63] These relationships are not merely auxiliary; they are, rather, constitutive of personhood. This truth was also spelled out earlier in terms of the 'open transcendentals' of perichoresis, substantiality and relationality: we, and all things, are what we are only in relation to others. Moreover, persons are best characterized, recall, in terms of the capacity to love in freedom, rather than by reason, consciousness or agency. It remains to be said, finally, that human personhood is an eschatological concept. We are persons-in-becoming, called to grow into maturity until the full realization of our personhood. Gunton writes: 'The human being is one who is both created a person and placed on earth to become a person through giving and receiving love, in different ways to and variously from family, friends, acquaintances, enemies.' We are created 'very good' as persons in the image of the tri-personal God, upheld in our personhood and directed towards its perfection in Christ by the Spirit.[64]

The image of God

When personhood is spoken of in this way, we are not a far leap from our second important anthropological concept: the image of God. Gunton, in fact, treats them somewhat interchangeably: 'To be made in the image of God is to be endowed with a particular kind of personal reality. To be a person is to be made in the image of God.'[65] Historically speaking, attempts to pin down the *imago Dei* have been hamstrung by the conflating of two critical questions: (1) what is a human being (the 'ontological' question) and (2) how is a human different from God and other creatures (the 'comparative' question)? What has often resulted is the view that we are fundamentally minds – and this makes us most like God and least like other creatures. The problem with this approach is that it has the wrong starting point. Rather than moving from ontology to contrast, it develops an ontology on the basis of the contrast. In this scheme – as exemplified by Augustine and much Western theology – human beings are often viewed as individual minds separated relationally from others.[66] In fact, Gunton would write: '[O]ur particular embodiment – the sense that in certain respects, however much that has to be qualified, we are our bodies – is inseparable from our being in the image of God.'[67] Far from being located solely in some immaterial aspect of humanity, the image of God is bound up with our physicality.

Gunton is more cautiously optimistic concerning the other two main options for the image of God: the functional and the relational views. Regarding the first (i.e. the exercise of dominion or stewardship), Gunton asserts that it is too narrow, not taking into account the reshaping of the doctrine by the New Testament's description of Jesus as the *imago Dei*. Surely Christ as the image means more than his exercise of stewardship over God's creation.[68] However, dominion can be a helpful summary of the image if it is patterned after Christ and takes the form of enabling creation to praise its Creator.[69] The relational view is (predictably) a more promising option for Gunton, even though he objects somewhat to the form it has taken in some theology, most notably Barth's. That God created humanity in a duality of sexes indeed implies that relationality is fundamental to human being. While this is suggestive, Gunton cautions that Barth's view reflects a binitarian theology underlying the anthropology, an emphasis on the Father–Son relation rather than a broader theology of communion.[70] However, in the picture of male and female relatedness, we truly do see a human echo of the divine being, which is being-in-relation: 'To be in the image of God is to be called to a relatedness-in-otherness that echoes the eternal relatedness-in-otherness of Father, Son and Spirit.'[71] Humans image God by being in many forms of mutually constitutive relationships – vertical and horizontal, with God and with the human and non-human creation. Here again we see that to be in the image of God is the equivalent to being a person. That is why Gunton is able to define the image of God along similar teleological lines. He writes: 'To be in the image of God is therefore to be called to represent God to the creation and the creation to God, so enabling it to reach its perfection.'[72] The image of God has a functional aspect, but in the end is primarily relational.

The central focus of the doctrine of the *imago Dei* is Jesus Christ, who is both the image of God himself and the means through which the image is renewed in humanity.[73] Yet to speak of the *renewal* of the image is to be reminded of its fallenness and distortedness. Here, according to Gunton, the typical question of whether the image was lost in the fall is a futile one since we no longer view the image as a capacity within human beings. The image of God is indeed distorted, and this consists in the fracturing of the aforementioned relationships. Idolatry – ascribing worth to the creation that belongs only to the Creator – is the root cause of the image's defacement. It results primarily in deformed sexual relationships and in the mistreatment of the created order, because God is displaced as the centre of the universe.[74] The image of God is still operative after the fall when we see healthy human community, love between men and women, and when dominion or stewardship are exercised in ways that praise the Creator and direct the created order towards its eschatological perfection. However, in all these relationships there is the admixture of goodness and sin. Redemption is the work of the triune God centred on Christ. Gunton puts it this way:

> Christ the incarnate, crucified, risen and ascended Son comes from the Father through the Spirit and in due time gives that same Spirit as the way by which the creation may through him return to the Father... The Son images the Father as through the Spirit he realises a particular pattern of life on earth... The representative bearer of the image becomes, as the channel of the Spirit, the vehicle of the renewal of the image in those who enter into relation with him.[75]

Renewal and restoration take the form of freedom from idolatry and for renewed relationships. The primary vehicle for this transformation is the church, which is the community in which deformed relationships are reformed in Christ by the work of the Spirit in the act of worship. As Christ – the ideal humanity – is held forth in word and sacrament, the perfecting Spirit moves the church towards and brings present instantiations of the eschatological realization of the image of God, which chiefly consists in restored relationships with the Creator, other believers, society and the created order generally.[76]

Freedom

More needs to be said of freedom – a topic of real importance to Gunton. His earliest extensive treatment of the subject came in his *Enlightenment and Alienation*, a critique of the Enlightenment's dehumanizing legacy.[77] He describes the Enlightenment as a quest for autonomy, and particularly freedom from limits imposed by outside sources of authority – especially an omnipotent and, therefore, freedom-denying God. If God is absolutely omnipotent, so the argument goes, then humanity is impotent; if God is absolutely in control, then humanity is merely servile. To gain freedom, humanity must break free from this God. We must be a law to ourselves, so to speak, finding laws to govern ourselves within our own rationality. To be dependent on anything external to ourselves is to debase humanity and make us merely passive participants in the world, all of which is an affront to freedom.[78] While Gunton concedes that the desire for freedom – even liberation from that kind of omnipotent deity – is commendable, he argues that the answer was sought in the wrong place. By rooting freedom in the inner self rather than God or even the outside world, the Enlightenment project led to the alienation of human beings from God and their world.

The beginnings of a proper concept of freedom take shape as attention is paid to the form of life modelled by Jesus Christ. In his temptation we see his freedom exercised not in the assertion of autonomy, but in obedience to the commands of another. 'Scripture is quoted at the devil,' Gunton writes, 'in order to show that this human being, however elevated, is only what he is in a relationship of subordination.'[79] A similar pattern can be discerned as Jesus approaches his death. As the authorities conspire to kill him, he makes it clear that he will go only because he chooses. Here we have a death imposed by the religious leaders and the Father alongside the authority to give and take up his own life. His life was characterized by freedom – freedom from false expectations, freedom to love others sacrificially – and this was both the source and result of obedience. Hence obedience to another, or what Gunton calls 'heteronomy', is not the enemy of autonomy. Sovereignty and servanthood are not finally paradoxes.[80] In Christ we encounter a God who does not just command from outside, but comes alongside us as a fellow human. Gunton writes: 'The very obedience and freedom of Jesus as a man is also and at the same time the freedom and self-giving of God to human existence.'[81] The Enlightenment rejection of God is unwarranted if God is conceived along these lines. This self-giving of God in Christ is, in fact, grace; it is the power of God for obedience and freedom, given within the structures of our reality rather than from without. Grace is liberating power through personal relation.

By describing grace thus, we have entered into pneumatological territory. There are three characteristic functions of the Spirit that are relevant to this discussion. First, the Spirit, as we have seen repeatedly, moves the creature towards eschatological perfection, even in the realm of properly exercised freedom. Second, the Spirit forms a community around Jesus Christ. Finally, the Spirit works within the believers in a way that respects the independence of the creature.[82] When taken together, we see that the Spirit liberates us by freeing us from our alienated pasts and moves us towards eschatological freedom through the community patterned after Jesus. As Gunton puts it: 'As he relates us to Jesus Christ, in whom alone there is no conflict of freedom and obedience, his authentic humanity becomes once again possible: a kind of autonomy.'[83] Jesus' way of relating to God, which is paradigmatic for all divine–human relations, is actualized through the ministry of the Holy Spirit.

So, what is freedom? Gunton offers a two-part definition: '(1) Freedom is that which I do with my own particularity, that which enables me to be and do what is truly and distinctively myself; (2) Freedom is that which others do to and with my particular being, in enabling me to be and do, or preventing me from being and doing, that which is particularly myself.'[84] Freedom is about personal particularity, but it is also a fundamentally relational term. In accord with what was said earlier, these two aspects come together in Jesus, who was enabled by the Spirit to be and do what was particular to him.[85] As his freedom came within a set of relationships, so ours is conferred through the vertical and horizontal relationships described in our discussion of the image of God. In communion with God through Christ and in the Spirit, and in fellowship with the community of Christ, human freedom is restored and realized.[86] Freedom is mediated and, like other divine gifts, is mediated chiefly by God's two hands.

Sin

Finally, a brief word on sin. It should not be surprising at this stage that Gunton describes sin primarily in relational terms. Sin is fundamentally a disruption in the relationship between God and personal creatures, as well as between personal creatures themselves. 'The essence of sin,' Gunton writes, 'consists in wanting to be like God otherwise than in the way he invites and enables us to be like him.' Sin is about the creature trying to act like the Creator, which is idolatry, and leads to the destruction of sound relationships.[87] While sin obviously concerns individuals, it is best, according to Gunton, to maintain that it is a social reality: it is mediated to us by our history and the social context in which we live our lives.[88] This view obviates the need to affirm a historical Adam or even a historical fall. What matters is that sin is transmitted to us historically and socially, and that humans *choose* to do that which damages relationships.[89] Sin is inherited socially and committed personally.

Conclusion

The world that God created is good, both in its materiality and immateriality. Any tendencies towards Platonism should be rejected as sub-Christian, tipping the hat more to Greek philosophy than biblical revelation. The goodness of the material world is established and vindicated by the work of the Son, who became material, and the Spirit, who perfects the material order.[90] Gunton's doctrine of creation is inextricably wedded to his doctrine of God. Thus, we can only understand and appreciate the true being of the world when we see it Trinitarianly. John Webster writes of Gunton's contribution on this score: 'Along with T.F. Torrance, Gunton was one of the few theologians of Barth's tradition to devote serious thought to theological description of the created order, and to believe that any such description must be undergirded by trinitarian teaching.'[91] Gunton sought to emphasize that the Creator, who is essentially relational, brings into being a good world that is relational at its core. From this commitment to relationality, he develops his important concept of the *imago Dei*, an account not without its own limitations. It is not entirely clear why a relational account renders the biblical material more faithfully than the traditional stalwarts, the structural and functional views. It might appear to some that identifying being-in-relation as that in God which we mirror – that which makes us in the image of God – is arbitrary. Why could not, for example, some function or act – God's being-in-act – be the thing reflected by humanity? Moreover, if you view the image of God along christological lines, as Gunton rightly does, it would seem that the non-relational views make viable candidates. If Jesus is the image of God, the pattern and provision for our being (re)made in that image, then what is it he exemplifies and restores? Surely Christ is not solely the pattern and provider of perfectly functioning relationships. Is it not possible that Christ is also the image of God as that human who exercises full and proper dominion over creation? Or might he be the archetypal human whose faculties, unaffected by sin, reflect God in some unique way as they are wielded for his worship? The point here is that Gunton's relational view need not preclude other perspectives. It might be asked whether his relational ontology overwhelms his reading of Scripture in a manner not too different from his forebears whom he accuses of viewing Scripture too much through Platonic or Aristotelian lenses.

Related to this is Gunton's relational concept of the human person. Here we are confronted with the same issue addressed at the end of the last chapter, namely, that of the migration of theological concepts from God to humanity and vice versa. The focus here will not be on projection *per se*, but rather on whether the language and conceptuality of divine 'personhood' can fruitfully be applied to human personhood. Fermer contends that *hypostasis*, defined as a concrete, particular, individual existence, cannot without much qualification be translated as 'person', which is what Gunton is accused of doing. Instead, *hypostasis* is a useful term because of its 'Spartan simplicity'; it provides us with a basic answer concerning what are the three relating within the Godhead, but not much else. Fermer's point is made clearly by Nicholas Lash:

> Not only does the concept 'person' misleadingly give the impression of telling us something about God which we would not otherwise have known, but the information that it seems to give us is false. For us, a person is an individual agent, a conscious centre of memory and choice, of action, reflection and decision. But when we say there are, in God, 'three persons,' we do not mean that God has, as it were, three minds, three memories, three wills . . . Amongst us, three persons would still be three people.[92]

The point is that when *hypostasis* is translated as 'person', the translation imports with it alien meanings never intended in the use of *hypostasis*. Fermer prefers to draw a distinction between 'person' and 'personal', a distinction that preserves 'the austere grammar of the Cappadocians' use of the term *hypostasis*, while distinguishing it from the concept of human personhood'. The *hypostaseis* of Father, Son and Spirit are able to express states that we might call 'personal', but by the use of the term 'personal' we avoid the language of consciousness endemic in discussions of personhood.[93] If we then apply to human persons the 'austere' meaning of *hypostasis* as it is applied to the Trinitarian persons – as 'distinctness', 'uniqueness' or 'particularity', for example – we come very short of providing a very personal and informative account of human personhood.[94] A second potential problem with Gunton's relational account of human personhood issues from his basic definition that persons are constituted by their relation to other persons. If persons are not relations, as Gunton argues, then what precedes the relation? As Fermer asks, 'Who or what is entering into relationship?' He elaborates:

> The answer would appear to be the *hypostaseis*, but they are said by Gunton/Zizioulas to be constituted, in the trinitarian context, by their relations. This may be acceptable in the unique case of God, the triune being grounded in a strong conception of *ousia*, but when it is appropriated

to the human realm it appears to be circular; for the implication is that relations precede the particular human person, begging the question of who or what does the relating. To argue that a relational concept of personhood is legitimated by the relational nature of the Divine *hypostaseis*, is to beg the question again as to how personal relations could ever have been established in the first place.[95]

There seems to be a lack of distinction between what may be called numerical versus qualitative identity. The former refers to the reality of the person, the latter to the qualitative characteristics of the person. While the latter may change, the former may not. Relationality is an aspect of personal life (as a quality), but it cannot be that which constitutes (numerical) personhood *without remainder*. Gunton seems to confuse categories, which, according to Fermer, is 'to sacrifice numerical identity at the altar of qualitative identity, and hence to deny a basis from which personal being can relate'.[96] Again, what is it that is able to enter a relationship in the first place? Bernhard Nausner, following Fermer, writes: 'The concept of particularity [as persons] cannot be dissolved into the concept of relations and vice versa. Relations are in need of parts. If this balance is lost we have nowhere to go.'[97] There must be something that we call a human person, comprised of a nature and capacities, that makes relationship possible. Thus it appears that relationality cannot be primary in an account of human personhood without falling prey to a further reductionism. Furthermore, by failing to have a stronger concept of divine *ousia* which grounds the relations, Gunton has a more difficult time describing the 'what' that precedes human relations. Therefore, against his own intentions, he loses the concreteness and particularity of persons essential to any account of relationality and human being.[98]

Some writers also raise the question of the absence of a doctrine of sin in Gunton's theology, partly because he devotes so little space to it in his writings.[99] Some argue that he reductively identifies the fundamental problem of modernity as wrong thoughts about the Trinity, rather than sin, rebellion and unbelief.[100] Others question if Gunton takes seriously enough the effects of sin on the created order. Speaking of sin's effect on humanity, Molnar writes: 'Barth also takes the problem of sin far more seriously than Gunton in that he believes our old sinful lives are doomed to death – they are not merely perfected, but brought from death to new life.'[101] Sin brings death, requiring resurrection. Gunton's preference for the idea of 'perfecting', while not excluding the need for a radical transformation by God, may tend to mute it. This raises the issue of the relation between sin, creation and providence in Gunton's theology. If creation has always been God's 'project', which is tending towards eschatological perfection, what effect, if any, did the fall have? One writer contends that Gunton is more apt to 'speak about creation as an ordered whole without the elements of sinful disorder'.[102] Since creation has always been bound for perfection, and is being carried there by the redemptive work of the Son and Spirit, it is fundamentally ordered. God's creation project *will* be completed. One author notes correctly: 'Gunton's theology of creation actually *is* his doctrine of salvation, and his soteriology could be accurately classified as a *creational soteriology*.'[103] By framing matters in such a way, Gunton brings creation, providence and salvation so closely together that there is no real space made for, or there is at least an apparent ambivalence towards, the question of sin's impact on God's project.[104] Yet this tight linking of creation and providence is also one of Gunton's most notable contributions, for it enables him to affirm the goodness of creation before and after the fall. Creation is not a failed project; rather, it is moving towards a good end. This world, which finds its true being in proper relationship to God and other personal beings, awaits the *eschaton*, when the fullness of this well-ordered relationality will be realized through the redemptive work of Christ and the Spirit.

4

The Knowledge of Faith: Reason, Revelation and Scripture

Gunton is no stranger to modern debates regarding the possibility of the knowledge of God and the source(s) of such knowledge. For him, however, the knowledge of God is a given. By this he does not mean something latent in the universe, discoverable by the powers of unaided human reason. Rather, knowledge of God is after the fact, *a posteriori*. God has given himself to be known in the Son by the Spirit. Thus, any talk about the knowledge of God brings us to the question (rather, fact) of divine revelation, and through divine revelation back to the doctrines of the Trinity and creation. In this chapter we explore Gunton's post-critical account of knowledge, beginning with his treatment of the age-old question of the relationship between faith and reason. In the course of our discussion we will encounter his key influences (Polanyi and Barth) along with his foils (various forms of 'dualisms'). The second half of the chapter examines his Trinitarian doctrine of revelation and how this plays out in his doctrine of Scripture. As always, the concept of mediation will play an important role in parsing what it means that the triune God gives himself to be known by his creatures.

Faith and Reason

Pre-Enlightenment

As early Christian cosmologies developed in dialogue with or opposition to Greek thought, so the church's view on the role of reason

The Knowledge of Faith: Reason, Revelation and Scripture 83

in attaining the knowledge of God took form. On the one hand, writers like Justin Martyr and Clement of Alexandria were fairly optimistic about the capabilities of human reason for knowing God and his ways. Tertullian, on the other hand, was more cautious, famously pitting Jerusalem and Athens against each other.[1] However, it is from Augustine that the characteristic form of future conversations derives. Gunton argues that Augustine bequeathed to the West three related dualisms – one directly, and the other two indirectly. The first dualism, the ontological (discussed in Chapter 3), concerns the division of matter and spirit, or time and eternity. What results from the elevation of spirit and eternity is the marginalizing of secular endeavours and duties – what Gunton calls the second dualism, the cultural versus religious dichotomy. Third, and most pertinent to our discussion, corresponding to the other dualisms, there is the epistemological dualism of faith and reason, a distinction Gunton claims was hardened through the work of Boethius.[2] What developed from Boethius into the Middle Ages is the so-called two-source theory, where faith and reason are seen as two parallel and non-contradictory springs of knowledge. Medieval theology sought a way to synthesize philosophy and theology, the Greek and the Hebrew, so to speak. 'In so doing,' writes Gunton, 'it developed a conception of reason as essentially religious, in that it was at one with faith in being a parallel source of knowledge of the one truth, which was divine truth.'[3] All truth is one, it was asserted; thus, both faith and reason would say the same or compatible things. In a thinker like Aquinas, for example, reason can accomplish quite a few things, such as knowing the existence and unity of God. Faith, on the other hand, is necessary to establish such truths as the Trinity and incarnation. In this schema, reason is indeed viewed optimistically, but it is always in service to faith, providing rational explication or philosophical foundation.[4]

The Enlightenment

While the Reformation and post-Reformation brought about a relative chastening of the powers of human reason, the Enlightenment radicalized the optimism of the medieval period.[5] Corresponding to extreme shifts in ontology (from the eternal to the temporal) and culture (from the religious to the secular) was a shift in epistemology that saw reason triumph over faith, thus marginalizing the latter as an inferior form of knowledge. The world created by the Enlightenment is the outcome of the choice of one side of the dualisms generated by the Augustinian tradition.[6] There are at least three specific features of the Enlightenment world that are pertinent to Gunton's constructive reappraisal. The first feature is its individualism. As is often cited, Descartes' search for epistemic certainty apart from anything except his intellect is representative of this age. All outside authorities must be rejected, so that only what can be demonstrated by the rational individual should be accepted.[7] Second is the spatial relation – rather distance – between mind and reality. The picture here is one of a static, spatial relation between the knower and the known. The subject stands at a distance from the object and relates to it as a disinterested spectator.[8] The third feature is foundationalism, the view that justified knowledge only proceeds from axioms derived intuitively or empirically. Anything that claims to be knowledge must be built from these foundational truths. Gunton summarizes:

> Knowledge is something (1) possessed by an individual, who (2) stands over against something which is conceived to be spatially distant. The spatial distance is bridged by bringing either the mind into conformity with the world ('realism') or the world into conformity with the mind ('idealism'). In either case, (3) the intellectual bridge between the two is provided by the foundational axioms which are conceived to link the mind with the world.[9]

It is in the face of these Enlightenment challenges that Gunton offers a constructive reappraisal of the relationship between faith and reason, principally through two voices – Michael Polanyi and Karl Barth. Both provide post-critical accounts of reason, one philosophical, the other theological.

Rehabilitating reason

Michael Polanyi

Gunton depends greatly on Polanyi's theory of personal knowledge as providing a way past critical epistemologies towards a healthy reappropriation of reason in theology. Two concepts or ideas loom large in Gunton's use of Polanyi. The first is the concept of tacit powers (or inarticulate faculties), which describes the ways in which we know things that defy explicit articulation. As Polanyi famously states: 'We can know more than we can tell.' For example, we know a person's face, but cannot tell how we recognize the person's face among millions of others. This knowledge cannot be put into words.[10] What is important for Gunton is that the use of these faculties only occurs in a person, thus making all knowledge, even scientific knowledge, personal in nature. 'There is no knowledge,' he writes, 'which is not subjective, when subjective means *requiring a subject*.'[11] Thus, Polanyi's insights call into question the depersonalization and false objectivity of Enlightenment thought and create space for a more personal understanding of knowledge. Second, and closely related, is the metaphor of 'indwelling', which refers to the tacit use of tools that help us understand our world. The obvious example is our body; we indwell our bodies in that they are the instruments by which we experience and come to know the world. Polanyi, explaining indwelling, writes:

> All parts of our body serve us as tools for observing objects outside us and for manipulating these for purposes of our own. Every time we make sense of the world, we rely on our tacit knowledge of impacts that the world makes on our body and of the responses of our body to these impacts. Hence, the exceptional position of our body in the universe. But hence also our capacity for assimilating to ourselves things outside, by relying on our awareness of them for attending to something else. When we use a tool or a probe and, above all, when we use language in speech, reading, or writing, we extend our bodily equipment and become more effective and more intelligent beings.[12]

It is from within our bodies and by extending our bodies through the use of tools, concepts, even presuppositions, that we make sense of the world.[13] A blind man, as a further example, must 'indwell' his walking stick if he is to perceive the world around him. The key point for Gunton is that 'the mind is not related to the world by clear and distinct ideas or relationships conceived in primarily mathematical terms, in a disembodied way'.[14] Rather, true knowledge is pre-propositional: there is a real relation between the knower and the known prior to conceptual expression.[15] This insight helps to overcome the problem of spatial distance fostered by Enlightenment thought in a few ways: (1) it obviates the divide between realism and idealism by arguing that the world can indeed be known (realism) by those who indwell it rationally (idealism); (2) it relativizes propositions, which tend to distance knower and known, as the only way to true knowledge; and (3) it opens the door to other forms of knowledge beyond the propositional. What Polanyi contributes is the notion that knowledge is a knowledge of acquaintance, of real relationship – a form of faith seeking understanding.[16] This insight sets the stage for Barth's contribution, as Gunton conceives it.

Karl Barth

Part of Barth's programme was to overcome the dualisms outlined earlier. However, while rejecting the form that epistemological dualism took in Kant, he views the latter's value in forcing theology to be clear regarding its understanding of reason and rationality, or more directly, the relationship between philosophy and theology. Barth's relationship with Hegel is also of importance. Although he was quite critical of Hegel's overemphasis on reason and ambivalence to faith, he at least found in the philosopher a conception of the rationality and knowability of God, *contra* Kant (and Schleiermacher). Moreover, Barth found Hegel's concern for truth both unique and commendable. Finally, Barth commends Hegel's rooting of truth in temporality and history. All these themes in Hegel are steps towards overcoming the epistemological dualisms and 'straitjackets' imposed by Kant and the Enlightenment, and are each taken up (not uncritically, of course) in Barth's approach to faith and reason.[17] Gunton further points out the conspicuous absence of Kierkegaard in Barth's treatment of nineteenth-century theology, describing Barth's attitude as 'ambivalent' towards the Danish thinker. The early Barth was undoubtedly influenced by Kierkegaard, but later came to reject the strong opposition of time and eternity and, correspondingly, faith and reason. 'According to Kierkegaard,' Gunton writes, 'faith is irreducibly paradoxical and the sworn foe of all attempts to rationalize.' While the adversarial character of this approach appealed to the Barth of *Romans*, he would later repudiate it as it perpetuates a two-source theory and the dualisms he tried to avoid.[18]

Thus Barth is situated somewhere between Hegel and Kierkegaard, a figure at once orthodox and modern in his approach. Gunton writes: 'To reduce faith to reason along with Hegel is to lose history in a gnostic and monistic synthesis. To throw faith in the face of reason along with Kierkegaard is certainly an improvement, but . . . faith can so easily turn into its opposite and generate a new rationalism.'[19] Faith and reason must be coordinated, but how? Here Barth turns to Anselm, a thinker who was not enslaved to a two-source view of truth or to philosophy in his theological construction. What resulted was a reversal of the traditional ordering of reason followed by faith. Instead, following Anselm, Barth proposed that faith, as the means by which one enters into a relationship with God, precedes and establishes the authentic use of reason.[20] The knowledge of God comes only in fellowship with God, only on the basis of God's self-disclosure through the Son and Spirit. Faith, as a way of expressing this relationship to God, is also a kind of knowledge, a knowledge that comes to us in the context of the Christian community, beginning with the apostles and prophets, and extending over time. The knowledge of faith requires no other foundation, no justification, other than the proclamation of the apostles and prophets. Barth's epistemology, however, is not without its problems. For example, Gunton argues that because Barth so emphasizes the difference between the knowledge of God and all other types of knowledge, he perpetuates the Kantian epistemological divide.[21] Nevertheless, Gunton concludes: 'In place of the static, propositionalist, individualist and foundationalist, we have a conception of knowledge which seeks to be dynamic, personal and communal.'[22] In Barth, as in Polanyi, relationship is the basis for articulate knowledge – whether of God or other objects.

Summary

Gunton summarizes in five theses the type of rationality to which Polanyi and Barth point, and which attend true knowledge of God. First, knowledge is relational. It is the personal knowledge of faith, and as such is outside the control of the recipient. It must be given. Second, knowledge of God has an intellectual component that is internally coherent and illumines other parts of reality. Third, knowledge is utterly contingent, being focused on the contingent event of the incarnation of Christ and the work of the Holy Spirit in bringing the salvation requisite for true knowledge. Fourth, the content of this knowledge is unique, requiring God himself to make it known. Finally, this knowledge is obtained and experienced within the Christian community.[23] Faith and reason cohere, as long as reason remains fettered to the faith that establishes its rationality. Talk of faith and knowledge points us to the question of revelation, the making known of the God to whom faith responds. This will occupy us in the next section.

A Theology of Revelation

The problem of immediacy

When Gunton takes up the doctrine of revelation, he returns to a familiar theme throughout his theology: mediation. One of the chief problems in modern views of revelation, according to Gunton, is the assumption that God relates to us without mediation, either

The Knowledge of Faith: Reason, Revelation and Scripture 89

to the mind or experience. Barth, the chief interlocutor through whom Gunton would develop his own doctrine of revelation, falls prey to a similar problem; for while not arguing for non-mediation in the human mind or experience, Barth holds to what Gunton calls a 'revelational immediacy', namely, 'a direct apprehension of the content of the faith that will in some way or other serve to identify it beyond question'.[24] Knowledge of God is accomplished by an alien and *immediate* encounter with the objective reality of God. The sovereign God acts freely to give direct apprehension of himself.[25] This belief in non-mediated revelation is expressed in Barth's insistence that revelation is *self*-revelation, and that God is freely revealed through God. To Gunton, mediation basically denotes 'the way we understand one form of action – God's action – to take shape in and in relation to that which is not God; the way, that is, by which the actions of one who is creator take form in a world that is of an entirely different order from God because he made it so'.[26] As this is applied to the triune God, mediation is summed up thus: '[A]ll of God's acts take their beginning in the Father, are put into effect through the Son, and reach their completion in the Spirit.'[27] Therefore, anything we might say about God's self-revelation must be construed along these lines. To be sure, God reveals God, but the precise nature of how that revelation is mediated by God and in God must be spelled out. Barth does not parse this out, resulting in a tendency to minimize aspects of the roles of Christ and the Spirit in mediating revelation.

Certainly Barth was aware of the centrality of Christology to any construal of revelation. However, if one holds too tenaciously to the principle that only God reveals God, Gunton asks, then what space is left for the *humanity* of Jesus, for example, to be revelatory? Is it possible for God to be revealed by that which is other than himself?[28] In Barth, revelation in Christ comes through his divine nature, not his humanity. Yet, according to Gunton, the Son is 'the focus of God the Father's immanent action, his involvement *within* the structures of the world, as paradigmatically in Jesus'.[29] Thus, self-revelation is somehow mediated through Jesus' human life and ministry in the world. He argues that one of the chief weaknesses of Barth's theology is that he buys into an 'Aristotelian principle' that only like can reveal like.[30] However, Gunton contends:

> The Fourth Gospel suggests a more subtle interweaving of revelation not only through the like – he who has seen me has seen the Father – but its counterbalancing by a theology of revelation through otherness. The Father is indeed made known by Jesus, but as one who is greater than he (14:28), and so beyond all we can say and think: one revealed by humiliation and cross, but revealed none the less as other.[31]

The Son, in his humanity, mediates revelation. Creation mediates the Creator. Barth fails to give an adequate account of this fact, often even setting up an either/or proposition: either God (construed generally) reveals himself (directly) or there is no revelation.[32]

As a result of his lack of specificity, the mediation of the Spirit is also given short shrift in Barth's theology of revelation. Barth follows Reformation theologies by more or less limiting the Paraclete's work to the application of the benefits of salvation or to the internal confirmation of Scripture's message. On this account, the Spirit's role in revealing or mediating revelation is negligible. Moreover, in Barth there is a tendency to blur the distinctive revelatory roles of the three persons of the Godhead. With respect to the Spirit, he fails to highlight that the Son's ministry of revealing the Father is carried out in the Spirit, thus making the Spirit a mediator of revelation in that distinct manner. Without an adequate theology of mediation, particular revelatory works of the Spirit wind up underappreciated. What this points to is the need in Barth (and many other theologies) to better specify the different patterns of mediation (in this case, of revelation) within the Trinity.[33] In the end, Gunton maintains that there is little room for mediation in Barth's theology of revelation – whether by Christ, the Spirit or creatures – and this contributes to the troubled relationship between Scripture and revelation in Barth's thought, as we will discuss later in the chapter.

The mediation of revelation

Gunton's account of revelation 'begins' with an attack on the perceived autonomy of reason over against revelation. Following Coleridge's saying that 'all truth is a species of revelation', he contends that all knowledge must be 'revealed' by the object of knowledge and received by an open subject, and that revelation is an ordinary part of the everyday ways we come to know things. Whether in personal relationships or in the varied forms of enquiry, this revelation is always mediated – through other people, our senses, theories, experiments and art.[34] Without such a general theology of revelation, he contends, we cannot give an adequate account of divine revelation. If God is to be known, he must give himself to be known and we must be open to receive it. Furthermore, a theology of divine revelation must coordinate the doctrines of creation, theological anthropology and pneumatology in a careful way, so as not to reproduce the ontological errors discussed in Chapter 3 and the epistemological errors described earlier in this chapter. To put it differently, a doctrine of revelation must account for the fact that (1) the created world is the kind of world in which revelation is possible; (2) human beings can appropriate it because we were created for such reception; and (3) the Spirit of truth enables human rationality to comprehend the truth of revelation.[35] The question now is *how* God reveals, and this leads us to the related concepts of a theology of nature, natural theology and general revelation.

Gunton is careful to distinguish the three concepts, which, in his estimation, are so often conflated. A theology of nature is founded upon the doctrine of creation and speaks to the kind of reality 'nature' is. Natural theology traditionally refers to the enterprise of attaining the knowledge of God by the use of unaided reason. General revelation denotes the making known of things about God from the things he has made. On the surface, both a theology of nature and general revelation are distinguished from natural theology by the latter's displacement of revelation by reason as the source of knowledge.[36] Natural theology, thus described, is an impossibility, since it presupposes an innate human capacity to appropriate revelation, an ability that simply does not exist.[37] Gunton goes a step further, arguing that both a theology of nature and general revelation, deriving from a doctrine of creation, are therefore only received by special revelation mediated through Scripture.[38] That we can say what nature is or claim that it reveals anything about the Creator is only made possible by revelation itself. Granted these qualifications, the structures of nature reveal at least three things about God's power and nature. First, the glory of God is made manifest through the world's otherness, not sameness. That the world is its own distinct reality points to the uniqueness or ontological otherness (or holiness) of God. Second, the world reveals God through its beauty, whether cultural or natural. Third, the world reveals God by manifesting patterns of relationality and particularity, unity and diversity, which find their basis in the triune God (as discussed in earlier chapters). Again, even these insights are derived from revelation and are not surmised by the strict deployment of autonomous reason.

Leaving behind his general theology of revelation and theology of general revelation, let us further specify Gunton's account of revelation, particularly as it relates to the work of the Son and Spirit. He follows Barth in seeking to centre revelation on God's saving action. He defines revelation proper as a unique event, bound up historically in the original encounters of prophets, priests, kings and apostles with God's redemptive action, and culminating in Jesus Christ as God's saving work incarnate. Whatever else might be defined as revelation must be done so only in a derivative and inferior sense. If revelation proper is *sui generis*, then the issue for us becomes one of mediation: what is the precise nature of this revelation of redemption in Christ and how is this unique revelation made accessible to us?[39] Let us address both of these matters.

Revelation is defined by Gunton as 'a form of personal relation of God to the world' and brings about the knowledge of the heart – the knowledge of faith – and not merely intellectual knowledge.[40] Although there is an intellectual component to revelation (and the knowledge that follows), it is not at the top of the hierarchy.[41]

The Knowledge of Faith: Reason, Revelation and Scripture 93

If revelation is in some sense redemptive, then 'heart knowledge' is superior to 'head knowledge'. Arguing from the Fourth Gospel, he writes that the knowledge of the Father mediated by the Son (e.g. John 14:9), and the 'truth' mediated by the Spirit (John 16:13) are not propositional, but personal. As a source of personal, relational knowledge, revelation is a gift, not a possession. Gunton argues that in John's Gospel, *gnosis* is found most often in its verbal form, so that 'knowing is something that is done as the result of a relation to God in Christ'. If this kind of knowledge is a gift, then it silences boasting and pre-empts presumption, for no one can take hold of this personal relation at a whim; it must be given.[42] Revelation, which engenders the knowledge of faith, is then what Gunton calls a 'success word' in that it 'presupposes that something has actually been conveyed from revealer to recipient'.[43] How does this take place? This takes us to the centre of Gunton's doctrine of revelation – the mediatorial work of the Holy Spirit.

If revelation is the past Christ event, but also somehow a present personal relation, then that which connects God to humanity, the past to the present, and Person to person, is the Spirit. Now, the Spirit's distinctive function in the economy and eternity, according to Gunton, is to establish and actualize particularity – especially of persons divine and human. Thus the particular humanity and mission of Jesus, which function as the very vehicles of revelation, are brought about by the Spirit from start to finish.[44] By emphasizing the mediation of the Spirit, Gunton seeks to draw attention to the revelatory necessity of Christ's human nature – his creatureliness – and vice versa. Unmediated revelation of the Father is not our reality; revelation comes to us through the incarnate Son, by the Spirit. A theology of mediation rightly recognizes that the triune God enables the created order – which includes Christ – to bear a ministerial function. 'This means,' Gunton asserts, 'that parts of the world are empowered to serve as mediators of God's creation of other parts.'[45] As this pertains to our main concern, the Spirit's *present* and *ongoing* mediation of revelation takes place primarily through communities, traditions and texts. Creaturely realities mediate the Creator through the creative Spirit of God.[46] It is at this stage that we might be able to make sense of Gunton's doctrine of Scripture.

A Stronger Doctrine of Scripture

In his posthumously published *Barth Lectures*, Gunton asserts concerning Barth's doctrine of Scripture: 'As a matter of fact I think he is wrong, I would want to have a stronger doctrine of scripture as the Word of God, myself.'[47] What lies at the heart of Gunton's critique was the issue of mediation. He maintains that there is little room for mediation in Barth's theology of revelation – whether by Christ, the Spirit or creatures – and this contributes to a troubled relationship between Scripture and revelation in Barth's thought.

According to Gunton, Barth's actualist vision of revelation, when specifically applied to the Bible, disposes him to place too much of an emphasis on how Scripture becomes the word of God today and too little stress on how it was *originally* inspired and received as the word of God.[48] If present revelation is located in subjective response, or revelational immediacy, then it is more difficult to see how it may be located in a text. In what sense, then, is the Bible inspired so that it becomes a unique vehicle of revelation? In Barth, the Bible's inspiration is not so much found in the authors' words, but in the act of God's self-disclosure to the person engaging the Scriptures.[49] The Bible is a 'witness' to the real thing, not the thing itself, since a creaturely thing cannot reveal God. Gunton takes issue with Barth's use of the witness metaphor, writing, 'Witnesses speak of what they see, autonomously and in their own strength, or at any rate . . . they are in external relation to that which they record.' He concludes that the metaphor of witnesses implies that the Spirit works from the outside to transform the human words of the writers into the words of God. This account neglects the Spirit's role in (1) forming a community around Jesus Christ, (2) enabling particular members of that original community to recognize what was redemptively significant in their encounter with Jesus Christ, and (3) empowering the apostolic authors of Scripture to write those words, making those words the medium of revelation.[50] In Barth, the Spirit merely mediates the subjective response of the contemporary hearer or reader. Barth's problem is – as is to be expected from Gunton – a 'deficient pneumatology'.[51] Therefore, without jettisoning the notion of the Spirit's work of quickening a proper response to Scripture, Gunton aims to develop a more robust account of Scripture's relationship to revelation.

According to Gunton, Barth's account of Scripture focused almost exclusively on Scripture becoming the word of God in the event of revelation, or present inspiration, and underemphasized original inspiration and original reception. He further charges that traditional treatments conflate inspiration and revelation, so that 'the text either replaces or renders redundant the mediating work of the Spirit'.[52] Much of Gunton's work on Scripture is spent attempting to specify the relationship between inspiration and revelation. Following Coleridge, he argues that it is one thing to say something is revelatory, and another to say that it is inspired by the Spirit. Coleridge writes:

> There may be dictation without inspiration, and inspiration without dictation; they have been and continue to be grievously confounded. Balaam and his ass were the passive organs of dictation; but no one, I suppose, will venture to call either of those worthies inspired. It is my profound conviction that St. John and St. Paul were divinely inspired; but I totally disbelieve the dictation of any one word, sentence, or argument throughout their writings. Observe, there was revelation. All religion is revealed . . .[53]

Gunton holds that this kind of distinction makes space for the human character of Scripture, and allows us to 'dispense with the need to wring equal meaning out of every text'. Put differently, inspiration does not negate the fallibility and limitations of the biblical authors; thus it cannot be straightforwardly equated with revelation.[54] Scripture is not revelation itself, a claim Gunton says is in line with the mainstream Christian tradition, but rather it mediates revelation. The important question has to do with the nature of that mediation.[55]

Revelation might be defined as making things known which otherwise would remain hidden. Inspiration is the unique form of the mediation of revelation that makes known, by the Spirit through the biblical writings, truths about God and his ways that could not be obtained elsewhere.[56] What makes the Bible unique as revelation (in some sense) is that it is the 'bearer of saving knowledge'; it mediates to us the salvation mediated by Jesus Christ.[57] Yet, how does the Bible come to be the bearer of this knowledge? This brings us back to Gunton's concern regarding the relation between inspiration and revelation, and underscores the need to identify and specify the peculiar character of inspiration.

The Spirit's involvement in inspiration must take account of at least two facets of the Spirit's work more broadly speaking. First, it must be highlighted that the Spirit is the one who forms communion, or community, with God and others. The church is constituted every time the word of the gospel is proclaimed and the Holy Spirit, through that word, calls the community into being – lifting them to the Father through the Son. Gunton frequently emphasizes the Spirit's role in liberating and opening people to exist for their Lord and one another.[58] Therefore, part of the Spirit's work as it relates to inspiration is to form a particular community, from and for whom the writings arise and are compiled. Gunton writes: 'If the Paraclete is the one who guides the community into all truth, as the Fourth Gospel promises that he is (Jn. 16.13), the Bible's inspiration may be perceived to derive from precisely this fact, that it is the book of a community.'[59] The Scriptures are the work of the Spirit inasmuch as they are the result of the Spirit's formation (and guidance) of the church. Second, we must consider that one of the Spirit's primary vocations is to bring us to Christ, who himself reveals the Father. He is the Spirit of Christ, the one who directs attention away from himself to the Son of the Father.[60] Any conception of inspiration must take account of at least these two factors. Hence, the inspiration of Scripture is to be found partially in the idea that the Holy Spirit enabled members of the original community to recognize and articulate what was redemptively significant about the events surrounding Jesus

Christ. This is precisely where Barth's witness metaphor falters. Witnesses can be autonomous observers, whereas the biblical authors are part of a community the Spirit has oriented around and to Christ, out of whom writings emerge that function as the unique medium of revelation – even the words of God in a sense – because of the Spirit's work. Gunton cites P.T. Forsyth approvingly: 'The Apostles were not panes of bad glass, but crystal cups the master filled.'[61] The words that arose from and were used to convey their experience of revelation are in some way intrinsically related to the revelation itself. Moreover, something must be said for the unique function the apostles had due to their proximity to Jesus. The apostles' role was to mediate revelation, and in doing so mediate salvation. Inspiration consists of the Spirit enabling these apostolic authors to write what they have written and to enable these words to be the unique mediators of revelation.[62] All this being said, there still must be a distinction made between the words of the apostles and revelation itself. The Bible is revelation, or better revelatory, only insofar as it brings us into contact with the salvation that is found in Jesus Christ, who alone grants us access – epistemically, relationally and salvifically – to the Father.[63]

The uniqueness and promise of Gunton's proposal arises from his distinct pneumatological emphases. If, as Gunton often remarks, the Spirit is the 'eschatological member of the Trinity',[64] the one who proleptically brings the perfection of the *eschaton* into the present, and if revelation is ultimately eschatological – God becoming *fully* known – then any revelation occurring in past and present time will occur through the Spirit, who enables a foretaste of revelation to take place and 'so mediates revelation that we may say that the mysteries of God are made known in our time'.[65] As the perfecting Spirit, his work in the production of Scripture is to direct people towards the Father's redemptive *telos*. The biblical authors write as those who are caught in the wake of God's salvific work, and are instruments of the Spirit's eschatological perfecting of the people of God. The Spirit is the agent of God's preparation of the human authors of Scripture. He preserves and even establishes their creaturely freedom to write as they would, while bearing them so that they record what would communicate God's work and ways. Still, however, this is too individual a picture of the Spirit's providential work. If the Spirit is the Spirit of communion, who incorporates a diverse people into Christ (1 Cor. 12:13), brings unity in Christ (Eph. 4:3) and leads the apostolic community into all truth (John 16:13), then it is not implausible to conceive of inspiration along more communal lines. Under the guidance of the Spirit, the original authors and communities interact concerning God's salvation in Jesus Christ, employing normal human faculties and ways of relating, to produce writings that may be called the word of God. The New Testament documents, for instance, emerge from and are fundamentally shaped by the engagement of the inspired author with his particular communities, so that inspiration need not be envisioned individually. Therefore, not only does God prepare a Paul, as B.B. Warfield famously asserted, but also the various communities of which Paul is a member.[66] As Gunton puts it: 'Revelation thus takes place in an ecclesial relation between inspired teacher and inspired taught.'[67] The Spirit's mediation of revelation in this scenario is perhaps more rich and complex; but the complexity helps to highlight how creaturely realities are God's chosen means to disclose his salvation in Christ. The words deployed in Scripture are ultimately, then, the word of God because of the proximity this community and its writers had to the event of revelation in Christ and the unique function they have in proclaiming his redemption. This is what Gunton calls 'the advantage of the contemporary'. The apostolic community testifies to Jesus in an utterly unique way, such that there is 'an intrinsic relation between revelation and the words used to enable it to come to expression'.[68] The words and phrases of the Bible truly matter, as they mediate redemptive revelation by the Spirit's handiwork. The precise nature of the intrinsic relation is not spelled out any further.

Conclusion

Gunton offers a fairly Reformed vision of revelation, placing a characteristically Reformed emphasis on the finitude and fallenness of humanity, and the consequent need for divine disclosure of the truth. It might be questioned, however, if Gunton is still too optimistic about human capacities. In one place, he writes: 'Revelation speaks to and constitutes human reason, but in such a way as to liberate the energies that are inherent in created rationality.'[69] Comparing Gunton and Barth, Molnar responds: 'From Barth's point of view, Gunton's analysis in this context underplays the seriousness of sin and the fact that revelation is offensive to us – it does not just release something inherent in created being – but rather completely transforms human reason in a way that goes against what we would consider reasonable apart from grace, faith and revelation.'[70] The issue here is not that Gunton lacks any recognition of the fallenness of human reason, but that he appears to soften the noetic effects of sin. Barth, like some in the Reformed tradition, might desire to see a more radical divide between fallen and restored rationality.

Some readers may also question the details of Gunton's polemics regarding revelation and inspiration. For instance, he makes the charge that the tradition tends to conflate the two. It is not entirely clear to whom and to what he refers. Certainly examples could be given of medieval, Reformation and post-Reformation writers who drew clear distinctions between inspiration and revelation, and even spoke well of the Trinitarian patterns of mediation involved in the production of Scripture. Bonaventure, for example, writes: 'Scripture does not take its starting-point in human inquiry; rather it flows from divine revelation, *coming down from the Father of lights, from whom every fatherhood in heaven and on earth receives its name.*'[71] It is from revelation that Scripture comes to be, coming principally from the Father. Lest we conclude that he does not think in terms of mediation, he adds later: 'The manifold meaning of Scripture is also appropriate to its source. For it came from God, *through* Christ and the Holy Spirit, who spoke through the prophets and the other holy people who committed this teaching to writing.'[72] To employ one of Gunton's favourite images: scriptural revelation comes to us through the mediation of the Father's 'two hands', especially through the various modes of the Spirit's inspiration. Revelation, inspiration and Trinitarian mediation are all here present. In addition, Richard Muller, in his magisterial *Post-Reformation Reformed Dogmatics*, provides several accounts of medieval, Reformation and post-Reformation writers who drew clear distinctions between inspiration and revelation, and even spoke well of the Trinitarian patterns of mediation involved in the production of Scripture.[73] Aquinas, for example, made the distinction between revelation and inspiration, and brought greater specificity to the modes of the Spirit's mediation. Inspiration, for Aquinas, refers to the work of the Spirit elevating the mind of the prophet and giving it a capacity for divine knowledge, while revelation denotes the actual presentation to the mind of inaccessible knowledge.[74] Whether one agrees with Thomas or not, he is aware of the distinction between the two related acts. Even in the twentieth century, the conservative B.B. Warfield, aware of the need to distinguish revelation and inspiration, retorts that this distinction is necessary in the case when revelation is narrowly conceived as 'an external manifestation of God' or 'an immediate communication from God in words'. In such cases, revelation is clearly not identical with inspiration. However, he contends:

> 'Inspiration' does not differ from 'revelation' in these narrowed senses as genus from genus, but as a species of one genus differs from another. That operation of God which we call 'inspiration,' that is to say, that operation of the Spirit of God by which He 'bears' men in the process of composing Scripture, so that they write, not of themselves, but 'from God,' is one of the modes in which God makes known to men His being, His will, His operations, His purposes. It is as distinctly a mode of revelation as any mode of revelation can be, and therefore it performs the same office which all revelation performs, that is to say . . . it makes men, and makes them wise unto salvation.[75]

Inspiration is a species of revelation, brought about by the Spirit of God, with the ultimate purpose of salvation in Christ. It not only records revelation, but is revelation; it not only records the redemptive acts of God in Christ, but is a redemptive act.[76] Thus, it is difficult

The Knowledge of Faith: Reason, Revelation and Scripture 101

to see how Warfield and many others miss the important features Gunton identifies as lacunae in traditional treatments. Here in Warfield – the ultra-traditionalist, some might say – we find triune mediation in various modes and a careful delineation of the differences and similarities between inspiration and revelation.[77]

Gunton's concern is to provide a Trinitarian account of knowledge that displaces the autonomy and supposed objectivity of reason and establishes relationships as the context in which knowledge arises. Reason comes into its own, so to speak, only in the context of 'faith' relationships. Even though he may be accused of overdoing it (or being unclear) in his claim for the utter contingency of knowledge, his treatment more than makes room for an account of revelation, indeed demonstrating the necessity of revelation for all knowledge – of God and everything else.[78] Gunton forcefully and successfully maintains that knowledge of God and everything he has created cannot be attained apart from revelation; therefore, natural theology is excluded at the outset. God must give himself to be known, and he does so through the Son and Spirit, as mediated primarily by Holy Scripture.

5

The Logic of Divine Saving Love: Jesus Christ

Largely due to his interest in the doctrine of God, and particularly how it is, or should be, shaped by an account of Jesus Christ, Gunton found himself in christological waters from as early as his doctoral thesis (discussed in Chapter 2). His later, more formal, work in Christology had three related concerns. The first had to do with christological method, chiefly the question of whether a Christology 'from below' or 'from above' did better justice to the subject matter. The second, less prominent concern, was to show that the one acting in space-time to restore creation is indeed God. This raises the question of the Son's eternal relation to the Father (and Spirit). Finally, he desired to more adequately depict the *full* humanity of Jesus, a humanity truly like our own – fallenness included. While Gunton is conventional at points, largely defending the tradition, he diverges from the main line in some stimulating ways, particularly in his treatment of Christ's humanity. However, let us begin with the question of method.

Issues in Christological Method

In his largest and most important treatment of Christology, *Yesterday and Today*, Gunton confronts the modern discomfort with classical christological formulations. This discomfort arises from at least three sources. First, there is the supposed problem of Greek philosophical language and concepts, and their attendant metaphysic. Creedal formulas import a static metaphysic that does little justice to the dynamism of the New Testament. Second, there is a perceived gap – an ugly ditch – between the primitive mythological worldview of the past and the conceptual sophistication of the present. A Christology that is funded by, for example, a belief in a three-storey universe is suspect to modern theologians. Finally, the methodological starting point of ancient Christology was 'from above', starting with another world, or God, and then speaking of immanent realities. For the modern, the starting point must be 'from below', taking seriously the created world.[1] Hence, the form and method of ancient Christology are, according to some, at odds with the modern view of reality. Therefore, if any continuity with the past is to be maintained, it will be after shedding its conceptual and methodological baggage. However, Gunton contends 'that certain changes of form entail also a change of content: and that it is very difficult to maintain a real continuity with earlier ages unless we can *at least in some ways* affirm their words as our words, even though necessarily we shall not use and understand those words precisely as they did'.[2] The concern of his volume is to substantiate this thesis, beginning with a discussion of so-called 'Christology from below'.

Christology from below

Although there is no one way of understanding Christology from below, its basic concern is to begin theological enquiry in the immanent realm rather than with the eternal Word; it 'aims to ground what it has to say primarily in the anthropological or, more generally, in that which has to do with time rather than eternity'.[3] Two forms of this method come under Gunton's scrutiny – those of Rahner and Pannenberg. The former begins Christology with a philosophical or transcendental anthropology, describing human being as that which is open to transcendence. Jesus, on this account, is first and foremost a unique, ideal instance of openness to God, and his divinity must be grasped in that light. His perfected and fulfilled humanity *is* God's existence in the world. Gunton raises at least two objections to this account 'from below'. First, he notes that it addresses only the humanity of Christ, but does little justice to the creeds' presentation of his divinity (i.e. 'of one substance with the Father'). The only way Rahner is able to maintain continuity with the tradition is to resort to a form of Christology from above, appealing to a notion of the Logos entering the human sphere. Therefore, his account is not strictly from below, but has to cheat somewhat.[4] In addition, his treatment of Jesus' humanity falls short of Chalcedon, as it obscures Christ's ordinariness, lowliness and true solidarity with us by its talk of Jesus' self-transcendence or perfect openness to transcendence. 'Rahner's weakness,' according to Gunton, 'is in his dependence upon an anthropology which, far from removing the dangers of ancient anthropology, reproduces them in another form, by creating a gulf between the New Testament picture of Jesus and forms of human self-assessment drawing heavily on existentialist and other modern traditions.'[5] A change of form engenders a change in substance. Other related forms of Christology from below fare little better. What are called 'degree Christologies' – those that hold that Christ differs from us in degree rather than kind – fail to maintain the commonness of Jesus' humanity, for they base his significance on the superiority of his possession of certain human characteristics. What results is something resembling a divinized man, rather than one who is of the same substance with our humanity.[6]

It is Pannenberg's formidable account that receives most of Gunton's attention. The starting point for Pannenberg is the assertion that a Christology from below grounds rather than expounds, establishes rather than supports, the Christian confession of the deity of Christ. If we are going to confess the divinity of Christ, we must arrive there through historical, empirical research, rather than presupposing Christ's deity and then seeking to manage the historical details of his life. The movement must be from the finite to the infinite, the temporal to the eternal. The resurrection is the key to Pannenberg's method, for in it we have an historical event open to investigation that carries with it its own theological interpretation. The resurrection did not need to be interpreted, since in the context of Jewish eschatological hopes the resurrection of Jesus would have had a clear meaning regarding his person and work. History and dogma, fact and meaning, converge in the resurrection. The main problem with this approach, according to Gunton, is that it employs the method it rejects. To argue that the resurrection carried its own meaning *to those with particular eschatological expectations* is to admit a dogmatic context for the interpretation of historical events and, therefore, to do something other than pure Christology from below. Moreover, without this context of meaning – assuming it is correct – it is difficult to see how one moves from the fact of the resurrection to the divinity of Jesus.[7]

For Pannenberg, the movement from history to theology is mediated by an appeal to 'universal history', the ultimate context for the meaning of all things. Gunton writes: 'For him [Pannenberg], all human intellectual inquiry presses towards the horizon of universal history. To inquire about any finite entity inevitably leads on to questions about the relation of the part to the whole. Accordingly, the quest for the meaning of the whole of history, for its overall and universal meaning, is part of the human intellectual process in general.'[8] All thought is, therefore, theological. The meaning of the whole of history will not be revealed until the *eschaton*, but the resurrection – as the link between history and the end times – provides the key to relating the finite human being to ultimate reality, that is, to God. Thus, like Rahner, there is an appeal to something other than immanent realities. In the one it is an appeal to Logos Christology; in the other it is the assumption that all thought is theological. However, Pannenberg rejects the Chalcedonian formula in favour of a Christology that is more consistently from below. What results is a Christ who is united with God in that he reveals the meaning of history, but not one consubstantial with the Father. Christ is divine only insofar as he connects us to the ultimate meaning of all things. Here is another form of the divinized man, according to Gunton, since all we can say about Jesus' divinity must be based upon his finite history.

Pannenberg's account pays too little attention to the gospel's claim that the historical action of Jesus finds its origin in the eternal saving love of God. As a result, a crucial tie is severed between Christology and soteriology.[9] It is true that he connects the person of Christ to the revelation of the meaning of universal history – a kind of soteriology, one might suppose – but such a view takes its shape more from Hegel than the evangel.[10] In the end, a strict Christology from below fails on two fronts. First, it cannot escape the docetic tendency it rejects in the Christology-from-above approach. In trying to describe Jesus using purely immanent principles, one ends up (at best) with a divinized man, one far superior to and quite different from those with whom he is supposed to identify. Second, this method is unable of itself to arrive at the saving significance of Jesus Christ. Therefore, one is compelled to impose on Jesus whatever significance is fashionable at the time. The method and form of Christologies from below yield content that is discontinuous with the New Testament and Christian tradition. Gunton concludes that if we are to know the meaning of Jesus, it must be given by God.[11] This leads to the second christological method under examination.

Christology from above

This second approach to Christology can be described generally as a method which begins with a concept of God and his relations to the world and then proceeds to understand the concrete historical particularities of the human life of Jesus provided by the New Testament.[12] According to Gunton, there are two forms of Christology from above. The first (Type A, as he calls it) derives its concept of God philosophically, while the other (Type B) does so theologically. He cites Origen as a classical example of Type A. According to the Alexandrian, Christ is the eternal Wisdom of God and, as such, is fully divine and incapable of possessing any bodily characteristics. There is a dualism here, pitting the eternal and temporal against each other. Although there was an incarnation, the flesh of

Jesus has no meaningful interaction with the deity, but is brought into union only by the soul acting as an intermediary. Thus, the Word and his flesh are juxtaposed, so to speak. Origen's account is funded and governed by varied philosophical assumptions. For example, he begins with a strong concept of the Father's unknowability and transcendence and determines that the Son cannot possibly reveal the Father. The Son is an emanation from the Father, somehow subordinated to him, and not possessing the fullness of the divine attributes such as self-existence. This *a priori* metaphysic determines what we might say of Christ's divinity. Moreover, the humanity of Jesus receives short shrift because Origen is controlled by his philosophical *a prioris* rather than the historical events of Jesus' life. What matters is making sense of the apparent impossibility of the eternal Logos becoming a man, rather than allowing the gospels' depiction of Jesus to shape his understanding of both God and the God-man.[13] Origen does have room in his method for a movement from below. Believers are able to ascend from an inferior belief in the incarnate and crucified Christ to a superior belief in the eternal Word. Yet it must be said, the movement from below is governed by the movement from above. The Christian's knowledge of Christ is put into the straitjacket of prior metaphysical commitments, something we also saw in the modern representatives of Christology from below.[14]

Hegel, a modern example of Christology from above (Type A), makes similar moves. He begins with a philosophy of Spirit and contorts the incarnation into little more than the human consciousness becoming aware of the existence of spirit. The life of Jesus offers pictorial representations of the more important philosophical concept of Spirit, rather than being the source from which an understanding of God derives. Yet, because the incarnation is about the elevation of the human self-consciousness, it might be said that Hegel's is also a Christology from below. The main point for both theologians – ancient and modern – is that philosophical systems constrict their accounts of Christology. Form and method are decisive for the content of their understanding of the person of Christ.

The Type B version of Christology from above 'moves *from* rather than *towards* explicitly theological judgements about Jesus'.[15] It can begin from a basic confession of Jesus' lordship and proceed to provide elaboration and justification of the statement of belief. Gunton writes: 'We can say that Christology from above in this sense might well take the form of faith seeking understanding; of a quest for rational expression and justification of something already believed on other grounds.'[16] Although no one operates purely from above, it must be said that the New Testament writers began with beliefs about the significance of Jesus before offering an account of his very human life. Ignatius provides an early non-canonical example of a similar approach, beginning with a confession of faith in Jesus' divine significance, but one that is in dialogue with the facts of Jesus' earthly life. Barth operates similarly. For him, theological enquiry begins in faith and, thus, from above. However, this faith derives from immanent realities that may be investigated historically (though revelation is required). Although the New Testament, Ignatius and Barth deployed different conceptual forms, their christological content was in continuity. They were all better able to hold together Christologies from above and below, as well as the link between Christology and soteriology, in a way the above views were not capable of doing. Nevertheless, Christologies from above and below, ancient and modern, display the same weaknesses: dualism and docetism. Both operate with the axiom that the temporal and eternal are so absolutely separate that there can be no meaningful interaction between the two. Moreover, they both produce a Christ that is less than fully human, whether in the form of degree Christology (from below) or that of Arianism (from above).[17] Their chief difference lies in the way in which Christ is distorted. Ancient Christologies tend to remove Jesus from history by eternalizing him, while modern thought tends to absolutize Jesus' temporality to the neglect of his relation to eternity. According to Gunton, 'Both methods, made absolute, determine the content and falsify the subject-matter.'[18] Thus, he concludes: 'If the form of Christology can no longer achieve the harnessing together of Christology from above (the inseparable and unconfusable theological content) and

Christology from below (the content deriving from Jesus of Nazareth) it is doubtful whether it retains the same content.'[19] Continuity with the past in terms of content is difficult to maintain without some continuity in form and method.

New Testament Christology

Christology from below is true inasmuch as it begins its enquiry with the man Jesus Christ. Views like those represented within the so-called 'quest for the historical Jesus' are a spin-off of this concern to develop a Christology from the life of the man from Nazareth. To Gunton (and several others) the quest was misguided and a failure on a number of fronts, most notably, in its allergy to the theological content of the New Testament texts. In failing to read Jesus within a theological framework – viewing him in terms of both time and eternity – one misses the New Testament's Christ.[20] The Christ of the four gospels is on both the divine and human side of reality. What we find in subsequent accounts of the 'two natures' or the incarnation are systematic, metaphysical expressions of Scripture's narratival and doxological descriptions of God's work in Jesus Christ.[21] Gunton claims that the Formula of Chalcedon, for example, is simply a sophisticated statement arising from the church's 'indwelling' of the New Testament, tradition and Christian worship.[22] There is no Jesus of history versus the Christ of faith, no primitive Jesus versus the church's Christ. Gunton contends that the difference between New Testament Christologies and later work is one of degree rather than kind. Although 'haphazard' in its descriptions of Jesus, the New Testament nonetheless had little problem moving back and forth between ascribing both humanity and divinity to Jesus.[23] Underlying this conception of Jesus is a view of history in which time and eternity are 'intermingled'. Such a stance undoubtedly derives from the Old Testament's concern to depict the acts of God towards Israel as concrete historical events, thus weaving together the temporal and the eternal. It is God himself who appears to Abraham and Moses at specific times and places. By sticking close to the Old Testament, New Testament authors are able to avoid the dualisms that cripple Christologies that are exclusively from below or above, both ancient and modern. In Jesus, then, we find God's action in real time and space. The idea of the incarnation, as a key example, derives its 'inner logic' from the story of God's relationship with Israel. Thus, rather than prematurely proscribing what may be said of the relation between God and the man Jesus, attention to the Old Testament – which is the fundamental presupposition of New Testament authors – enables us to make sense of the faith of the church and see this faith as consonant, rather than at odds, with 'primitive' Christianity.[24] Jesus can be, and is, both God and man; he is God's action as he is human. Gunton sums up his argument thus:

> In so far as a Christology wishes to make use of the New Testament, it can only be as the intellectual quest of those who seek understanding of the faith in the present Christ which has been received in worship, biblical exploration, experience or some other means. This is because the New Testament knows of no other Jesus than the one who was past but has become present and will be in the future. It also knows of no other Jesus than the one whom it understands from the beginning as God's presence in time. The temporal ('below') is from the outset charged with the life of the eternal ('above') . . . To seek the Jesus of the New Testament is to seek a human and earthly figure whose intrinsic meaning is to be expressed in expressions employing the word *God*.[25]

The New Testament's Christology is about the eternal dwelling with the temporal, indeed *as* the temporal.

The logic of divine saving love

When we speak of Christology as from 'below' or 'above' we are employing spatial metaphors, which do not always prove helpful in this enquiry. If, for example, our understanding of space is dictated by the sense of sight, then it will be difficult to imagine how two realities can occupy the same space. They must be mutually exclusive. The effect is obvious when translated into the realm of Christology: the co-presence in space of both God and man becomes inconceivable.[26] However, if our understanding of space is shaped by hearing, rather than sight, we can see in the example of music how two or more things can share the same space. A musical chord consists of three individual notes occupying the same space, retaining their identity, while becoming a new thing.[27] Notwithstanding, the fundamental issue for Gunton in christological method – as alluded to above – is the relationship between time and eternity. Ancient and modern theologians come to Christology with a shared conception of time and eternity, and this conception determines the form and content of their treatment of the topic at hand. The ancients absolutize eternity, while moderns absolutize time; the ancients deemed the eternal as the real, while moderns view the temporal as the most real. Yet both see time and eternity as mutually exclusive and incompatible. Moreover, both hold to what Gunton calls an 'alienated doctrine of time', which consists in an overemphasis on the fleetingness and disorderliness of time. In short, what results is a view that time is in itself resistant to order and rationality. The ancients escaped this irrationality and chaos by an appeal to timeless eternity; modern thinkers, like Kant, view the mind as that which brings structure and order to temporal reality. A dualism exists that makes it difficult to imagine the co-presence in time of God and man, or the 'perichoresis' of time and eternity, in Jesus Christ. Christological heresies of all sorts arise – Nestorianism, monophysitism, Apollinarianism – when it is axiomatic that time and eternity cannot co-exist while themselves remaining intact.[28]

As discussed above, 'the New Testament interweaves the temporal and eternal, seeing the one to be the locus of the other'. There is, Gunton observes, 'a logic to be discerned within the temporal events that make up the career of Jesus'.[29] This logic is what Gunton calls 'the logic of divine love': that in the story of Jesus Christ, we can discern the eternal love of God within this world of space and time. 'Jesus,' he writes, 'is God's love taking place in our time and history.'[30] Eternal divine love takes the form of initiative, revelation, judgement and restoration – ultimately the healing of our existence in time – in the temporal life of Jesus Christ.[31] In fact, Gunton would argue, the language of pre-existence is meant to convey that the love expressed in the life and ministry of Jesus is continuous with the eternal love of God. Put differently, in Jesus we see what Gunton would in later work call *'the communication of actions'* – that Jesus' acts are at once God's actions and those of a human being.[32] Hence the love displayed in this one human life is the manifestation of eternal divine love.[33] Now, since God's love is a saving love, the question of the relation between Christology and soteriology must be raised briefly.

Methodologically speaking, one's understanding of the shape of salvation determines, to some degree, what type of Christology arises. Gunton offers three instructive examples of figures whose soteriology enabled them to see the divine and human in Christ more clearly. Irenaeus' Christology, for example, is founded on the premise that salvation consists in the restoration of humanity through a human life. Thus, his theology of recapitulation is of a piece with the affirmation of Christ's full humanity alongside his deity. Similarly, in Anselm we find humanity as the cause of moral and cosmic disorder, thus requiring the *man* Jesus Christ to make satisfaction and restore God's just order. Finally, Barth offers the best example in his section on the 'judge judged in our place' (*CD* IV/1). Here Barth describes the Son as fully identifying with humanity in its fallen state. As both man and God, Jesus displaces every human and establishes God as supreme Judge, and in doing so liberates each person from the burdensome task of trying to justify himself or herself. The Son takes on humanity and is the one judged (or, in cultic terms, sacrificed) in order to renew the human condition 'from within' and bring us to God. Again, we see incarnation and salvation interwoven: if humanity is to be restored, it must be from within; therefore, the Saviour must be a man who is also God's saving and reconciling action (since only God can save and reconcile). Thus the incarnation, the coming to be of divine–human reality that is Jesus Christ, is not merely the logic of divine love but, according to Gunton, the logic of divine *saving* love.[34]

The Eternally Begotten One

Two principles were at the centre of debates over Christology in the early centuries, both of which have to do with the nature of salvation. The first principle holds that since salvation can only be wrought by God, Jesus, in some way, had to be God in action. The second holds that since human salvation requires a fully human saviour, Jesus had to be fully human.[35] It is the first of these concerns that we take up in this section, namely, the divinity of Christ. The interweaving of soteriology and Christology is critical for maintaining a balanced portrait of the natures of Christ. On this score, Gunton commends Calvin's account of the mediator as exceptional for its relentless pursuit of ontological answers by asking soteriological questions. For example, when Calvin asks, 'Who but life could swallow up death?' he is trying to draw out the saving significance, indeed the necessity, of Jesus' divinity.[36] The point is, again, only God can save. In order to preserve this axiom, a doctrine of divine impassibility must be upheld, one that is biblically, rather than philosophically, determined. Gunton writes: '[U]nless God is impassible in one sense, his very being is at risk on the cross, so that the cross rather than being his saving *action* becomes something that happens to him, beyond his power. History then controls God, not God history.'[37] Similarly, kenosis cannot be conceived as the Son abandoning certain divine attributes for a season. 'If it is not God, one fully God, but a depotentiated divinity that meets us,' Gunton writes, 'then the gospel is void, for that holds that in Christ the fullness of Godhead dwells bodily.'[38] The fundamental point is that in Jesus we have *God* – the unchangeable and impassible Creator – acting, entering history to save and direct his creation to its proper *telos*.

While it is true that Jesus is God's action in the world, in what way is he related to the Father in his being? Put differently, what is Jesus' eternal way of being God? This, of course, raises the matter of the eternal generation of the Son, a dogmatic portrayal of Jesus formalized in the patristic era. Early expressions of this doctrine tended to falter because they (1) tended to depersonalize the relationship between

Father and Son by focusing on the Logos rather than the Son and (2) tended towards abstraction rather than allowing the economic actions of Father and Son to shape their conception of the eternal relation between the two.[39] Hence this doctrine must be carefully articulated, lest it fall into the same ditches. To begin, Gunton writes:

> To say that Jesus Christ is begotten is to use a metaphor, for clearly, whatever else is the case with his being begotten in time in the womb of Mary, he is not there *eternally* begotten. To say that God the Father is the negation of this – that he is unbegotten – is to contrast the ways of being of the Father and the Son, their *tropoj u'parcewj*. It is to specify an inner-trinitarian difference, and remains metaphorical in the respect that its use is transferred from the finite to the infinite realm.[40]

Of course, we must say that language of eternal begottenness derives from Scripture, but how is that the case? The New Testament speaks of Jesus as God's Son, the one by whom God's presence is made real in time; the one in whose face we see the Father (2 Cor. 4:6). He is declared the mediator of creation (Heb. 1:1–2) and the unique Son who alone has seen the Father (John 1:18). We are undoubtedly pushed by Scripture to say more of Jesus' relation to the Father than that he was temporally begotten or temporally sent. The very divine works attributed to Jesus Christ – creation and redemption – signal that he is in some sense eternally related, even intrinsic, to the being of God. This is a key point for Gunton. He writes: 'The only-begotten Son is also the lamb who takes away the sin of the world. The one who is the object of the worship of heaven in Revelation is the lamb bearing the marks of slaughter upon him. It is not a Logos with no relation to Jesus whom we confess but "One Lord Jesus Christ . . . Begotten not Made."'[41] There is surely a tension here: on the one hand, the Son was before there was a Jesus; yet Jesus Christ is intrinsic to the being of God. Both must be affirmed, however much the tension is felt. For the present purposes, once we say that Jesus the Son is intrinsic to the being of God, we are led by the hand to the affirmation of his eternal begottenness, for the answer to the question, 'In what sense is the Son eternally the Son?' is simply: He is the eternally begotten One.[42]

An issue raised by the above tension is the relation between the economic and immanent Trinity, as well as the temporal and eternal Sonship of Jesus Christ. Gunton does not want to collapse the one into the other, yet desires the former to shape the latter. He thus offers four theses designed to safeguard the doctrine of eternal generation, while allowing the economy of creation and salvation to inform it. First, he notes, 'the purpose of developing a notion of the eternal Son of God is that it enables us to speak of one who is God in a different way from God the Father'.[43] The Son's eternal way of being is reflected in his being sent by and subsequent obedience to the Father. Second, the notion of eternal generation enables us to specify the kind of relationship that exists between the Father and Son. There is a subordinationist strand here with which we must reckon. The Son's eternal relationship to the Father is like that of a created father and son – he is begotten, commanded, submissive – but, Gunton asserts, 'must be construed only on the basis of what happened in the conception, birth, ministry, death, resurrection and ascension, all realized in and by the Spirit of God, of the actual man Jesus of Nazareth'.[44] Whatever it means for the Son to subordinate himself to the Father must be shaped by the history of Jesus Christ. This leads us to the third, and indeed striking, thesis: the Holy Spirit is central to a proper doctrine of the eternal generation of the Son. Already intimated above was the idea that the submission of Jesus to the Father, which shapes an account of their eternal relationship, was a work of the Spirit. The Son, in the freedom of the Spirit, subordinates himself to the Father. Gunton goes a step further, though admittedly cautiously. He suggests that since the Spirit is the agent of the begetting of Jesus in Mary's womb, it is possible that he is also the agent of the Son's *eternal* begottenness. 'The Son,' he concludes, 'is the kind of eternal Son that he is by virtue of the way in which he is related to the Father by the Spirit in the eternal triune love.'[45] Finally, the relationships between the three persons are mutually constitutive. While the Son and Spirit are subordinate to the Father and his constituting action 'in the eternal *tacij*', the peculiar actions of the Son and the Spirit, and the mutuality and reciprocity of the persons, make each what they are eternally.[46] These four theses help to uphold the traditional doctrine of eternal generation, while allowing the life and ministry of Jesus – rather than philosophical constructs loosely tethered to Scripture – to give it its decisive shape.

In the Likeness of Sinful Flesh

We turn our attention to the other material concern in Gunton's Christology, namely, rendering an adequate account of the full humanity of Christ – something he believes to be a weakness of Western theology.[47] He contends that a proper incarnational Christology must meet two preconditions: 'The first is that in some sense or other the incarnation must be conceived to be an expression of the very nature of God and not, in Rahner's way of putting it, a merely external miracle . . . The second is that the outcome be a real and not a docetic or passive humanity.'[48] It is the latter precondition that will be our focus in this section.

While the New Testament witnesses to Christ as the agent of creation, it also depicts him as part of the creation, a real human creature. As such he is constituted by his genetic make-up, history and the society in which he came to be. Christ as a creature finds his being in relation, to God and other creatures. 'We are what we are,' Gunton avers, 'we experience the particular outcomes of our lives, in part because of the shape our relationships take with other people and the world. In that respect, Jesus was as we are, a creature in relations of "horizontal" reciprocal constitution with other people and the world.'[49] Jesus' solidarity with creation generally and humanity specifically is a central feature of Gunton's Christology. The weakness of Western Christologies is connected to the way the concepts of *anhypostasia* and *enhypostasia* have been interpreted.[50] While we must confess that the subject acting as Jesus Christ is the eternal Son of God, this has at times been overstated or overplayed so that the humanity of Jesus is 'swallowed up'.[51] In developing his remedy to this sometimes docetic christological tendency, Gunton leans heavily on the work of Edward Irving.[52] Chief among Irving's contributions is his insistence that Christ took on *fallen* human nature, that his condescension was total, and his communion with us unqualified. He writes: 'For he condescended to dwell in concert and communion with flesh; to look up through fleshly eyes; by fleshly senses to converse with the great wickedness of the earth; and, through the faculties of the human soul, to commune with every impious, ungodly and blasphemous chamber of the fallen intellect and feeling of men.'[53] Irving adds: 'If Christ had not a reasonable soul, His human feelings and affections were but an assumed fiction to carry the end which His mission had in view; and His sufferings and His death were a phantasmagoria played off before the eyes of men, but by no means entering into the vitals of human sympathy, nor proceeding from the communion and love of human kind.'[54] At stake here is the reality of Christ's participation in our life, our experiences, our struggles, our fallenness. He argues that if Jesus had a human mother and was born into human history, there was no other humanity for him to take than that common to all people. 'His body,' Gunton summarizes, 'necessarily consists of matter that partakes of the fallenness of the world.'[55] Sinful flesh does not entail actual sinfulness in Christ, particularly if a distinction is made between *nature* and *person*. In his human nature Christ was subject to the effects of the fall. However, in his personhood, Christ was entirely sinless.[56] Moreover, soteriology hangs in the balance, as the patristic dictum – what is not assumed is not healed – is taken seriously only if we allow for Christ to have taken on the fullness of our humanity, rather than some sanitized form.[57] In fact, Christ's flesh is connected to all material things, so that his fallen flesh represents the whole of the fallen created order. As Adam in his body represented the whole earth, so Christ represented the whole of the fallen cosmos. Christ, then, took to himself the sin common to all humanity, creation even, and obtains victory over it by giving himself (and creation in him) fully over to the Father's will.[58]

Hand in hand with the tradition's refusal to accord to Christ full humanity is the minimizing of the role of the Holy Spirit in Christ's life and ministry. Irving's uniqueness rests largely on his placement of the Spirit at the centre of his incarnational Christology. Returning to the issue of Christ's sinlessness, Irving locates this reality in pneumatology rather than Christology. This enables him to read the gospel narratives in a more straightforward manner. For example, at his baptism Jesus identified with his people as one partaking of their same flesh, yet also receiving the anointing of the Holy Spirit, thus empowering him for life and ministry. Moreover, in his temptations, Jesus was subjected to real temptations common to fallen flesh, but overcame by the power of the Holy Spirit. His whole life – a normal life that passed through the normal life stages – as well as his ministry of healing and miracles is carried out in the power of the Spirit. The Spirit is not a substance infused into Christ, but rather, what Gunton emphatically calls, a *personal other* to whom Christ yields. As Jesus obeyed the Spirit's leading, he was enabled to fulfil God's purposes, and in doing so leave us an example we can actually follow.[59] The tradition has two basic positions concerning Christ's sinlessness. The first holds that Jesus was *non posse peccare*, unable constitutionally to sin, while the second holds that Christ was able to not sin, *posse non peccare*. Gunton offers a third option, namely, that Jesus was 'enabled not to sin' by the Spirit.[60] This view secures a humanity for Jesus that is truly like our own, sin excepted. This talk of the Spirit has bearing on the matter of Christ's wills. Does Christ have one or two wills? Gunton contends, along with the tradition, that Christ must have two wills, but he modifies the tradition in order to safeguard Christ's humanity. He writes:

> Clearly, there are two wills involved, and one accepts the decision of the other. But there are not two wills *within* Jesus, only two at work in his career, his will and the will of his Father. The incarnate Lord, through the Spirit and assisted by the ministering angels, accepts the will of his Father and goes to the cross. The Father's will is fulfilled by the free human willing of his incarnate Son in the power of the Spirit.[61]

By stating the issue thus, he affirms a form of monothelitism (although it appears he evades the issue somewhat). Jesus is a true human and thus has one will, a human will. Notice that the same pattern described above is here repeated: Jesus does what he does and is what he is primarily by the ministry of the Holy Spirit.

We conclude with what Gunton calls 'the marks of the human', his attempt to summarize what we must say about Christ's humanity, particularly as it is presented in the gospel narratives and the letter to the Hebrews:

1. The miraculous events of Jesus' life – conception, resurrection, ascension – must be construed as central to his human history, not merely as indicators of his divinity. Part of the significance of the resurrection, for instance, is that it is truly human life that is restored and transformed. Jesus becomes the first among fellow humans to be raised by God's power.[62]
2. Jesus' authority to speak the word and restore the created order 'by reclaiming it for its King' derives from the Holy Spirit. 'The rule of God is mediated by the words and actions of a genuinely human agent.'
3. The temptations of Jesus, though quite real, never resulted in any disruption in his relationship with the Father and the world. By the Spirit, he faithfully endured temptation, unlike fallen humanity, and this is part and parcel of his humanity.
4. Jesus is not some idealized man, but rather a particular Jewish man whose particular history is bound up with that of a particular people. Specifically, he is, in some way, in the line of prophets, priests and kings of Israel.
5. We must be attentive to the ascension of Jesus, recognizing that it is the man Christ Jesus who rules at the right of the Father, continuing (or consummating) his work of restoring the kingdom to God.[63]

In the end, Gunton concludes that the uniqueness of Jesus' humanity, of which his sinlessness is but a part, derives chiefly from the unique manner in which he was directed and empowered by the Spirit, rather than by some special endowment granted at conception.[64]

Conclusion

Gunton by and large defends the christological consensus of the tradition, but calls into question some of its tendencies. He rejects the modern disdain for dogmatic construals of Christ, those that favour a Christology solely 'from below', but is sympathetic with the concern to root whatever we say about Jesus Christ in his life and work in the economy of creation and salvation. This sympathy no doubt leads him into some idiosyncratic territory, chiefly in his understanding of the agency of the incarnate Son and the fallen nature of Christ's flesh. Gunton stresses the humanity of Jesus and the concomitant centrality of the Holy Spirit, so that he is unwilling to see any of Jesus' actions as deriving from anything but the human nature. Several scholars question whether that is too reductive an account of Christ's agency. Molnar contends that in the five central seasons of Christ's life – virgin birth, baptism/temptation, death, resurrection and ascension – Gunton's account fails to do justice to the biblical mystery of Jesus Christ. The chief contention is this: 'Gunton's emphasis on Jesus' humanity sometimes appears to eliminate the significance of his being the Word incarnate and at times actually tends to separate the actions of Word and Spirit instead of seeing these actions in their *perichoretic* unity.'[65] A few examples will suffice to illustrate this point. With respect to the virgin birth, Gunton fears that too much emphasis on the Word's agency makes Jesus' actions appear pre-programmed and determined in advance, that is, not authentically human. Thus Christ's future obedient actions are enabled by the agency of the Holy Spirit, rather than the Word. But does there need to be an either/or proposition: *either* his actions are enabled by the Spirit *or* they are inauthentically human (because enacted by the Son)? Could they not be the actions of the Son, though enabled by the Spirit, even if we cannot unravel the mystery? Gunton, following Owen's Spirit Christology too closely, attributes all the divine operations to the Spirit. Thus it would appear that the Word somehow ceases to be divine, or his divinity is radically suppressed, at the incarnation. In this way, Gunton 'relegate[s] the action of the Word into a corner and leave[s] the rest to the Spirit'.[66] He presents the matter as a zero sum arrangement – it is either all the Spirit or all the Word – rather than seeing the Word and Spirit acting together. Similar things may be said with respect to other episodes in Jesus' earthly career. One more should suffice. Regarding Christ's death, Gunton would emphasize that its efficacy is chiefly bound up with Christ's obedient self-offering as a human empowered by the Spirit.[67] While true, the emphasis may have shifted too radically. Molnar asks: 'Is it because of Jesus' free obedience, even as enabled by the Spirit, that redemption is achieved? Or is it because the offering he made to the Father was an offering made by the Son of God himself in the flesh?'[68] The problem is, again, the too-strict separation of Word and Spirit in the actions of Jesus.

On a related note, in Gunton's treatment of the wills of Christ, he stresses that there were not two wills operative *within* Jesus, but rather one internal and one external. The former is Jesus' human will, the latter the Father's will. Hence the divine will in Jesus' life and ministry is the Father's rather than the eternal Son's. This is a place where Gunton's lack of clarity on the matters at hand proves problematic. It appears obvious, Alan Spence protests, that 'it was not the Father who took human form and lived a life of obedience to God'. He goes on: 'It was not the Father who cried out in prayer in Gethsemane or who suffered on the cross – these were the actions of the eternal Son of God incarnate.'[69] Again, Gunton displays a reticence to allow the eternal Son any significant place in the works of Jesus, for fear that the humanity of Jesus be subsumed by his divinity. Nevertheless, it is possible – indeed desirable – to affirm that the actions of Jesus Christ are willed by the Word in a way that does not undermine or negate the authentic agency of his humanity. Is this not the mystery that is the incarnation?

Perhaps the most controversial issue in Gunton's Christology pertains to his affirmation of Jesus' fallen human nature.[70] There is certainly a long history of refutations of the view Gunton borrows from Irving, but a few arguments may suffice to show the difficulty of the position. First, Donald Macleod contests that it does not follow that for Christ to be like us, he had to partake of fallen human nature. There will always be continuities and discontinuities between Christ's humanity and our own, even on Gunton's (or Irving's) account. Jesus had a body and soul; he shared our temptations, sorrows and pains; he was reared in a particular social, spiritual and cultural environment – these are the continuities. He, however, never sinned, had a unique self-consciousness and was filled with the Holy Spirit beyond measure. 'Any of these [differences], let alone all of them together,' Macleod writes, 'would be sufficient to break the continuity between Christ and us.' On a related note, second, to be fully human like his brothers and sisters, Christ did not have to partake of fallen human flesh, unless fallenness is intrinsic to human being. Protology and eschatology tell us differently: Adam was fully human before sinning, and we will ultimately be fully human even when unable to sin in the *eschaton*. Third, and with increasing importance, it must be asked how the human *nature* of Jesus Christ could be fallen without implicating the *person*. Unless we want to separate the nature from the person – thus giving the nature independent agency – we are compelled to say that as the nature goes, so goes the person. Finally, what is it to be 'fallen' if not 'sinful'? There is no real, meaningful distinction. We must, therefore, ascribe to Christ the sinfulness of nature that inheres to all humanity post-fall.[71] Oliver Crisp extends the argument, noting that even if one rejects inherited guilt as part of original sin, original corruption is enough to render Christ a sinful human being, which would imperil any orthodox view of the atonement. Moreover, this sinfulness of Christ's human nature would certainly be abominable in God's sight, since corruption entails a deformity of soul that would disqualify Christ from heaven. It is one thing to contend that Christ's human nature exhibited or experienced the effects of the fall (as Gunton wants to emphasize); it is quite another thing to say he had a fallen human nature.[72]

Gunton's Christology will probably not find a hearing in some quarters due to the unorthodox nature of some of his moves. However, his attention to the humanity of Jesus and the relation of pneumatology to Christology is part of what makes the paths he travels promising for further christological reflection, even reflection on the work of Christ, the topic of the next chapter.

6

Metaphors and Atonement: The Work of Christ

The Christian doctrine of atonement is an attempt to articulate what exactly has taken place with the advent of the God-man. For Gunton, God's action in Jesus is manifold and incapable of being conveyed exhaustively. Fittingly, he never provides a thoroughly worked-out *Cur Deus Homo*. However, he does seek to offer a rational, even if not exhaustive, account of the atonement. While Gunton's writings on the work of Christ do engage the well-worn paths of atonement theology in the tradition, his essays are by and large attempts to make sense of three sets of metaphors – victory, justice and sacrifice – asking what it means that Christ achieved a victory, fulfilled justice and offered a sacrifice when he died on the cross. The bulk of this chapter takes up Gunton's treatment of these atonement metaphors and how they uniquely depict the work of Christ. The chapter concludes with reflections on how these metaphors help to resolve (or at least properly handle) lingering tensions within atonement theology.

On Metaphor

From very early in Gunton's explorations of the doctrine of atonement, he recognized the need to make sense of biblical and theological language if the atonement was going to have much currency in the modern church. At the heart of the issue is the question of the function of metaphors. Are metaphors mere images, largely inadequate – even obscuring – ways of describing the world? Such was the view during much of the modern era, according to Gunton. For some rationalist thinkers – Hobbes, for example – metaphor is a misuse of language; it is incapable of communicating the truth. If we describe metaphor as the use of old words or concepts in new ways, or as 'teaching an old word new tricks', to borrow from another writer, then the rationalist problem with metaphor comes to light. Metaphor implies change; therefore, the meaning of words is no longer stable, clear and literal. In this light, metaphorical language cannot be a vehicle for truth, especially theological truth. It may be helpful as an ornament, or as an instrument in one's rhetorical toolbox, but it cannot accurately convey reality. 'The outcome,' Gunton writes, 'was a belief that what cannot be translated from metaphorical into "literal" language cannot be held to be true.' He concludes: 'On such an account, metaphor is disqualified from being a means of our rational interaction with the world: *unless it ceases to be metaphor, it cannot tell the truth.*'[1] Gunton's treatment of atonement is by and large a formal opposition to this dogma. His attack begins with a rehabilitation of the concept of metaphor generally, before attending to the specific metaphors deployed in the Christian doctrine of atonement.

Borrowing from recent studies in the philosophies of science and language, Gunton advances the claim that metaphor is necessary for our understanding of the world, and this in at least two ways. First, metaphor often precedes new discoveries by providing pictures or concepts – 'linguistic equipment' – by which the world is better understood. For example, when Descartes spoke of the universe 'as if it were a machine', this enabled new discoveries in classical physics. The second, and more satisfying, relationship between metaphor and our knowledge of the world sees language and discovery developing simultaneously, with metaphor serving as the vehicle of discovery. While this resembles the first view, the accent here is on the conversation between word and world. Language changes in order to accommodate the world, but as it does so, it provides 'epistemic access' to reality. 'It follows,' writes Gunton, 'that if it is to be a means of articulating what was not known before, it must change.'² Metaphors, then, represent the transfer of one image drawn from human experience to a new context, thus enabling the discovery or expression of the way the world is.³ The main point for Gunton is that metaphors are not ornamental, decorative, obscuring or odd, but are rather indispensable ways in which we make sense of our world. It is the dynamic, rather than static, nature of the metaphor that makes it a fit vehicle for describing reality. The literal use of words has no privileged status, especially since many terms that are now 'literal' began as a metaphor (e.g. muscle and *musculus* ['little mouse']). What matters in the end is whether or not language – literal or metaphorical – successfully captures human interaction with the world.⁴

As we shift our focus to theological language, and ultimately to the language of atonement theology, we find a similar dynamic at play. To be sure, language used in theology will differ from its use in, say, the natural sciences since theology's subject is God.⁵ However, just as our interaction with the world forces changes in the language we use to describe it, so an encounter with God's action in the world animates a shift in our descriptions. Theological language accommodates to the new world created by God's action. Turning to the metaphors of atonement, we might say that these are the ways in which the early church described reality as a result of the radical change in the world instituted by the history of Jesus Christ. 'Language that is customarily used of religious, legal, commercial and military relationships,' Gunton observes, 'is used to identify a divine action towards the world in which God is actively present remaking broken relationships.'⁶ The transformed world exerts pressure on our language so that words drawn from our everyday lives are transferred to a new context and become the vehicles for discovery and understanding of the new reality. The atonement metaphors derive from a dialogue between God's action and our use of language. As a response to divine action in Jesus, everyday language is commandeered and decisively transformed so that these metaphors employed illumine our lives, and might even be said to have a revelatory function.⁷ The basic point is that, contrary to some contemporary writers, the metaphors we will be discussing in subsequent sections – victory, justice and sacrifice – are not mere pictures or impressionistic accounts of redemption, or even futile attempts to name the ineffable, which can be readily corrected or easily dismissed.[8] Rather, when read as metaphors and not literally, they are the instruments by which we grasp reality, the new redemptive reality inaugurated by the ministry of Jesus Christ for us.[9] These metaphors convey the actuality of the atonement.

Atonement in Three Metaphors

The concept of atonement is one way of expressing the Christian doctrine of reconciliation. Gunton defines atonement broadly as 'the acts by which relations between God and creatures, disrupted by human offence, can be restored'.[10] This work takes place within what Gunton calls a 'fourfold matrix' of relationships, that is, between God, the sinner, human society and the cosmic order.[11] Sin caused a breach within all the above relationships that must be repaired through atonement. Since creation, as we saw earlier, is fundamentally relational, the atonement is about the restoration of creation, which consists of mending those relationships broken by the fall. Scripture depicts this work of reconciliation through various metaphors, none more privileged than the other. It is our task, through Gunton, to make sense of what it is these metaphors communicate specifically about the atoning activity of Christ and what it accomplished exactly. We begin with the metaphor of victory.

Victory

It was Gustav Aulen's *Christus Victor* that revived modern interest in the so-called 'classic theory' of the atonement, which states that the atonement is a divine conflict and victory over the evil powers that enslave humanity, so as to reconcile humanity to God. Aulen argues that a legal understanding of the atonement came to dominate in the

West, resulting in the relative loss of the classic view. Legal notions of satisfaction are inadequate largely because they are rationalistic, a futile attempt to explain away mystery and somehow reconcile divine love and justice. The 'Christ as Victor' view is to be preferred, with all its apparent contradictions.[12] Much of Gunton's discussion of the victory metaphor is carried out in conversation with Aulen's seminal work. While applauding the renewed emphasis on otherwise neglected themes in Western atonement theology, Gunton calls into question Aulen's implicit equating of a quest for rationality with an arid rationalism. Certainly the classic theory should not be accepted *because* of its contradictions. Rather, Gunton asks incisively:

> Is it possible to give some rational account of the way things are without either succumbing to rationalism and so *explaining away* pervasive features of human life or in a positivist manner simply throwing paradox in the face of the reader? If theology is concerned with truth, it cannot evade the question of rationality; but how may it do so without rationalizing away recalcitrant features of the human condition like those noticed by Aulen?[13]

The answer returns us to the question of metaphors and their ability to communicate truth – in this case 'victory' and the associated concept of 'demons'. Atonement metaphors, like victory, give us access to God and his action in the world, offering a rational account of them. The issue is what exactly it means to say that Jesus won a victory for us. How much is that metaphor communicating?

Aulen argues that the life, ministry, death and resurrection of Christ are conceived by New Testament authors primarily as a divine victory over demonic powers. For example, Revelation 5:5 speaks of 'the Lion of the tribe of Judah' as conquering. In John 16:33 Jesus declares that he has 'overcome the world'. Satan is described as falling 'from heaven' (Luke 10:18), even thrown down to the earth (Rev. 12:7ff.). Thus, this account is warranted, according to Gunton, since at various points Jesus' work is depicted as a battle with a divine victory.[14] However, Aulen overlooks two critical features of the victory motif in the New Testament. First, he misses that the victory won by Christ is ongoing in the life of the Christian community (e.g. Rom. 8:37). Second, and more important, he ignores that Jesus' victory is as much human as it is divine, in fact being divine inasmuch as it is human. The paradigmatic example of this human–divine triumph is the temptation narrative in Luke's gospel. There Christ is tempted to misuse human power and commit idolatry. Instead, he overcomes by refusing to be enslaved by the demonic; his refusal to succumb to temptation is his victory. This pattern of standing up to temptation, of refusing to misuse power, culminates in the cross, which becomes the decisive conquest over all that enslaves human life. Human submission to divine authority is the divine victory over all that would deny such authority.[15] Therefore, if qualified in this manner, the victory metaphor helpfully – though not exhaustively – conveys what was accomplished by Christ's atoning work. It is not a theory *per se*, but one of a few accurate portraits of a manifold act.

More needs to be said about that over which Christ gains victory, namely, the demonic. Gunton contends that, unlike the apostle Paul, the Fathers displayed a wrong-headed tendency to personify the devil. What resulted were various forms of the so-called ransom theory of the atonement, wherein Christ's victory is conceived as a defeat of a personal devil who accepts Christ as a ransom payment leading to the release of humanity from Satan's dominion. In this view, the devil, believing Christ to be a mere human victim, is deceived and ultimately undone by the power of Christ's divine nature. Such theories, according to Gunton, are problematic for a number of reasons, but chiefly because they tend to read metaphors too literally. Metaphors collapse into myths, so that the main thing conveyed by the metaphor is obscured by a fanciful, often detailed, story about events in the supernatural realm.[16] When the New Testament speaks of devils and demons, it is employing 'mythical language in a non-mythological way'. Principalities and powers represent the political, social, economic and religious power structures of the old world order. They are earthly, this-worldly realities rather than personal beings that inhabit another world outside our own. Gunton writes: 'The texts present us not with superhuman hypostases trotting about the world, but with *the metaphorical characterisation of moral and cosmic realities which would otherwise defy expression.*'[17] Gunton tries to take a *via media* between fundamentalism (his own term), which personalizes demons, and reductionism, which would view the demonic as earthly and/or psychological without remainder. Here again he stresses that we must distinguish between metaphor and myth. The language of 'demons' or the demonic gives an indirect, though accurate, description of reality and, therefore, does not need to be demythologized. In fact, these metaphors are the best way to depict the tension between the personal and cosmic dimensions of the demonic.[18] The demonic is the corruption of the good; it is another way of speaking of the objective reality and pervasive character of evil. A person is demonic when he or she worships what is not God and becomes enslaved to the moral, psychological, social and cosmic forces in the world. His or her slavery is both moral and metaphysical.[19] 'The language of the demonic,' Gunton concludes, 'is language which enables us to bring to expression the fact of the subjection of human moral agents to forces they are unable to control.'[20] If we are to retain a notion of Christ triumphing over demons, it must be conceived as a victory over powers along these lines.

Thus, contrary to the Fathers, Christ's victory is not over otherworldly forces but earthly structures and ways of being that keep humans in bondage. Following Aulen, Gunton views the whole life of Christ – culminating in the cross – as atoning, as victorious over the demonic. Healings and exorcisms, for example, are part of the process of freeing humanity from bondage to forces outside its control. The cross is the victory of God over moral and cosmic forces through a human moral victory. Jesus defeats the demonic by refusing to exercise power demonically: 'It is an exercise of authority which, because it does not *succumb to* the typical human temptation to violence, is a submission which consists in a refusal to submit.'[21] What appears a defeat is really the victory of God. What, then, is the significance of viewing the atonement as a 'victory'? First, it reframes our way of understanding what it means to be victorious, thus providing what

Gunton calls a 'new vision' of human life. One is not victorious by being violent and slaughtering an opponent. Victory is about refusing to use power demonically, so that evil might be overcome by good. Thus the concept of victory undergoes a shift in conversation with reality – in this case, redemptive reality. Second, Christ's victory opens up a new vision of the world. No longer is the world characterized by bondage to the demonic. Jesus' life, ministry and death heal and re-order the distorted cosmos by re-establishing the rule of God over the created order. Finally, the metaphor of victory enables us to speak of God as a saving God. Through it we are given real knowledge of God's action and being, as the one who conquers through the human life of Jesus Christ. This God decisively changes our circumstances in anticipation of the final reconciliation of all things to himself.[22] Herein is real victory, God's victory, conveyed most realistically by metaphor.

Justice

Western atonement theology, according to Gunton, has been characterized by a fixation on law and justice. There developed a tendency to view the relationship between God and humanity largely in terms of the satisfaction of legal obligations.[23] This shift in emphasis is problematic for at least two reasons. First, the legal view tends to highlight the quantity of the penalty to be paid for lawbreaking. Jesus is then said to bear that penalty, calling into question the justice of God. One's penalty, let alone the penalty of millions, cannot justly be transferred to another. Even if it were possible, while the penalty might be obliterated, the offenders remain untouched and unchanged. Second, the law and its penalties are often conceived mathematically or 'externally', resulting in a view that the atonement is little more than a transaction, rather than a loving restoration of relationships. Thus, God is about law more than love, and the relational, covenantal aspects are obscured by the judicial.[24] A proper view of the atonement as judicial must avoid the quantifying and transactional elements of much of the tradition.

To this end, Gunton turns (surprisingly) to Anselm, the poster child for juridical views of the atonement. Rather than joining the bandwagon of critics who see Anselm as nothing but a slave to medieval feudal notions of honour and justice, Gunton commends him, but only if he is read correctly. Not only is Anselm to be lauded for dismantling inadequate ransom theories of the atonement, but he also provides a notion of satisfaction that evades the charge of depicting the atonement as a mere transaction. Indeed God is likened to a feudal lord, not in his arbitrariness, but in his role as the upholder of justice – in God's case, universal justice.[25] For God to be just, he must not ignore violations of his moral order. This leads to a second key aspect of Anselm's treatment – the sinners' moral obligation to God. Human beings fail to meet the demands of God, incurring a debt they are unable to pay, but one that must be paid. Therefore, God is presented with a dilemma of sorts: punish or provide 'satisfaction' from elsewhere.[26] Gunton summarizes Anselm's position:

> The assumption underlying Anselm's argument – and it is probably a necessary assumption for Christian theologies of atonement – is a belief in universal moral order and God's responsibility for upholding it. The human breach of this moral order has led, on the one hand, to human moral incapacity to atone, because of the infinite weight of accumulated offence; on the other, it has led to a situation in which God must either punish or provide some alternative (such as satisfaction) if his purposes in creation are not to be frustrated. Anything else (for example, the mere remission of sins) would involve an offence against universal order, and so be unjust, even (or especially) for God. Punishment would consist in annihilating the human race and so would involve an abandonment of God's purposes in creation; satisfaction requires a counterbalancing act of restitution which maintains that order.[27]

What is noteworthy here is that satisfaction is not synonymous with punishment. Gunton observes that satisfaction is the way in which God *avoids* having to punish. This is different from what would later be called the penal substitutionary view of the atonement, in which

Christ is punished in place of sinners. There is a substitution here in Anselm, but it is not primarily penal.[28] Satisfaction denotes the action by which God sets right what was thrown into disorder by human sin. As stated above, satisfaction has to do with God not abandoning his purposes for creation, but rather bringing them to fulfilment. Rather than the picture of a vengeful God, we have a good, loving God who desires to restore humanity to its proper place and function. Gunton writes: 'The deficiency of much traditional treatment is that it makes it appear that God has to be reconciled rather than himself being the author of reconciliation.'[29] The 'transaction' that actually takes place involves God the Son freely offering himself to the Father as an act of grace, not legality. This death, as an act of free grace, is of infinite value, far outweighing the mass of sin committed by humankind, and is accepted by the Father. The accent in Anselm and in a proper account of satisfaction is on the giving over of Jesus Christ, offered as God *and* man, embodying divine love *and* free human obedience, for the purpose of rectifying the ruptured moral order of God's universe, rather than on punishment justly exacted.[30]

Anselm, it should be noted, does not fully escape the earlier charge of making the atonement seem external and non-transformational. Salvation is indeed portrayed disproportionately as the remission of penalty. However, what he does offer is a notion of sin as more than personal offence or legal transgression, but also as 'cosmic disorder' requiring a salvation that encompasses the personal and cosmic – a justice that is nothing less than the putting right of the universe.[31] This vision calls into question Luther's understanding of the justice of God and his related treatment of justification, which were too concerned with individual sin and forgiveness, to the neglect of the aforementioned dimensions. If the justice of God is 'the form of God's action in saving human beings in and with the cosmos', then the justification of sinners is but one aspect of that greater work.[32] Luther is of course correct in viewing justification (or the justice of God) as divine action, something done for us by God. The parameters of that action, however, need to be expanded to include the entire created order. Gunton appeals to recent biblical scholarship on 'the righteousness (or justice) of God', which describes the concept as centring on the notion of God's faithfulness to the world he has made.[33] In the end, the family of metaphors connected with justice simply conveys that in Jesus Christ God is reordering the universe, setting aright all that has been upset by human sin – particularly relationships between God, humanity, human society and the cosmos.

Sacrifice

The last metaphor, Gunton observes, connects least naturally to modern readers, not least because of the seemingly primitive and savage character of blood sacrifice.[34] Gunton's task is to rehabilitate the metaphor of sacrifice so that it performs the function of other metaphors: to give expression to the way things are in the world. He asks how sacrifice might uniquely convey the work of God through Christ. At a basic level, sacrifice performs a function similar to victory and satisfaction, that is, 'the ordering and reordering of human life both in relation to God and in the cosmos'.[35] What is the disorder for which the sacrifice of Christ is the remedy? In the case of victory, sin conceived as bondage was that from which Christ set humanity and the cosmos free. The metaphor of justice views the problem as lawbreaking and moral disorder, which are set right by the satisfaction of the God-man. With respect to our present metaphor, the problem is pollution, which only a sacrifice can remove.[36] Although sacrifice may seem irrelevant to moderns *prima facie*, Gunton contends that it is a universal feature of human experience, as much as is our instinctive abhorrence of dirt, sickness and death. The language of sacrifice is regularly deployed – in ancients and moderns alike – to speak of that which restores cleanness.[37] What do we make of the metaphor when applied to Christ's life and death?

In the Old Testament, sacrifices were carried out for a variety of purposes and the idea was interpreted both literally and metaphorically. What all sacrifices held in common, however, was their context: God's deliverance of Israel.[38] Whatever a sacrifice was, it could not be understood divorced from the backdrop of Yahweh's saving of a people for himself. In the New Testament, metaphorical uses of sacrifice abound. Praise and good works are sacrifices (Heb. 13:15–16), as are living bodies (Rom. 12:1), for example. When applied to Jesus, 'sacrifice' is certainly used metaphorically, since there is, for example, no priest offering him or altar, but soldiers and a cross. This does not mean that Christ's death is not a sacrifice; but we must understand what is meant exactly by the employment of this particular metaphor to describe his work. In fact, Gunton writes, 'we *understand* from the life and death of Jesus what a sacrifice really is'.[39] The fluidity of Scripture's use of sacrificial language signals that literalism will not get us very far in understanding the atonement as a sacrifice. As a metaphor birthed from the dialogue between language and the ultimate reality of God's saving work in Christ, sacrifice sheds new light on God and human life in his world. First, because sacrifice is finally understood with reference to Christ's death, all animal sacrifices are rendered obsolete. The metaphorical sacrifice of Jesus replaces the literal sacrifices of the old order, which could never do what Christ's did. Second, in Christ there is a conjoining of offerer and offering, priest and sacrifice. A central feature of Jesus' sacrifice is that it is a voluntary self-giving, a willing offering up of his whole life to the Father for the sake of sinners. Here we do not find a victim of punishment, but rather a deliberate giving over of oneself to God, for God's purposes. Thus, sacrifice is neither passive, nor confined to a bloody death. It must include the notion of a properly oriented human life, one lived faithfully before God. Finally, we find in Jesus' sacrifice not only his self-giving, but the Father's giving of his Son.[40] In the Old Testament, sacrifices were typically gifts given by the people or priest to God. However, Gunton writes, 'when Christ is described as a sacrifice, the notion of gift remains, but both the nature of the giver and the means of the giving are understood very differently'. Christ is a sacrificial gift, yes, but the primary giver is God, not the people or priest (e.g. Rom. 8:32). God, in Jesus, provides the means by which our covenant relationship to him is restored.[41]

This leads us back to the charge that much Western theology betrays a transactional and external understanding of the atonement. If the sacrifice of Christ is a gift of God and a self-offering of the Son for the sake of relationship, then the atonement is more than a legal transaction enacted by two opposing factions. Yet, this matter still remains underdeveloped. For help in filling out this understanding, Gunton appeals to one of his favourite sources: Edward Irving. At issue for both Gunton and Irving is the inadequacy of mathematical or quantitative conceptions of sin and redemption, that is, that sin is the accumulation of wrong acts or a debt, and salvation is the balancing of the ledger. Such conceptions, as we saw, leave the sinner unaffected. There must be a connection between the past event of atonement and the present reality of the Christian. Sin, according to Irving, 'is not a thing, nor a creature, but it is a state of a creature – the second state of a creature, in which it is not subject to the law of God, neither indeed can be'.[42] Accordingly, salvation must address the state – the fallen state – of the creature in a manner more sufficient than a legal exchange.

Irving's solution is to lay stress on the full humanity of the Son, which would include the taking on of the fallen flesh of all humanity (as we saw in the previous chapter). According to Gunton, the logic is straightforward: 'If salvation is really to be communicated to us, then our flesh must be healed. And it must be healed as it is, that is, as infected . . .'[43] Christ's body, formed by the Spirit of fallen flesh, is representative of all human flesh. This body, however, is continually kept from sin by the Holy Spirit, so that it becomes the firstfruits of restored humanity and the basis for the salvation of all fallen humanity. Quoting Irving: 'As unfallen creation stood represented in unfallen Adam, so fallen creation stood represented in Christ; and as in Adam's fall all together fell, so in Christ's resurrection shall all be made alive again. *This is the first part of imputation*: that He freely came under, without any obligation of whatever kind, the load and burden of a fallen world's infirmity and sin.'[44] Imputation loses the notion of transferred punishment – from us to Christ – and gains the sense of willing, gracious self-offering for the sake of restoring humankind, providing for it a new beginning.[45] The sacrifice of Christ is, then, the representative offering of perfect human worship to the Father, in fallen flesh, by the power of the Holy Spirit. His life is more than one man's life, but rather is the 'concentrated summation of humanity'. Therefore, Gunton concludes: 'That one offering can stand in for the others because, in anticipation of the eschatological presenting of all God's people spotless before the throne, it takes the representative and random sample of fallen flesh and offers it, through the Spirit, perfect to the Father.'[46] Moreover, this offering enables the rest of humanity to offer true worship to God. The key, again, is the Holy Spirit. The same Spirit that enabled Jesus to worship the Father in spirit and truth is given by Christ to empower believers to respond properly to God. In this way, past atonement is connected to present worship, thus signifying the true healing of fallen humanity. Sin, remember, is contamination, and this contamination is fundamentally the relational disorder common to all creatures. Atonement heals the relational breach by reorienting human life, indeed all creaturely life, to the Father – a task beyond the power of all save Christ and the Spirit.

The metaphor of sacrifice has little to do with any notions of penal substitution, but rather points to three interconnected ideas about redemption. First, the sacrifice of Jesus is the gift of God, the expression of God's love for all he has made. Second, sacrifice denotes Christ's offering of true human worship in place of our false worship. Finally, the metaphor is concerned with the restoration of broken relationships and the reorienting of creaturely life towards God.

Summary

That last point, in fact, links all three metaphors, for all share that common emphasis on restored and reordered relationships, even though they depict sin and its effects differently ('victory' views sin as bondage to powers, 'justice' as lawbreaking, and 'sacrifice' as defilement or pollution). Moreover, inasmuch as atonement has to do with the righting of the cosmos, all the metaphors address universal concerns by appealing to universal features of human life, thus shedding light on every aspect of life in the world. Therefore, they function as more than mere metaphors, but rather as transcendentals that illumine all reality.[47]

Atonement and the Triune God: Towards a Theology of Reconciliation

Gunton's analysis of victory, justice and sacrifice provides a starting point – an important one – for a fuller Christian understanding of the atonement. However, there remain further questions and tensions in the doctrine that must be addressed. The first has to do with placing the atonement within its proper eschatological context; the others are concerned with addressing recurrent questions regarding the atonement.

Atonement and eschaton

The atoning work of Christ must be set within the broader context of creation, not simply redemption. The victory, justice and sacrifice of God are the means by which creation is restored, not back to its original state, but to its intended end. Creation, remember, has a *telos*, and it might be summed up as: to unite all things in Christ (Eph. 1:10). If God purposed from the very beginning to perfect creation through Christ, then the work of Christ should not be conceived primarily as a rescue act, though it is that. For Gunton, we have an either/or proposition: *either* eternal love for the creation is the primary motivation for sending Christ, *or* sin is the impetus. It is clear that the three metaphors observed have everything to do with the overcoming of sin and its effects. However, sin cannot be seen as the ultimate cause of the atonement of Christ, but rather the immediate or formal cause. Since evil is that which hinders creation from becoming what it is intended to be, it must be decisively defeated by God in Christ.[48]

Moreover, as all the metaphors have to do with reordering and renewing creation, they are inescapably eschatological in orientation. For example, although the life and death of Christ signalled the decisive victory of God over the powers, this victory still awaits its final consummation. Similarly, if the justice of God in Christ centred on the turning of creation back to its Maker, then surely this reorientation awaits the final day when the created order will be fully in step with the Creator.[49] Finally, the metaphor of sacrifice points to a chief goal of creation that we encountered in Chapter 3, namely, the offering of the perfected created order back to God. The gift of Christ's sacrifice makes possible the living sacrifices of the rest of humanity. However, this living sacrifice is ultimately only an eschatological possibility, for it is at the *eschaton* that humanity will be holy and blameless (Col. 1:22).[50] As Jesus offered a perfected form of human life to the Father, so all his brothers and sisters will willingly offer up this form of life. Through these metaphors we are enabled to conceive of the atonement and its relationship to the 'project' of creation both eschatologically and Trinitarianly; 'The purpose of the Father achieved by the incarnation, cross and resurrection of the incarnate Son has its basis in the creation by which the world took shape, and will find its completion in the work of the Spirit who brings the Son's work to perfection.'[51] The purposes of the Father for creation are advanced by the Son – as a victory, the restoration of just order, and cleansing sacrifice – and are brought to completion by the Holy Spirit.

Objective or subjective?

In what has been said, it is clear that Gunton believes the atonement to have accomplished something objective, altering creation's status and being before God. This is of first importance. However, what do we make of subjective views of the atonement, those that argue that Christ's life and death primarily present an example of love or devotion to be imitated, or demonstrate the love of God which should stimulate responses of love in the creature? It is clear that Scripture presents Christ as an example to be followed, at the very least in his self-sacrificial love and fidelity to the Father.[52] Gunton, however, takes issue with subjective and exemplarist accounts of the atonement as totalizing accounts, for at least three theological reasons. First, exemplarist accounts neglect the christological backdrop that makes sense of why Christ is an example in the first place. Gunton writes: 'Jesus is an example because he and he alone is the incarnate Son who by the enabling of the Holy Spirit remained unfallen where we universally fall.'[53] Christ is what he is by virtue of his unique, though authentic humanity, and imitation is only possible because of the work carried out by this unique person. The call to imitate is empty divorced from its dogmatic context. Second, such accounts often ignore the significance of the death and resurrection of Christ, something the gospel writers obviously believe is critical for interpreting the life of Jesus. Jesus' death is the culmination of a life of obedience, and this death has saving significance. He is not an example of a noble person who suffers a tragic death. Rather, his life was destined for Jerusalem; it was a life lived for redemptive death. This leads to a third reason for rejecting subjectivist views: they tend to trivialize evil. If evil could be overcome by a mere decree (as many subjectivists argue), then evil is not all that serious a matter. It is subjective theories, Gunton contends, that propound a 'legal fiction' rather than objectivist, substitutionary accounts, since nothing changes in the transgressor if forgiveness is merely a declaration of God.[54] Exemplarist views fare little better, for sin is dealt with simply by following the pattern of Jesus' virtuous life. Yet according to the three metaphors, sin is slavery, disruption of the moral order and pollution – all of which are quite objective, affecting every sphere of life in this world. These are not so easily remedied by a mere decision, whether God's or our own, for sin is a theological problem, not solely a moral one. What is needed, then, is the redemption and renewal of humanity and the rest of creation, which consists primarily in healing personal relationships between God and all he has made.⁵⁵ The triune God is the source of this transformation.

Universal and particular

By speaking of the atonement in such cosmic terms, Gunton contends, along with the whole Christian tradition, that what is quite particular – the work of one Jewish man at a particular time – is also universal in nature. The so-called 'scandal of particularity' is overcome, he suggests, by one basic, though multidimensional, axiom: 'If the acts by which the particular Jesus-history is distinctively what it is are acts of God, then it is in some way or other made or shown to be universal by the one who is the author of all meaning and truth.'⁵⁶ God is *the* universal reality; therefore, what he does is of universal significance. There are a number of ways in which the universality of the atonement might be established. First, by claiming that the ministry of Jesus is the outworking of God's eternal plan to bring all creation into fellowship with him, the particular is made the means of accomplishing the universal. Second, the resurrection of Jesus is universally significant, as representing the first sign of the renewal of the whole created order. Third, by identifying Jesus of Nazareth with the eternal Son of God, we see that the one through whom everything was made is the very same who lived and died for our salvation. The universality of Jesus derives from the fact that everything created is in some relation to him, since he is the mediator of creation *and* redemption.⁵⁷

While more could be said, all these point to the basic fact that God accomplishes universal purposes through particularities. This point is lost, according to Gunton, in Western discussions of the relation between election and atonement. Rather than affirming universality as the goal of particularity, the regnant Augustinian account limits the benefits of the atonement to an elect few.⁵⁸ In such a view, the salvation of the elect is the goal, so that the view reaches a dead end at particularity, often denying the universal concerns the atonement is meant to address. Gunton reminds us: 'The atonement is a particular event which is decisive for the outcome of things, for it concerns the decisive act of God in the midst of time to reorder the teleology of, to recreate, a world that through evil had become threatened with a loss of its teleology. It is there that talk of the universality of the atonement must be located.'[59] The tension of universal and particular in atonement theology is not resolved by the denial or stressing of one or the other. Ultimately, the universal is rooted in the God who acts for the sake of the whole universe; the particular is rooted in the time-bound character of the work of reconciliation carried out by Jesus of Nazareth.

Substitution or representation?

It is fashionable in some circles to view Jesus as our representative rather than our substitute. In many instances this is an attempt to avoid the notion of penal substitution. Some accounts have Jesus representing humanity before God in his ideal God-consciousness, or obedience, or penitence, but fail to take seriously both sin and the demand for objective justice, and thus the death of Christ. Sin, conceived as radical relational disorder between Creator and creatures, is not remedied solely by Christ standing in our place as an ideal human. Objective measures needed to be taken to heal the breach, and only God could take such action.[60] Claiming this does not require assent to penal views of substitution, but there must be some form of substitution, of Christ bearing the consequences of sin for the purpose of restoring those broken relationships. Gunton offers three brief arguments against penal views: (1) they treat the legal metaphor in isolation from the others; (2) they read the metaphor too literally and personalistically; (3) they create a separation between the action of God and the actions of Jesus.[61] Nevertheless, he writes, 'The fact remains that reconciliation on the biblical understanding requires an exchange, and that exchange is centred on the death of Christ, which accordingly involves that suffering is endured for and in place of those who merited it.'⁶² Jesus is our substitute in that he does what we cannot do ourselves. Yet, his substitution, according to the New Testament, finds its climax at the cross and resurrection, for there 'the real evil of the real world is faced and healed *ontologically*', not merely symbolically.⁶³ He undergoes God's judgement for us, but does so willingly and not as a hapless victim. Hence we must say that he is both our representative and our substitute. As representative he conquers, upholds God's just order and is holy, where we are defeated, disobedient and corrupted. As substitute he offers himself in death to his Father as that valuable gift which alone could restore the fallen creation.⁶⁴ Both concepts are required to do justice to the atoning work of Christ.

Conclusion

Gunton's contributions to atonement theology are significant, not least because of the way he gave atonement metaphors the status of revealing truth about God's work through Jesus. The points at which his theology raises questions might be transparent to many readers, but let us briefly examine three.

First, Gunton makes no attempt to find a unified 'theory' of atonement arising from Scripture. He does not privilege one metaphor over another, but rather views each as presenting a window into the reality of the atonement. One of his students makes the claim that the weakness of his proposal is that he fails to coordinate the various metaphors, thus offering a coherent treatment of the atonement.⁶⁵ While he might gesture that the metaphor of sacrifice may be 'the heart of the doctrine of the atonement',⁶⁶ Gunton does not work that out systematically. Writers like Henri Blocher remain unconvinced by the approach adopted by Gunton of seeing all metaphors as fundamental equals. Rather, Blocher argues persuasively that the judicial metaphor is the central and unifying one – as 'the least metaphorical of all'.⁶⁷ And this leads to a second concern, namely, Gunton's treatment of the theory of penal substitution. He rejects the view as being too 'mathematical' and transactional, leaving those forgiven 'untouched' and 'unchanged'. What may appear to be a problem for penal substitution accounts is a misunderstanding or misrepresentation of the judicial view.[68] Gunton's concern is reminiscent of Calvin's opponent, Osiander, who asked whether God leaves untransformed those whom he justifies. Calvin responds: 'This is exceedingly easy to answer: as Christ cannot be torn into parts, so these two which we perceive in him together and conjointly are inseparable – namely, righteousness and sanctification. Whomever, therefore, God receives into grace [i.e. justifies], on them he at the same time bestows the spirit of adoption [Rom. 8:15], by whose power he remakes them to his own image.'[69] Calvin saw no conflict between forensic, judicial notions of Christ's work and its effects, and the more regenerative concerns of Gunton (and Osiander). One does not cancel out the other. Blocher sums up the matter well:

> The vision of Christ our *Head* and *archēgos,* who leads us in the transition from death to life, into the New Creation of which he is the New Adam, who thus effects, through the agency of his Spirit, a real ('ontological,' if you will) change in believers, is not an alternative interpretation of salvation (as C. Gunton seemed to think). On the contrary, it is the fruit of his substitutionary work. Because there is no longer any condemnation, God having condemned sin in the flesh of Christ, the law of the Spirit of Life unleashes the energies of the New Creation (Rom 8:1–11) – 'it breaks the power of *cancelled* sin.'[70]

Christ bearing the penalty for our sin is the basis of the subsequent benefits, such as sanctification and the power to live a cruciform life. One author observes that it may be Gunton's emphasis on 'perfection' that moves him to conflate justification and sanctification, making his soteriology appear more 'process-oriented' than, for example, a Reformed account.[71]

Furthermore, does penal substitution necessarily paint a picture of a God more concerned with justice than love, as Gunton suggests? Of course, some versions of penal substitution may appear to posit a divide between the Father and Son, where the former acts out a cruel and seemingly unjust punishment on an innocent. However, we might follow Kevin Vanhoozer's point that Jesus' death is best seen from within a covenantal, rather than merely legal, framework. Therefore, the atonement is about making right covenantal relationships. God's concern is not merely to enact a judicial transaction, but to act with integrity and justice to bring about proper legal and interpersonal relationships between him and his people.[72] When this context is coupled with the fact that Jesus is the Lawgiver and Judge – the God – who voluntarily gives himself to bear the penalty for his people, this just act can simultaneously be viewed as a loving act, rather than that which drives a wedge between the Father and Son.[73]

Finally, it might be noted briefly that Gunton's treatment of the demonic reveals not a little modern bias against forms of the supernatural. It would be difficult to convince many Christians in the global South, for instance, that the demons are merely structural or institutional realities rather than personal beings. Like the writers of the New Testament, many rightly see that the principalities and powers over which Jesus triumphed, both in his earthly ministry and death and resurrection, are personal in nature, having intelligences of their own.[74] Justyn Terry fittingly notes that Gunton's view does not provide 'an adequate account of Jesus' own encounters with the devil and his demons, nor does it sufficiently affirm the victory of Christ in those encounters'.[75] It should be said, however, that Gunton's rendering of the victory motif could be preserved without much loss, even if one rejects his turn to the characteristically modern hermeneutic of demythologizing.

Gunton has done theology a great service in showing that while the work of God in Christ is hardly reducible to language, it is nevertheless capable of being presented in words and concepts comprehensible to its beneficiaries. The New Testament presents the work of Christ in metaphors; therefore, if we are to gain epistemic access to the atonement it is going to come through such metaphors. In their own ways, the images of victory, justice and sacrifice accurately render the problem addressed and the solution offered by the atonement. In Christ our slavery to oppressive powers has ended, our disruption of the moral order has been righted, and our pollution has been cleansed. The healing of the relational disorder that characterizes the presence of sin has been inaugurated, awaiting fulfilment in the *eschaton*, as the Spirit brings to completion the work of the Son for all that God has made.

7

The Real and Ideal Community: The Church

Definitions and descriptions of the church no doubt abound. The signature move in Gunton's ecclesiology is the relentless attempt to root the nature and calling of the church in the being and action of the triune God. As we have seen elsewhere in Gunton's theology, it is God that determines every reality, the church included. Before we speak of programmes or polity, the very nature of church must be grasped, and this is inextricably bound to who God is and what he does. Of chief importance for Gunton, and a consistent thread throughout his work, is the issue of relationships, within God and the church. If God is a communion of persons, this speaks to the core of what the church is. Our course in this chapter, therefore, will be to first examine three related areas that contribute to a fuller understanding of the Trinitarian heart of Gunton's ecclesiology: (1) the theological ontology of the church, (2) the place of pneumatology, and (3) the role of a proper Christology. Following from these we will address the eschatological dimensions of the church and, finally, its sacraments.

In Search of an Ontology

In Gunton's clearest and most explicit treatment of the church from the perspective of ontology, he argues that the inadequacy of theologies of the church derives from the fact that most are not seriously and consistently rooted in the triune being of God.[1] Unlike the patristic attempts to clarify the church's understanding of God's triunity and the two natures of Christ that resulted in a distinctive Christian ontology, no such attempts were made in ecclesiology. Instead, theologians conformed their ecclesiologies to models found in the world around them. In the East, where neoplatonism was influential, the urge to think in terms of hierarchy proved most compelling. The ecclesiologies of the West similarly adopted alien conceptualities, the chief of which derives from Augustine, of whom Gunton writes: 'A conception of the church as the community of believers is undoubtedly important for him, but it is overlaid by developments deriving from the church's change of status after Constantine.'[2] At that time, the church no longer consisted solely of believers, but appeared to be a mixed conglomeration of saved and lost, which led to two developments. First, since the church was no longer constituted by the faithful, there emerged a greater stress on the institutional nature of the ecclesia built around its hierarchical head. Second, there developed a Platonizing distinction between the visible and invisible church, where the latter was envisaged as the true church, the elect, only known to God.[3] East and West, failing to extend the insights of the doctrine of the Trinity to the ontology of the church, thus filled the vacuum by setting up rival ontologies along the lines of a neoplatonic graded hierarchy (East) and/or authoritarian legal–political structures (West).[4]

A Cappadocian and Puritan contribution

For Gunton, the doctrine of the Trinity, as it appears in the Cappadocian Fathers, provides a more satisfactory ontology upon which to build a doctrine of the church sufficient to the needs of today. The Cappadocians assert that the being of God consists in free personal communion. Following John Zizioulas, Gunton writes, 'The nature of God is communion.'[5] Indeed, communion is an ontological category. The being of God, he adds, is 'a community of energies, of perichoretic interaction'.[6] The threefold *koinōnia* that is God is not a static hierarchy, but a dynamic community. The point for the church is that it reflects the being of God by displaying *koinōnia*. The church, Gunton notes, is to be a 'finite echo or bodying forth of the divine personal dynamics'.[7]

In order to flesh out this insight, he contrasts the Trinitarian understandings of Augustine and the Cappadocians. The former, as we saw earlier, is modalist in direction and tends to conceive of the persons of the Godhead as posterior to an underlying being of which they are 'outcrops', so to speak. What Augustine neglected was the Cappadocian contribution, which stated that there is no being anterior to the persons. The being of God, in contrast, *is* the persons in relation to one another.[8] These different construals of the Trinity result in correspondingly different ecclesiologies. Augustine's doctrine of the church views the being of the church as ontologically prior to the 'concrete historical relationships of the visible community'. The real being of the church, in this scheme, underlies the relations of persons rather than being a function of them.[9] Gunton elsewhere describes this difference as basic to that between an institution and a community. The former exists independently and is logically prior to the persons who become part of it; the persons who join it are at best secondary if not irrelevant to it. By contrast, the latter, the community, is 'constituted by its members by virtue of their free relatedness to each other'.[10] The main point is that the actual relations of concrete historical persons constitute the primary being of the church in the way that the hypostases-in-relation constitute the being of God.[11]

Gunton finds support for his view from the Puritan John Owen, whom he deems to be the first to develop an ontology of the church-as-community.[12] Owen writes: '(1) The material cause of this church, or the matter whereof it is composed . . . are visible believers. (2) The formal cause of it . . . is their voluntary coalescency into such a society or congregation, according to the mind of Christ. (3) The end of it is presential local communion, in all the ordinances and institutions of Christ . . .'[13] And elsewhere he notes: 'By the matter of the church, we understand the persons whereof the church doth consist, with their qualifications; by its form, the reason, cause, and way of that kind of relation among them which gives them the being of a church.'[14] The association of actual believers in free voluntary relationships with one another is what constitutes the church of Christ. The community is the church. Owen's shift, furthermore, from Aristotelian terminology (i.e. material and formal cause) in his earlier work to traditional Trinitarian vocabulary (i.e. persons, relation) in his latter work signals, for Gunton, an ecclesiology shaped and understood in the light of a doctrine of the triune God. Owen's great achievement, then, is his contribution to the understanding that the church is to reflect on its own level the kind of being God is eternally – as a communion, a being-in-relation.[15] The weakness in Owen, however, is that his conception of the church as a voluntary community may collapse into a secular and individualistic understanding of freedom unless controlled pneumatologically.[16] The Cappadocians, according to Gunton, provide the necessary safeguard by presenting the Holy Spirit as the 'perfecting cause' who sovereignly frees persons to be for God and for others in Christian community and thus to become what they are meant to be. In short, it is the Spirit who calls the community into being.[17]

Open transcendentals and the nature of the church

A description of Gunton's ecclesial ontology would be wanting if his 'open transcendentals' were not taken into account.[18] The three interrelated transcendental concepts native to the being of God, remember, are perichoresis, substantiality and relationality.[19] By way of review, the first, perichoresis, refers to the idea that the three persons of the Trinity exist only in reciprocal eternal relatedness. 'God is not God,' Gunton writes, 'apart from the way in which Father, Son and Spirit in eternity give to and receive from each other what they essentially are. The three do not merely coinhere, but dynamically constitute one another's being.'[20] Perichoresis implies free and ordered 'interrelational self-formation' and, for God, 'eternal interpersonal life'. This abundance and order in the divine life is part of what constitutes reality in the created order, of which the church is a part. God is what he is by virtue of the 'dynamic relatedness' of Father, Son and Holy Spirit, and reality at all levels displays this relatedness, its own perichoresis.[21]

The second transcendental, substantiality, refers primarily to the particularity of the persons in the Godhead.[22] 'God is what he is,' Gunton observes, 'only as a communion of persons, the particularity of whom remains at the centre of all he is, for each has his own way of being . . . Therefore . . . the particularity of created beings is established by the particularity at the heart of the being of the creator.'[23] Substantiality affirms that particulars are truly particulars because everything is created by God to be and become what it distinctively is and not something else.[24]

Lastly, relationality refers to the notion that all things are what they are by being particulars constituted by many and various forms of relation. In God these relations exist eternally between Father, Son and Spirit, in which there is a giving to and receiving from that is constitutive of the other. In the created universe, all things, personal and non-personal, have their beings constituted by their relationships to everything else.[25] Thus, the three concepts – perichoresis, substantiality and relationality – go hand in hand to describe a new kind of ontology, an ontology of communion rooted in the doctrine of the Trinity.[26] This ontology is the point of departure for any understanding of the nature of the world and, for our purposes, the church.[27]

The ideal versus actual church

An important question emerges from the above discussion, namely, what does the ontology of the church have to do with its *actual* being? Drawing on Colossians 1:18, Gunton responds by pointing out that the church's connection to the cosmic reconciliation wrought by Christ makes the church a 'community of the last times', called to realize in its life the beginnings of the reconciliation of all things. Through the proclamation of the gospel and the celebration of the sacraments, the community is temporally oriented to the being of

God. Proclamation turns the church to the Word, whom it is called to echo, and the sacraments direct the church to the love of the Father as it is mediated by the Son and Holy Spirit.[28] Thus the church echoes the life of the Trinity when it is enabled by the Spirit to order its life to Jesus Christ.

It should be clear from his reading of Augustine and the post-Constantinian church that Gunton opposes the notion of an invisible church. Neoplatonic, monistic and authoritarian ecclesiologies locate the true church in something other than the actual people that comprise it. His rationale for rejecting this kind of 'invisible church' may be understood as follows: since to be the church means to be voluntarily in communion with those who are ordered to Jesus by the Spirit (i.e. concrete individual believers), then the church must always be a visible entity. We know a true church when we see a community that freely orders and disciplines its life so that it echoes the community of the Trinity – one where perichoresis, substantiality and relationality are freely acknowledged and lived out.[29]

To sum up, what we find in Gunton is an attempt to derive an ontology of the church, not from the surrounding environment, but from the uniquely Christian starting point – the being of the triune God. The Cappadocian Fathers provide a conception of the being of God as a communion of persons – persons-in-relation – that has largely gone unnoticed in the West, to the detriment of the church. God, when conceived as the free relations of particular persons, provides a basis for an understanding of the church as a voluntary group of individual believers, drawn together by the Spirit to actualize who they were created to be.

The Transcendent Spirit and the Church

Also among Gunton's criticisms of traditional ecclesiologies is that they fail to take seriously the work of the Holy Spirit. He writes: 'It would be possible, as an exercise in cynicism, to write a history of the Church as the story of the misappropriation of the doctrine of the Holy Spirit.'³⁰ Christ promises the Spirit to the church, yet too often in history, the works and judgements of churches and individuals have been identified with the work of the Spirit. Two issues lie at the heart of this mistaken identification. First, there has been a failure to recognize adequately the particular identity and work of the Holy Spirit. Second, there has been a corresponding failure to ascribe transcendence and freedom to the Spirit. Both deficiencies underlie the anaemic ecclesiologies characteristic of the West.[31] One of the gifts of the Cappadocians, according to Gunton, is that they developed a way to distinguish between the types of action characteristic of each person of the Trinity without destroying the unity of divine action *ad extra*. Gunton finds in Basil, particularly, the invaluable distinction of the Father as 'original cause' of all things, the Son as the 'creative cause' and the Spirit as the 'perfecting cause'. Although they do not provide us with a doctrine of the church, the Cappadocians do provide a conception of the Spirit that is concrete enough to allow clearer thinking about his relation to the church.[32]

Following Zizioulas, Gunton affirms that the drive towards institutionalism, that is, the identification of church structures with the Spirit, results from the church giving more weight to the historical work of Christ over the ongoing work of the Holy Spirit. Following a Cappadocian distinction, Gunton identifies the Son as representing God's immanence in history and the Spirit as God's transcendence. 'He [the Spirit] is God's *eschatological otherness* from the world,' Gunton writes, 'God freeing the created order for its true destiny – and so, to use Basil's terminology, its perfecting cause.'[33] A second and related ecclesiological point is that the Son *institutes* the church, while the Spirit *constitutes* it. This distinction is essential lest the Spirit be seen merely as the 'fuel' that drives the all-important institutional vehicle.[34] In such a case, the Spirit and the community are only auxiliary to an already-given reality.

What is meant by the Spirit's constituting of the church? The church, according to Gunton, must be more than just the voluntary association of individual believers. The freedom to join the Christian community is wrought by the Spirit and is different from the autonomous notions of liberty so characteristic of secular society. The Spirit, as the 'transcendent other', liberates by calling people into relation with Christ through the medium of the church. He frees people by bringing them into community, enabling them to be with and for others whom they do not choose.[35] Gunton goes on to say:

> The Spirit respects our liberty, because he is not an internal, immanent causality forcing us into the Church, but a personal 'other' coming alongside us to set us free for others, just as he was alongside Jesus in his temptation in the wilderness . . . [T]he positive gift of freedom is to be free in and for community: because to be free *is* to be in community: anything else is a denial of what it is to be human.[36]

The church is constituted every time the word of the gospel is proclaimed and the Holy Spirit, through that word, calls the community into being – lifting them to the Father through the Son.[37] Through the Spirit the biblical narratives concerning Jesus' victory, sacrifice and justification become constitutive of the life of the community and create its self-understanding.[38] Moreover, every true act of worship in the community is a fresh forming of the church, since the church is a community 'that must, ever and again, take place: it must be constituted in the present as the people of God'. When, by the Spirit, the church offers true worship, *then* it is truly the church.[39] This is what John Colwell calls Gunton's ecclesiological 'occasionalism': that the church must ever be constituted afresh by a free and sovereign work of the Spirit.[40] Thus for Gunton it is fitting to say that whenever a new member is called into this community and this body worships through the proclamation of the gospel, the church is formed anew by the sovereign Spirit, whose work in relation to the church is to call it into existence by liberating people to freely exist for their Lord and one another.[41] The Spirit is not a force helping an institution accomplish its agenda, but a person who acts unfettered to bring all of creation, the church included, to its intended end.

The Church's Christ-Shaped Orientation

Two factors need to be considered when attempting to discern the christological dimensions of a doctrine of the church.[42] First, as mentioned above, the church was instituted by Jesus. The issue, then, is the character and manner in which the church was instituted and their effect on the present. If, on the one hand, Jesus' choosing of twelve disciples was a reconstituting of Israel, then the emphasis in ecclesiology would be on the creation of a historical community. On the other hand, if Jesus was setting up the disciples as first in a line of authoritative clergy, then a more clerical ecclesiology will emerge. Gunton questions both readings and strongly opposes drawing a direct line between past historical occurrences and consequent ecclesiologies.[43]

The way forward lies in the second factor to be considered, namely, that of the significance of the dogmatic Jesus for ecclesiology. This concerns the way in which the church is seen to be patterned after or shaped by the life of the God-man.[44] A Christology that overemphasizes the divine Christ – the omniscient and infallible One – will issue in an ecclesiology with an inflated self-understanding. Gunton wants to place a much-needed stress on the ecclesiological significance of the humanity of Jesus. He asks: 'If our christology take [sic] on board the full implications of the contingency and fallibility of Jesus, what of the church?'[45] Jesus, as a truly human being, partook of the same contingency, fallibility and defectibility as all humans, yet he did not sin. However, his sinlessness was not due to some 'inbuilt divine programming', but to his 'free acceptance of the Spirit's guidance'. How can the church, full as it is of sinful people, Gunton asks, 'claim more for itself than it claims for him'?[46] Following Owen, he limits the immediate operation of the eternal Word on Jesus to his assumption of human nature. The humanity of Jesus remains authentically human and is not overcome by the immanent reality of the Word.[47] It is the Spirit, not the Word, who is the source of the particularity, freedom and contingency of Jesus' humanity. This pattern has implications for our doctrine of the church. The same Spirit who constitutes the church (granting its own particularity and freedom) will give the church a 'christomorphic direction', according to Jesus' true humanity and, thus, not the authoritarian and infallibilist shape of the past.[48] It is this checking of Christology by pneumatology that is so crucial to Gunton's perspective on the ongoing role of the second person of the Trinity in the church.[49]

The Humanity and Eschatology of the Church

A recurrent theme throughout this chapter is that the church is a human reality. Earlier we briefly encountered Gunton's caution against institutionalizing the Spirit by identifying the church's judgements with his work. In the last section, his emphasis on the humanity of Jesus as necessary for not divinizing the church was outlined. I now turn to a more focused examination of Gunton's concern for a proper recognition of the humanness of the church.

Limits need to be placed on what might be expected of the church, as a failure to do so often evinces an over-realized eschatology, which can be seen in at least three ways.[50] First, excessive claims are made for the church's ability to represent or be the kingdom, which has led to innumerable political embarrassments and historical blemishes on the church.[51] Second, an overemphasis on law and ethical teaching without a corresponding emphasis on justification by grace indicates, at the very least, that the function of the law and the place of virtues need a clearer explanation in light of the reality of the *eschaton*.[52] The third sign is an overweighting of the theology of the body of Christ, specifically as it takes shape in Lutheran theology. Since the first problem was somewhat addressed in the previous sections, we will focus on the last two.

Gunton provides a thoroughgoing Trinitarian response to those who suggest a disjunction between justification and an ethic of virtue.[53] His main goal is to see how the doctrine of the immanent Trinity shapes what it means to be human and, subsequently, what it means to be the church. First, he outlines a Trinitarian doctrine of the created order, wherein the Father (as originating cause), Son (as creating cause) and

Spirit (as perfecting cause) create a world that is truly other but remain intimately involved in it, moving it towards its *telos*.[54] As part of the creation, human beings also have a *telos* and this is to be actualized through the work of the Holy Spirit as it was in the human life of Jesus.[55] Next, Gunton outlines the nature of virtue. 'God's "virtues",' he writes, 'are God in the perfect coincidence of being and act.'[56] Actions flow from and manifest being. However, since human beings (the church included) are badly formed, any ethic of virtue must take into account the need for redemption.[57] Third, this leads to the notion that personhood is an eschatological concept. Human beings are directed to an end which exceeds their beginnings.[58] To become what we are becoming, then, involves training in virtue, and this occurs within the church as the place where one is reoriented to the eschatological promise of perfection in Christ.[59] Yet for the church to be a school of virtue it must first be the community that proclaims the forgiveness of sins wrought by Christ's death as the only basis for the healing of the will. Thus, justification precedes sanctification.[60] Finally, he concludes, the church is a school of virtue only in the sense that it has been justified by Christ, enabled by the Spirit to share in Jesus' relation to the Father, and freed by the same Spirit to be for one another and for the world in increasing measure. Virtues are provisional perfections, reminding us of what we will be one day.[61]

The other sign of an over-realized eschatology is the overweighting of the theology of the body of Christ. Gunton argues that Lutheran Christologies that tend to view Christ's physical body as ubiquitous are not as successful in making room for the work of the Holy Spirit in the church because there is too close an identification of the church with Christ. This view, at least as represented by Robert Jenson, too easily lapses into seeing the church as the actual body of an ever-immanent Christ.[62] However, 1 Corinthians, Gunton argues extensively, emphasizes a strong distinction between Christ and his body. For example, the 'until he comes' of 1 Corinthians 11:26 suggests that there is actually a *real absence* of Christ and, thus, he remains transcendent over the church as its Lord.[63] It is when, like Calvin, one views the body of Christ as physically circumscribed that greater space is given for the distinctive work of the Spirit in the church (rather than primarily in the elements). Furthermore, 1 Corinthians 15:23 makes a distinction between Christ's resurrection and our own, thus calling attention to the distinction between Christ and his church.[64] Here, as elsewhere, Gunton emphasizes that the church is an eschatological reality. Its worship and life are bracketed by the remembered gift of the Son for the life of the world and the anticipated gift of the Son's handing over of all rule and authority to the Father (1 Cor. 15:24).[65] In the meanwhile, Christ's presence is realized only through an anticipation that is formed by the eschatological Spirit. Membership in the body of Christ ultimately belongs to the age to come. The line between present experience and eschatology must not be blurred.

The Sacraments

The sacraments are the church's way of giving expression to the reality that the Word became flesh, that is, visible, tangible, created reality. That the Word was involved in the created order should inform our view of the sacraments. The common definition of a sacrament as 'an outward and visible sign of an inward and spiritual grace' is inadequate primarily because of its implicit dualism, which serves to diminish the material aspects in favour of the 'spiritual', the work inside the individual believer rather than the historical and communal. 'Jesus' life and death,' Gunton writes, 'are not the outward sign of something invisible, but the invisible become visible, God in action not only inwardly but also outwardly.'[66] Jesus Christ is the only true sacrament – a created reality that is 'unambiguously' the presence of God – and our sacraments are derivative of this. However, insofar as our sacraments proclaim Christ and bring us into communion with God through Christ, they are true sacraments.[67] The basis of both baptism and the Lord's Supper, as we will see, is ultimately Christ's life and death, which had as its aim the creation of a new people. Hence, to understand the sacraments correctly we must place them within the context of the cross and the community that flows from it. If nothing else, the sacraments are crucicentric and communal in orientation.

Baptism

Gunton's account of baptism is set forth as a response to increasing calls for believer's baptism, or what he calls 'rebaptism'. He contends that while it is true that much traditional paedobaptism has had an air of institutionalism to it, the converse falls prey to an overly individualistic conception of the sacrament. In fact, he argues that contemporary visions of rebaptism are often mere products of the Enlightenment ideal, where 'the reason or experience of the individual are what is decisive, over against and if necessary in opposition to the traditions and life of the *community* as a whole'.[68] However, a proper theology of baptism cannot be developed in isolation from the Christian community. Gunton writes: 'While baptism is in part the concern of the particular person, it is not primarily a matter for the person as *individual* but for the person in relation to other people in the community of salvation, the covenant people of God.'[69] Given Gunton's relational ontology of God, the world and the church, it is not surprising that he presents individualism as the chief enemy to the proper administration of the sacraments. Typically coupled with individualism was the church's negative concept of the human condition, in which all people are contaminated by Adam's sin and as a result are destined for hell. Taken together, baptism came to be conceived in a negative light – as that which removes the stain of sin from the individual and frees him or her from damnation – rather than as that which brings the individual into a new relation with God and his people.[70]

What does a positive account of baptism – especially paedobaptism – look like? Rather than appeal to specific Scripture texts or early church practice, which, in Gunton's view, are inconclusive, we must devise the doctrine from what he calls 'the logic of the gospel'.[71] By this he refers to that which the gospel requires or invites, which may not be easily read directly off the pages of the Bible. This logic begins with the death of Christ as its basis. 'We baptize,' Gunton writes, 'because Christ died on the cross for the sins of the world.'[72] Baptism and cross are connected in Jesus' acceptance of John's baptism in the Jordan. Since Jesus did not receive baptism as an act of personal repentance, we must find the meaning of his baptism elsewhere. His baptism, rather, is an anticipation of his death on the cross. Gunton observes: 'The significance of this baptism is – among other things – that it signified Jesus' identification of himself with Israel under the judgment of God represented and proclaimed by John, and that it points forward to his acceptance by death of the judgment of God on human sin.'[73] Through this baptism that culminates in a death, Jesus redeems and restores a new people to God. We are brought into a relationship with Christ by being a part of his people, and we are made a part of his people through baptism. We do not baptize because Jesus was baptized *per se*, but because he died on the cross to receive God's judgement on our behalf. Therefore, again, the cross is the basis of baptism. At least two conclusions follow from this. First, just as the saving death of Christ happened apart from our knowledge or faith, so there is an objectivity to baptism, or as Gunton puts it: 'It is not first of all the expression of the faith of an individual or some invisible inner cleansing.' Baptism, like Jesus' death, is primarily a public and communal act whereby God welcomes someone into the covenant community. Second, just as Christ died only once, so baptism can be received – and incorporation into the body of Christ can happen – but once.[74] Understood thus, baptism derives its validity from God and not from the individual recipient.

Since nearly all would agree that baptism may only occur once and that it incorporates us into Christ, the debate regarding infant baptism centres on the question of ecclesiology. Specifically, who comprises the church and, therefore, who is permitted to undergo baptism? To argue that the church consists of only adult converts is to have an 'impoverished' view of the church, since we are making church membership dependent on those who have had a particular experience or made a certain decision.[75] The ecclesiological question then becomes a pneumatological one: who are those brought into the body of Christ by the Spirit and therefore permitted to give and receive the Spirit's gifts? Of course, through conversion the Spirit engrafts people into Christ, but he also moves parents to bring their children to be baptized and brought into the covenant community. There the children give and receive the Spirit's gifts on the way to salvation in Christ. To restrict who may be baptized is to limit the ways in which the Spirit works and to diminish the true catholicity of the church. With each baptism the church becomes a new creation (2 Cor. 5:17), which consists in a new set of relationships including infants and children. These children are not ancillary, but are one of the Spirit's instruments of perfecting the new creation that the church is. As such, it is only those children who will enter into a relationship with the Christian community that should be baptized.[76]

The Lord's Supper

Gunton does not devote much space to the Lord's Supper, but what space he does give focuses on the communal or relational dimension of the sacrament. His most direct treatment takes place in conversation with Paul's first letter to the Corinthians, where the apostle's chief concern is the way the members of the congregation live towards one another as those in Christ. Their relationship to God and one another is to reflect their new allegiance and must be consonant with their new identity, which was clearly not always the case. Incest, legal battles, meals taken in idol temples and arguments over spiritual gifts all betray the fundamental relational problems in the church. Drawing on 1 Corinthians 10 – 11, Gunton contends: 'The problem is not of failing to believe theoretically that the bread and wine are the body and blood of Christ; it is their behaviour to one another.'[77] The blood and body (1 Cor. 10:15–16) refers to the cross and the church respectively. Paul is exhorting the Corinthians to pursue fellowship, through the meal, with the church rather than with idols and those who worship them (10:14). Similarly, the body that is 'discerned' or 'recognized' (11:29) is the body of Christ, the church, rather than bread. The judgement that follows from not 'discerning the body' (10:29–31) has to do with members destroying churchly relationships rather than mistreating the elements.[78]

In order to avoid the complete moralizing of the Lord's Supper, Gunton is at pains to remind us (again) that the root of the meal is, first, the death of Christ. The action that brings us into relation with God and one another in the first place is the cross, which the Lord's Supper is meant to proclaim.[79] Second, communion is founded on the triune communion that God is in himself, which overflows into creation and the church. The meal is to represent reconciled and whole relationships that are a finite echo of the eternal *koinōnia* of the Trinity.[80] Whatever ethical dimensions there are to the Lord's Supper, they are rooted in the very being of God and are thus profoundly theological. What, then, of the elements? The bread and wine derive their significance from the eschatological and anticipatory features of the Lord's Supper. Just as fellowship around the Table anticipates the perfecting of human relationships that is to come, so the incorporation of created and cultural artefacts – bread and wine – foreshadows the time when the whole created order will be caught up into the praise of its Maker. The elements matter not because they are somehow transformed into or transfused by something else.[81] Rather, they are critical as signs representing and anticipating the reordering of all things that began on the cross. Thus both sacraments have everything to do with cross and community, redemption and relationships. The decisive action is God's, not immediately in the soul *per se*, but mediately through the cross and by the various works of the Spirit in extending its benefits.

Conclusion

In his effort to bring the doctrine of the Trinity into meaningful contact with the doctrine of the church, Gunton delves into the closely related areas of theological ontology, pneumatology and Christology.

His is a careful attempt to root the nature of the church in the being and action of God. In order to situate his proposal Gunton expresses a distaste for Augustine's contribution to Trinitarian thought and, consequently, ecclesiology in the West. His set-up of Augustine as foil raises some questions, as should be expected. Is it fair to say that Augustine's ecclesiology is an offshoot of a monistic theology? What alternative readings of his doctrine of the church might be offered in the light of Augustine's essentially Nicene Trinitarianism? Augustine's ecclesiology is more complicated than simply being about the hierarchy or the invisibility of the church. For him, the church is primarily founded upon the reality of the triune God who himself created the church.[82] Building upon that foundation, there are various dimensions to his ecclesiology. First, the church is referred to as transhistorical, spanning from the Old Testament era until the present, comprised of all those who have placed their faith in the revealed God.[83] The Old Testament situation differs from that of the New in that since Pentecost the church is a concrete and universal community, the proper environment for the nurture of faith, and the way to salvation.[84] Second, the church is the 'body of Christ', a gathering of renewed persons into communion with Christ. The body is constituted whenever persons freely assent to be the body of Christ by serving God, one another and the kingdom.[85] Furthermore, the church is so intimately united with Christ that it really becomes his body on earth, comprising together the '*totus Christus*' (the whole Christ), the expression of the fullness of his humanity – although remaining a fully human entity itself.[86] Third, the church is made up of the people, but people are united to Christ and one another only by the Holy Spirit. Fourth, the church is a mixed body, consisting of true and false believers as well as believers who operate from sometimes pure, sometimes impure motives. Augustine is quite realistic about the church. He acknowledges that the church exists between the times, but also recognizes that it is oriented towards its perfection.[87] It is in the process of growing from a mixed body to the perfect body of Christ. The true church, in one sense, is purely an eschatological reality. A more adequate reading of Augustine, therefore, is that the distinction between the visible (the oncrete community of believers) and invisible (the hierarchy, institution or underlying reality) church is not necessarily *ontological*, but rather, *eschatological*. It is not that the being of the church is anterior to the concrete historical relationships of the visible community, but that the true and mixed historical church is on its way to becoming the pure church, with false 'members' excised and true members glorified. The whole community is called to be the church, but really it is only those who are for God and one another that constitute the church.[88] This more charitable reading of Augustine gives one pause when considering Gunton's set-up. Furthermore, the New Testament speaks of an invisible and eschatological assembly – the church of the firstborn whose names are written in heaven, those who presently partake in the worship of the New Jerusalem (Heb. 12:22–24). Indeed the author of Hebrews, at various points, hints at this eschatological dimension of the invisible church: we share in Christ now, *if* we continue to hold on to the truth of the gospel till the end (e.g. Heb. 3:14). Put differently, we are the true church if we demonstrate ourselves to be so in the end. Thus, the invisible church is an eschatological reality known only to God. Moreover, in Colossians 1:18 and throughout Ephesians, Paul speaks of the *ekklēsia* as a heavenly and eschatological reality. The church is the assembly of all those who are currently seated in the heavenly realms in Christ Jesus (Eph. 2:5–6), over which the cosmic Christ is head (1:22–23; Col. 1:18).[89] The point here is that talk of an invisible church need not be rooted in a blind acceptance of Platonic dualism, but rather can find resources in the biblical material. In the light of Scripture, Gunton's critique of Western ecclesiologies, at the very least, requires some nuance.

A second question has to do, as at the end of Chapter 2, with terminology: are 'communion' and 'community' interchangeable terms, as they appear to be for Gunton?[90] Whether due to imprecision or intentionality, Gunton does not preserve what seems an important distinction. Community commonly carries with it individualistic notions of the persons, in which individuals with their own wills and self-consciousness join together to form a society of sorts. This conception is absent in the works of at least one Cappadocian, Gregory of Nyssa, who, for example, speaks of the 'communion' (*koinōnia*, sometimes rendered as 'community') of persons and 'communion of substance' as a way of emphasizing the *unity* of the divine nature – particularly in the light of contemporary controversies.[91] The latter phrase, 'communion of substance', should immediately alert us to the fact that the divine *ousia* is distinct from and not reduced to *koinōnia*. Rather, *ousia* is the source of unity, that which is common to all three persons of the Godhead.[92] Moreover, not only does Gregory not begin with persons or prioritize persons over substance (*contra* Gunton), but when he does refer to persons (*hypostasis* or *prosopon*) it is a severely limited term without individualistic overtones.[93] For him the term 'communion' serves to maintain the mystery of union and distinction in the Godhead. Therefore, as helpful as the existence of 'community' in/as the being of God might be for expounding an alternative ecclesiology, it may be, once again, in danger of reading too much creaturely reality back into the Trinity.

Earlier we mentioned briefly what was called Gunton's ecclesiological occasionalism. Colwell, in a wonderful treatment of Gunton's ecclesiology, observes this tendency in several of Gunton's forays into the doctrine of the church. Repeatedly Gunton remarks that the church comes into being, or becomes an echo of its eschatological reality, through its participation in word and sacrament, but only by the work of the Spirit. This action of the Spirit is unpredictable; it cannot be presumed upon, but happens 'from time to time' – to borrow a phrase used regularly by Gunton.[94] Therefore, the church cannot presume at any time to be the church, if the transcendence and freedom of the Spirit are to be maintained. But Colwell asks whether this occasionalist account of the Spirit's presence and work 'displaces presumption but at the price of uncertainty and caprice'.[95] One of Gunton's concerns, remember, was to prevent too close an identification of human, churchly acts with the action of the Spirit. This concern is expressed in his discussion of Christ's presence at the Eucharist. According to Gunton, we cannot presume that Christ will be present at the celebration of the meal since his presence is mediated by the free Spirit. However, it can be asked whether this perspective mutes the promise of Christ that he will be there when the church gathers. 'Divine promise,' Colwell writes, 'can be the basis of a humble assurance of faith without succumbing to presumption and manipulation.' He goes on: 'This does not mean that Christ's mediated presence in and through the Eucharist is immediate and automatic; instead it is a being-given presence, mediated afresh by the Spirit, a mediated presence that can be anticipated and trusted – though never manipulated – since it is a *promised presence*.'[96]

The point is that the presence of Christ and the work of the Spirit, which are constitutive of the church, can be expected in the human act of worship – in this case, the Eucharist – because they are promised. Therefore, we need not place divine and human action, church 'constitution' and 'institution', in opposition, as Gunton seems to do, in order to make space for the Spirit's sovereign activity.

What emerges from Gunton's attempt to bring together the doctrines of the Trinity and the church is a portrait of the church as a communion – persons-in-relation – shaped by the Spirit according to the pattern of Christ's humanity and the triune relations. The church is an *imperfect* and *incomplete* sign of the present and coming kingdom of God; it is a Spirit-endowed *human* reality. It is with these eyes – those able to view the present state of the church in the light of its appointed *telos* – that we are to relate to the body of Christ. Though a human reality, the church, in its act and being, is an anticipation of the new creation, when all relationships will be reconciled and restored, indeed perfected. In the following chapter, we will extend our discussion of the *eschaton* and the agent of the *eschaton*, the perfecting Spirit.

8

Perfecting Cause and Perfected End: The Spirit and Last Things

The challenge of writing a separate treatment of the Spirit in Gunton's work is a challenge endemic to every good systematic theology, namely, the close interweaving of doctrinal loci and the resulting difficulty of isolating one feature from another. Nevertheless, it is noticeable that, unlike with other doctrines, Gunton himself does not treat the Spirit separately in his only systematic summary of Christian doctrine, *The Christian Faith* (though, admittedly, this may be due to his contention that the Spirit is 'self-effacing', as we will see). The act and being of the Holy Spirit became an increasingly pervasive theme in Gunton's work, perhaps beginning in his early forays into Christology and maturing in his later work on the doctrine of creation. Whatever the case, it would become clear to him that many deficiencies in Western theology can be traced to foundational weaknesses in pneumatology. A failure to delineate the nature and works of the Spirit inevitably leads to a misconstruing of the way and being of God, since the Spirit is the second 'hand' of the Father who mediates all his works in the created order. The aim of this chapter is to fill out the picture of the Spirit sketched in earlier chapters (on God, creation and Christ, for example) and to offer a rough outline of the features of Gunton's eschatology. The Spirit is the eschatological member of the Trinity, the one who brings all God's works to their perfected end and, as such, is the agent of the *eschaton* and the primary subject matter of eschatology. Talk of the Spirit inevitably converges with talk of eschatology. Thus, these two final loci will be treated together, beginning with the doctrine of the Spirit.

Problems in Pneumatology

The doctrine of the Spirit has been a problematic feature of (especially) Western thought. While Gunton does acknowledge some weaknesses in the Eastern Trinitarian tradition, he maintains that pneumatology in the West is more problematic, displaying at least four characteristic weaknesses: (1) the failure to identify the particular works of the Spirit, or to distinguish between the Son and Spirit; (2) the immanentizing of all the works of the Spirit; (3) the effective subordination of the Spirit to the Son; and, ultimately, (4) the failure to recognize the transcendence, freedom and eschatological orientation of the Spirit.[1] As is to be expected, these problems find their root chiefly in Augustine.

The first pneumatological weakness derives from Augustine's failure to distinguish the actions of the persons of the Godhead. Gunton quotes Robert Jenson approvingly: 'For Augustine, the three "persons," over against us, are functionally indistinguishable. Thus Augustine could no longer conceptualize the saving relation between God and creatures by saying that the Father and Son are transformingly present in the Spirit, as the Greek originators of trinitarianism had done.'[2] While Gunton does maintain that a tension must be preserved between the unity of God's triune action and distinctions in the actions of the persons, he contends that too strong a principle of inseparable operations (*opera trinitatis ad extra indivisa sunt*) has rendered it difficult to say anything about the Spirit's distinct action in the economy, and thus about his distinct being.[3]

This Augustinian weakness contributed to the second tendency stated above. By failing to identify the distinct actions of the Spirit, the temptation was to define the undefined in whatever way comports with contemporary sentiments. Thus, the Spirit's work came to be identified as a process or force, immanent in the individual, church, or some other institution. Gunton offers three examples of this immanentizing tendency in modern thought.[4] First, Barth is charged with being overly traditional in his treatment of the Spirit. Like the Reformers before him, he tends to limit the Spirit's work to the application of the benefits of Christ to the believer. Since the Spirit's act reflects his being, Gunton concludes: 'Because the function is defined so narrowly – almost wholly christologically – such a move maintains an effective *ontological* subordination of Spirit to Son and militates against an identification of the Spirit's specific *persona*.'[5] Second, he accuses the modern charismatic movement of the opposite error, namely, separating the work of the Spirit from the Son. In this case the Spirit is seen as the (at times) impersonal cause of religious experiences such as speaking in tongues, healing and conversion, in a manner divorced from Christ and his work.[6] Third, the influence of Hegel on modern thought has led to the tendency to identify the Spirit as the force that operates within the created order or human culture to bring about certain historical and cultural developments. The Spirit is the *Geist*, which is largely indistinguishable from the present order of things. While these three treatments of the Spirit differ materially, they share a common tendency: they each internalize the action of the Spirit – for the first two within the human person, the latter within creation or culture.[7] All these are failures to account adequately for the Spirit's relation to the Son, to creation and to humanity. In short, these are failures to identify the particular personhood and action of the Spirit.

The root of these modern Western shortcomings is Augustine's doctrine of the Spirit in *De Trinitate*. The first problem arises from Augustine's identification of the Spirit as love and gift. While not entirely unjustified, it is not apparent that the Spirit is any more the love and gift of God than the Son (whom God 'gave' to the world). Thus, these forms of identification do not adequately distinguish the Spirit from the other persons of the Trinity. Furthermore, there is little scriptural warrant for such an identification of the Spirit. What results, according to Gunton, is a muting of other salient features of the Spirit's work found in Scripture. Augustine's 'speculative drive' creates a separation between what the Spirit is in eternity (i.e. love and gift) and what Scripture shows him to be in the economy of creation and salvation (as we will discuss later).[8] The second problem in Augustine derives from his use of the psychological analogy of the immanent

Trinity. In this schema, the Spirit is the will whose function is to bring the contents of the memory (the Son) to the understanding (the Father). Thus, the Spirit's function within the Godhead is chiefly to unite the Father and Son as the bond between two persons. As in the case of the concepts of love and gift, this identification of the Spirit neglects other features of the Spirit's operations. Gunton concludes that the deployment of these concepts led to the characteristic weaknesses of Western pneumatology described above. If the Spirit is simply the unitive love of Father and Son, he will be effectively subordinated to the Son (the third weakness mentioned at the outset of our discussion). If the Spirit is likened to the will, the tendency will be (and was) to view the mind as the location of the Spirit's work – whether the human mind or the mind of the universe – and thus to internalize or immanentize the Spirit (the second weakness, detailed above).[9] What these tendencies amount to, according to Gunton, is a failure to recognize the true otherness, transcendence and freedom of the Spirit – common features in Scripture's testimony to the Spirit's work in the economy, as we will see.

The Spirit in the Economy

A discussion of the Spirit's work in the economy will focus on at least two areas: (1) creation and incarnation, and (2) the church.

Creation and incarnation

With few exceptions, a typical weakness of the tradition is that it did not connect the Holy Spirit to the work of creation in any meaningful way, preferring to focus on the Spirit's work in fostering piety.[10] However, in the opening words of Scripture we find the Spirit of God in creation, 'hovering' over the chaos (Gen. 1:2). The presence of chaos signals that the work of creation is unfinished (a theme that is picked up in Genesis 1:28 with the commissioning of humanity to 'subdue' the earth and the reality of a garden in chapter 2). Whatever is understood by the Spirit's 'hovering', this appears to be an indication that the Spirit will be involved in making the world what it was created to be, in perfecting it. Psalm 33:6 places the Word and Spirit together, as God's 'agents' of creation. Psalm 104:29b–30 attributes creation and the sustaining of creation to God's Spirit. In Ezekiel 37, the Spirit is the agent of eschatological renewal, bringing the dead to life. Thus the Spirit's action as it relates to creation is at least twofold: to maintain creation and to perfect and renew it.[11] The Cappadocian notion to which Gunton often appeals, namely, that the Spirit is the 'perfecting cause', finds its warrant in passages like these, which also provide the building blocks for a doctrine of *Spiritus Creator*.

A full doctrine of the Spirit in creation, however, must take on board two further dogmatic points. First, it must be connected explicitly to Jesus Christ and, therefore, human redemption. Gunton argues:

> This is needed to save us from the kind of pneumatology of creation that attributes to the natural order itself either some intrinsic significance apart from those who have been granted dominion over it or some power to save itself apart from the incarnation. The word spoken in the beginning is, after all, the Word who became man first for human salvation and only after that for the reconciliation of all things.[12]

This connection between human salvation and the renewal of creation is the point of Romans 8:19–23, where we are told the creation eagerly awaits the full redemption of the children of God (we will return to the question of the Spirit's work in the human sphere later). Second, one must ever keep in mind that the Spirit's action in creation is inseparable from the work of the Father and Son. Upholding this truth prevents us from 'making the Spirit a kind of individual agent in relation to the created order'.[13]

Gunton brings these biblical and dogmatic strands together in proposing three points of focus for a christologically oriented doctrine of the Spirit's role in creation, derived mainly from the gospels. The first has to do with the incarnation. The opening chapters of Luke are in continuity with the Old Testament tradition (discussed earlier) regarding the Spirit. Here the Spirit acts transcendently to bring forth life in the womb of Mary and forms Jesus to be the particular kind of human being he will be for the sake of the world. The incarnation represents a particular use of the created order by God to form this man, which implies for Gunton a reaffirmation of humanity as the climax of God's creative acts. Only by the Spirit's formation of a man, *this* man, will the relative chaos of the cosmos be subdued. 'Where the Spirit is,' he writes, 'there is the end breaking into the present with the renewal of life signalled and begun by the conception of this particular child.'[14] The Spirit's renewal and perfection of the created order begins in the womb of Mary.

The second point has to do with the saving work of Christ. The insight from our earlier chapter on Christology, that it was by the Spirit that Christ did the will of the Father, must be advanced and applied to the present task. If in the gospels sickness and disease, demons and life-threatening storms represent the slavery of the created order to inimical forces – powers that prevent it from becoming what it is meant to be – then the healings and exorcisms performed by Jesus serve to redirect and reorder creation, as harbingers of the eschatological perfection of the cosmos and its freedom from the 'bondage to decay'. Now, the gospels are clear that these works were performed in the power of the Spirit, so that we are able to say that the Spirit is once again the agent of creation's perfection, working in concert with and through the ministry of the Son. Gunton concludes: 'We must say that through his Son and Spirit, his two hands, the Father both prevents the creation from slipping back into the nothingness from which it came and restores its teleology, its movement to perfection.'[15]

Following from this, the third focus of a christologically oriented account of the Spirit's work in creation centres on the resurrection of Jesus. Romans 8:11 speaks of the Spirit as the Father's agent of Christ's resurrected life. The same Spirit that gave life to the first Adam gives new life to the second Adam. It is in the resurrection of Christ that we see the firstfruits of the new creation – both continuous and discontinuous with the old.[16] Again, it is the Spirit who takes creation to its appointed destiny: resurrection life. The repeated theme emerging from these three points of focus is that the Spirit is the sustainer and, especially, perfecter of the created order, he who freely directs creation to its appointed *telos* chiefly through the ministry of Jesus the Son. This is his primary work in the economy of space and time.

Applying these insights specifically to the human creature, Gunton contends that the Spirit's primary function is to liberate people to be themselves, to live out their calling as human beings. Gunton holds that 'to be free is to live according to the law of one's being'. Contrary to some modern views of freedom that see it as individual autonomy, to be wrested from some external authority and wielded for one's own purposes, he views this freedom as a gift to be received and not something to be grasped at. From where does this gift come? It is from the Spirit of the Lord that we experience liberty (2 Cor. 3:17). How the Spirit relates to human freedom is, however, a tricky matter. Gunton writes: 'The dispute within theology about freedom is at bottom a dispute about who the Spirit is and how he operates.'[17] As mentioned earlier, one of the problems in modern Western pneumatology is its inclination to conceive of the Spirit as something immanent, the possession of an institution or individual, rather than as a free, infinite, transcendent and divine other. The conception of God as immanent leads not to our liberation, but our enslavement. Gunton observes: 'The closer the world is tied up with the immanence of God, the more it loses its otherness and therefore its autonomy and freedom to be itself.'[18] Now, as we saw in a previous chapter, all personhood – divine and human – is constituted or given in relation to others. If freedom is to live fully according to one's being – to be fully human, so to speak – then freedom comes only in community; and since human community is comprised of fallen and finite creatures, freedom to be with and for one another must be received repeatedly as a gift; it is not intrinsic to, nor a possession of, human beings as such. As a free and transcendent Other, the Spirit is able to constitute our being as persons and free us to be what we are meant to be, particularly towards other people.[19] This argument is grounded, once again, in the relation of the Spirit to the incarnate Son. Gunton begins: 'It was only in virtue of his relation to this other that Jesus realised his divine and human calling.' He elaborates:

> The Spirit's activity in freeing Jesus to be himself – as is instanced in the temptation narratives – provides a model for human liberation in general. Jesus' particular calling was to be one kind of Messiah rather than another: to be in certain definite relationship to the people of Israel, and so ultimately to the whole of humanity. Human freedom, so far as we can speak of it in general, is that which enables people to be constituted as *particular* persons in free and social relationships.[20]

This is what Gunton often refers to as the *particularizing* role of the Spirit: the establishment and freeing up of persons to be what they are meant to be in particular. As the Spirit enabled Jesus to be a particular kind of person within a particular set of relationships to fulfil a particular calling, so the Spirit liberates us to fulfil our human callings within the context of mutually constitutive relations with others. 'Freedom is freedom,' he writes, 'when it is received as a gift, from God and from each other.' And it is only by the Spirit, 'the Father's liberating otherness', that the perfection of the age to come is realized in the present – not in autonomy, but in free relationships with others.[21]

Church and worship

Talk of community and relatedness no doubt leads to the question of the Spirit's action in and with the church. Since some of this ground was covered in an earlier chapter, brief comments will be limited to three areas. First, the Spirit's liberating action within the church takes an additional form to that expressed above regarding human community generally. Here Gunton again draws attention to the particularizing action of the Spirit, observing that each person in the church is able to be what they are called to be for others only as the Spirit grants particular *charismata* to each person. The gifts of the Spirit are given to strengthen the church community in its worship, common life and mission, which function as anticipations of the eschatological right ordering of all relationships.[22] The Spirit's work is to free the church to grow into adulthood by enabling each part to do its particular work (Eph. 4:16).

Second, in a sermon on John 15:26, Gunton offers several ministries of the Spirit to the church: (1) the Spirit is the one who brings the presence of the risen Christ to the church after the ascension of the Lord. It is only by the Spirit that the One who is physically absent is made real to us; (2) the Spirit, as Paraclete, comes alongside the church, strengthening it to live out its calling; (3) the Spirit leads us to the truth that is Jesus Christ and, through him, eschatological life; (4) by the Spirit we are enabled to worship the Father through Christ. Gunton writes: 'We have what can be called a descending and ascending movement: the Spirit comes from the Father, through Jesus, so that we can ascend to God the Father, also through him.' The overall point of these reflections is that worship is a gift of the Spirit who enables sinful creatures, through Christ, to do what would otherwise be impossible.[23]

Third, this renewed and perfected worship takes shape in the context of the community gathered around Jesus, paradigmatically so in the celebration of the Lord's Supper. The Lord's absence occasions the sending of the Spirit, who brings this community together to remember Christ ('Do this in remembrance of me'), proclaim his death that establishes the covenantal bond between the Father and the church ('this blood is the new covenant'), and all this in anticipation of the perfection of all things in the *eschaton* ('until he comes'). What is noteworthy for Gunton is that in the bread and wine used in the Lord's Supper we see a glimpse of full redemption in Christ – not just people, but natural, even manufactured, realities. He writes: 'In offering worship through a Christ so represented, the Church offers not only itself as a "living sacrifice, holy and acceptable to God" (Rom 12:1–2 ESV) but also the whole created order, in anticipation of its final perfecting when all things are "brought to a head in Christ."'[24]

It is the role of the eschatological Spirit to perfect the church's worship and use it as a vehicle and sign of the perfection of all created things through the risen and ascended Lord.

The Eternal Spirit

In moving to an account of the Spirit in the immanent Trinity, a basic methodological principle must be observed: the operations of the Spirit in the economy form the basis of any account of his eternal personhood and being. We do not leave behind what we have just discussed, but rather must take it up fully in our treatment of the eternal Spirit. Indeed, the chief problem of Western accounts of the Spirit in the immanent Trinity is this neglect of the Spirit's work in creation and redemption. For example, Augustine's view of the Spirit as a link between the Father and Son is derived from Platonic categories rather than economic ones. What results is a picture of the Spirit as 'a link in an inward-turned circle', or as that which completes the intra-Trinitarian self-love, rather than as he who frees people to move outward towards others (as we saw briefly above).[25] In effect, what Augustine was attempting to do is speak to the distinct personhood of the Spirit, which can be both commendable and problematic: commendable because there are three distinct hypostases; problematic because there ever lurks the danger of tritheism – an overemphasis on difference and distinction within the Godhead.[26] How then are we to speak of the distinct personhood of the Spirit?

The tradition of distinguishing between the Son and Spirit in terms of begottenness and procession, though apparently uninformative on the surface, is helpful for understanding the relationships within the Godhead. Gunton remarks:

> The advantage of maintaining the defining distinction to be between begotten and proceeding is that it enables us to denote a difference between a person conceived in terms of a genetic metaphor and one conceived to subsist in a distinctively different pattern of relationships. In such a

way we are able to locate conceptually but apophatically the fact that there is an immanent distinction corresponding to the distinction in the economy.[27]

What becomes important is allowing the economy of creation and salvation to shape our account of the Spirit's eternal personhood, rather than some generic and philosophical notion of love or gift. However, when notions of the Spirit's transcendence, freedom and perfecting agency in the economy are taken on board, an account of the Spirit as love might indeed be salvaged, even rendered useful as a further specification of his eternal procession. Gunton borrows from Richard of St Victor's insight that divine love cannot be contained within the relationship of Father and Son – as the closed-off and merely reciprocal love between two parties – but must be oriented to community. That being the case, the role of the Spirit within the Trinity is to perfect the love of Father and Son by moving that love outward. He writes: 'Corresponding to the eschatological movement of the Spirit *ad extra* there is within the divine eternity one who perfects the love of God as love in community. To be God is to be intrinsically related to the other in communion, and the Spirit is the one who enables this communion to be.'[28] This is a revised version of the Augustinian depiction of the Spirit, but one that is shaped by an account of the Spirit as God's eschatological otherness. As the one who perfects creation by bringing creatures into right relations among themselves and with their Creator – primarily by freeing persons to love others – the Spirit also perfects the love of the Godhead by not only being the bond of love between the Father and Son, but also opening that love towards that which is not God.[29] To the Spirit's eschatological movement *ad extra*, there is a corresponding movement *ad intra*: the Spirit liberates all things to be in a community that embraces the other. The Spirit's work in the Godhead becomes the basis for his (and the whole Godhead's) work in the world.

Perhaps, before moving on, I might insert a few comments about Gunton's treatment of the *filioque*. As has been hinted elsewhere in this volume, Gunton is quite critical of this development in Western theology. Three dangers in particular lurk with the affirmation of the *filioque*. First, if the Spirit proceeds from the Father and Son, there is a tendency to subordinate the Spirit to the Son and therefore 'reduce him to the margins'. All the Spirit does in this configuration is apply the benefits of Christ's work to the church or individual.[30] The corresponding weakness, second, is to underplay the full humanity of Jesus. As discussed in the earlier chapter on Christology, an emphasis on the Spirit's empowerment of Jesus' life and ministry, rather than one on the eternal Word, enables us to do better justice to the humanity of the Son. A lack of such an emphasis has only done damage to Christology. Finally, the spectre of modalism surrounds the doctrine of dual procession. Gunton puts the matter this way:

> If the Father is the one from whom the Son is begotten – in the Spirit – and from whom the Spirit proceeds – indeed, through the Son – our enquiries come to an end. There is a final, if mysterious, explanation for the way things are. But suppose that the Spirit does come from the Father *and* the Son. Can we avoid at least toying with the question of the reality which gives the Father and the Son their underlying unity? In other words, a double procession is an invitation to seek a deeper cause than the Trinity, and thus a modalism, even though it may not necessitate it, because while there remain two apparently ultimate principles, however unified in communion, discontented minds will seek that which underlies them.[31]

The solution for Gunton is to see the Father as the underlying source of unity, processions and missions within the Godhead.[32] This is at least one way of avoiding the potential modalism that impairs Western Trinitarianism.

Returning to the issue of the Spirit's distinct personhood, it could be noted, admittedly, that even Gunton's revised Augustinian account still gives us too little by way of information about the Spirit. However, he asserts that we must be apophatic to the degree that the

Scriptures compel us to be so. Gunton notes repeatedly that the Spirit has a 'self-effacing' or 'humble' character, pointing away from, rather than towards, himself.[33] Drawing on John's gospel, he observes that the humility of the Spirit can be seen in at least three ways: (1) by not teaching about himself, or on his own authority (John 16:13); (2) by bringing people to the truth that is Christ himself (16:13); and (3) glorifying Jesus rather than himself (16:14). In these ways, the Spirit effaces himself to point to the Jesus who brings us to the Father.[34] It is thus his distinct personhood to direct us to others and not himself, and in doing so leave us with minimal content regarding his distinctive character. However, in the end, according to Gunton, the Spirit may be identified as the distinct Other who proceeds from the Father (not the Son), and perfects the Father's relationship to the Son and to the world.

The End of All Things

Talk of the Spirit as the perfecting cause leads us naturally to consider that perfection to which the Spirit brings the created order. While eschatology is normally understood as the study of last things, Gunton is careful to distinguish between eschatology and futurology. The former is certainly concerned with the future, yet it is not limited to it. The end – the *eschaton* – breaks into present time, which, as we saw, is a chief work of the Spirit. Therefore, the study of eschatology must reckon with present as well as future realities.[35] Put another way, the 'end' to which the Spirit leads creation must be conceived both chronologically and teleologically. The Spirit is indeed sustaining, bearing and directing creation to a particular end date, so to speak. Yet this guiding activity, as we saw, has a particular *telos* – perfection in Christ. It is the teleological element of the 'end' that is brought forward chronologically by the Spirit, so that we experience the 'end times' in the present. With these qualifications in place, we can turn to Gunton's albeit brief formal treatment of eschatology, which centres on three issues: death, resurrection and judgement.

Death

Death is not identical to mortality, the latter referring simply to the limits of creatureliness. Rather, death represents 'the meaninglessness and failure that dogs all human life'.[36] It is 'to have no sense of time'.[37] Gunton is careful to emphasize the materiality of human life, so that once the breath of life is taken away from the body we are truly dead – 'food for the worms or carrion birds', as he puts it. Christians should adopt a more 'Hebraic' and thus biblical view of the human person, in which we are a whole rather than the conjunction of soul and body. In that light, death is conceived as the end. For Gunton, there appears to be no intermediate state – at least that is not Scripture's main line. Rather, he writes: 'For Scripture, death is not the escape of the soul upwards to heaven; it is a state in which the body decays in expectation of its renewal and resurrection in the life of the age to come.'[38] There is universal recognition that all creatures will die. Even secular ecological 'prophets' who speak of the looming end of the earth demonstrate this awareness that death is the lot of all things creaturely. The failure of such prophets, and most modern views of death, according to Gunton, is that they either take death too seriously or do not take it seriously enough. On the one hand, death is indeed final; it is the returning to dust of the human creature and the virtual dissolution of all else – a serious matter indeed. On the other hand, the seriousness of death is not felt fully unless one views it in the light of the resurrection. Gunton writes:

> There is no resurrection without death, which is also of eschatological significance because it represents the end of life, of relation to God and the other, and therefore the extinction of hope. If we recall once again the essentially embodied nature of our being human, we shall continue to bear in mind that our bodies come from and will return to the dust of the earth, and can be rescued thence only by a wholly eschatological act.[39]

It is only in the light of the need for eschatological transformation that we see clearly the radical nature of death. Death is not something to be taken lightly, nor can it be avoided; naïve optimism on this front only engenders what Gunton calls 'cheap hope'. Yet, since the reign of death is something that will ultimately be overcome, it must be encountered with the seriousness one gives a soon-to-be defeated enemy.[40] It will not have the final say, but since it necessitates that climactic eschatological event – the resurrection – it must be treated with gravitas as a critical aspect of any discussion of eschatology.

Resurrection

The resurrection is God's 'transforming completion' of embodied human life. Gunton contends that a proper account of the resurrection should include three features. First, it must be distinguished from doctrines of the immortality of the soul because the latter's stress on the immaterial, immortal soul leads it to overlook the reality that it is the whole human person that God aims to perfect. 'The doctrine of the resurrection,' he writes, 'is not first of all about immortality, but about God's purposes for his creation, and especially his human creation.' This is a repeated theme in Gunton, namely, that eschatological redemption is not summed up in immortality. Eschatology – and in this case, the resurrection – is about teleology: the Spirit is carrying human persons and all creation to their appointed end, their *telos*. Second, the perfection of humanity occurs only through a radical transformation, so that there will be both a continuity and discontinuity with our present physical existence.[41] The risen Christ provides the paradigm. In bodily form he appeared to Paul on the Damascus road, to the disciples on the road to Emmaus, ate with his disciples, but was also able to appear and disappear mysteriously. Gunton concludes: 'He clearly had a body, but one that God had transformed, raised into the conditions of the life to come.'[42] Finally, and this must be emphasized, the resurrection of Jesus involves all of the creation, which now is in 'its bondage to decay' (Rom. 8:21). By the rest of creation we mean not just non-personal creatures themselves, but time and history themselves, extending even to all churchly, social and political structures. The resurrection is the firstfruits and harbinger of 'universal 'salvation', when all of creation will be brought into the glorious liberty of the children of God by the Spirit of God.[43]

Judgement

According to Gunton, our understanding of final judgement has everything to do with how we conceive of divine justice. Justice can only be understood rightly when viewed in the light of the work of Christ, which is prefigured in God's dealings with Abraham and Israel. As we saw in an earlier chapter, the judgement enacted and the justice displayed on the cross sets to right God's creation. In that light, judgement must be portrayed positively, even if there is to be some measure of a dialectic of exclusion and inclusion, destruction and salvation, inherent in a responsible treatment of judgement. That being said, Gunton raises three 'problems' regarding divine justice as it pertains to final judgement. The first arises from the story of Abraham's plea for the city of Sodom (Gen. 18). Here, Gunton observes, the underlying assumption is that it would be *wrong* for God to destroy the unrighteous city if a 'representative number' of righteous people could be found within it. Put differently, 'God has failed if he has to impose retributive punishment . . . To do justice is not to punish offenders but in some way to allow them to be treated mercifully through the good offices of the just.'[44] Divine justice, and therefore judgement, has to do with overcoming evil rather than punishing wrongdoers, with restoration rather than retribution.[45] The second 'problem' concerns another scriptural plea, this time from the martyrs: 'How long, Sovereign Lord . . . until you . . . avenge our blood?' (Rev. 6:10). Although the writer does not explicitly approve of the plea for vengeance, according to Gunton, the oppressed saints do need to be granted some form of justice if God and the cosmos are to be described as just.[46] The third problem arises from the fact that the one who judges is also the one who saves. Jesus bore the judgement of God for humanity, and this indicates that whatever judgement believers endure has to do with their correction and cleansing, not their condemnation.

What about unbelievers? The story of Abraham and Sodom suggests that God's purpose is for universal salvation through the representatively righteous. Two important questions emerge. First, in what sense does the judgement on Jesus have universal relevance? God was certainly reconciling the world to himself in Christ (2 Cor. 5:19), but this reconciliation is yet to be actualized. One of the fundamental weaknesses of Barth's treatment of universal reconciliation is that he locates it in the 'already' rather than the 'not yet'. Gunton writes: 'Jesus does indeed do something for the whole human race; but the *perfecting* of that *complete* work continues to depend on its realization in time by the work of the Spirit who brings particular people into the community of the reconciled. Reconciliation is thus universal in intent, but not yet fully realized.'[47] Christ has fully borne God's judgement and completed humanity's redemption, but this work will be perfected in the future. Second, will everyone be saved ultimately? On this point Gunton is uncommitted.[48] His tendency is to present God's dealings with humanity in the brightest of hues. Therefore, as we have seen, if judgement means the destruction of the sinner, then it represents a 'divine failure'. Yet, he notes, we cannot ignore that Scripture maintains to the end (Rev. 20 – 22) the possibility that some could become so hard-hearted as to exclude themselves from the kingdom of God. That is not the overriding emphasis of Scripture, however. 'God's justice is to be seen,' he writes, 'in the fact that the old law of punishment does not have the last word, but rather that everything possible is done to see that all are given a way to share the goodness of God . . . God's justice *means* God seeing to it that all are called to share his mercies.'[49] This potential universalism does not necessarily undermine human freedom once we allow that all who are raised from the dead – good *and* evil – will be transformed in mind, body and will, so that none will be brought to the kingdom 'kicking and screaming'.[50] In the end, all by God's grace may freely will to be in the kingdom. God will demonstrate his justice by not allowing anyone created in his image to remain unperfected, thrown into the 'rubbish dump' of history.[51] 'The end,' he concludes, 'is life, whatever form of life that entails.'[52] Thus Christian eschatology is positive: death, resurrection and judgement conspire, through the working of the eschatological Spirit, to bring creatures to their perfected end. This is good news indeed.

Conclusion

The failure of much Western pneumatology is in its refusal to allow the economy of creation and redemption to sufficiently inform its understanding of the being and act of the Spirit. Gunton's insistence that there be a closer correspondence between the immanent and economic Trinity is of a piece with his criticisms of the likes of Augustine. If the economy does not decisively shape our pneumatology, undoubtedly something else will – something sub-Christian. When we look at the Spirit's actions, we find that his unique work is to perfect all things within the Godhead and in the created order. Undoubtedly Gunton's suggestion that the Spirit is the agent of the Son's eternal begottenness will raise some eyebrows, not least because of its speculative feel. For Gunton, the Spirit is not merely the love between Father and Son, but rather the one who perfects the love between the two. Paul Cumin, commenting on the logic of Gunton's view, observes: 'Without such an agent in the Trinity, God would be an immediate duad of Father and Son, and – with a nod to Coleridge – we can suggest that for Gunton such a thing would be ontologically nothing more than a homogeneous monotheos.'[53] This may be too bold an attempt to discern the *how* of the Godhead rather than remaining content with the *that*, namely, the mystery of God's tri-personality.[54] It may further be asked whether this configuration of intra-Trinitarian relations does much to highlight the distinct personhood of the Spirit. The Spirit perfects the loving relation of Father and Son, but seems external to that relation. Is the Spirit himself loved? One might also wonder if the problem we faced regarding the

Son's lack of agency in the economy is now brought into the inner life of God. The Father through the Spirit begets, and the Spirit perfects the mutual love of Father and Son. But what of the Son? Is he merely – for lack of a better term – passive? Is the second 'hand' of the Father too strong as to diminish the first hand?[55]

Pneumatology and eschatology converge precisely because the Spirit is the eschatological member of the Trinity. It is in the latter locus that another concern – an important one – arises from Gunton's treatment: the question of universalism. Since there is a whole history of literature speaking to the doctrine of universalism, I will only offer a couple of questions regarding Gunton's account. Justice, according to Gunton, has to do with restoration *rather than* retribution, inasmuch – it seems – as sin has more to do with the disordering of relationships than with lawbreaking. God's judgement has ultimately to do with the restoration of order to the cosmos. One has to wonder if this is not too reductive an account of sin, justice and judgement. Certainly judgement has something to do with restoration, but at the expense of retribution? Herman Bavinck writes:

> In order to appreciate the fact of eternal punishment, it is above all necessary, therefore, to recognize along with Scripture the integrity of the justice of God and the deeply sinful character of sin. Sin is not a weakness, a lack, a temporary and gradually vanishing imperfection, but in origin and essence it is lawlessness (*anomia*), a violation of the law, rebellion and hostility against God, and the negation of his justice, his authority, even his existence.[56]

Sin, he goes on to say, is to be measured by its intrinsic quality – as rebellion against the authority of God. Just as a crime committed in a fit of rage can lead to the death penalty or a lifetime of shame, so a crime against the majesty of God is justly punished with an eternity of shame. As most of the Christian tradition has affirmed, justice brings with it severe punishment for sin, not just restoration from it, and this is an affirmation of God's goodness rather than an affront to it. One wonders if Gunton's view of judgement is too controlled by an overly determined understanding of what creation's perfection might involve, and not enough by Scripture's depiction of sin as lawbreaking and justice as punishment. Related, then, is the question of whether reconciliation/perfection necessarily entails universal salvation. Since for Gunton creation is a project that has the goal of eschatological perfection, taking the form of a proper relatedness to God and all creatures, it is inconceivable that anything created would not fulfil its end by the work of the Spirit. However, one could fault Gunton for claiming to know too much about the *telos* of creation in the particulars. In this case, does perfection necessarily denote reconciliation in terms of union with God? Has God's creation project and indeed his judgement failed if he fails to bring all into saving union with himself? Clearly most of the tradition has not thought so. It seems that a stance of reverent ignorance regarding some of the details of creation on the front and back end, protologically and eschatologically, is advisable. Although Gunton might overreach in his account of final judgement, it is the very instinct to more closely integrate pneumatology with creation and creation with eschatology that is most promising. In the resurrection and even final judgement, the Spirit will complete the restoration and reconciliation of creation to its Maker, thus bringing creation to its perfected end.

9

A Concluding Commendation

The aim of this book was to provide a synopsis and modest synthesis of Colin Gunton's theology. Along the way, I presented some questions and criticisms posed to various aspects of Gunton's thought to alert readers to potential problems, tensions and unresolved issues in the work of this stimulating theologian. I recently stumbled upon a blog article written by theologian Mark Thompson that had as its title the provocative question: 'Has Colin Gunton's Theological Project Really Failed?' In the article he is responding to Bernhard Nausner's article (cited at various points in this book)[1] that deemed Gunton's project, though laudable, a failure, largely because of its misconstrual of Trinitarian language and its misapplication to questions of human personhood. Nausner is not alone in this criticism: one notices, for example, that he borrows significantly from Richard Fermer's earlier critical article (which Gunton encouraged the author to publish).[2] These authors along with several others have shown that there are some problems with Gunton's relational ontology as well as his use of historical sources. Given such critiques of some of the central features of Gunton's thought coming from a range of eminent scholars (many of whom were friends of his), is his project at all salvageable? Is it a failure? Thompson correctly and decisively responds:

> My own assessment is that any suggestion that Gunton's theological project has failed is premature. Gunton has been a catalyst for a new generation of scholars who are to some extent 'filling in the details' which Colin himself skipped over in his excitement about the possibilities which trinitarian theology suggested, not only for the rejuvenation of the academic

discipline of theology but also for a new and substantial Christian engagement with contemporary culture.[3]

At the outset of this commendatory postscript it must be said that Gunton's work is more than salvageable. This is not to discount the weighty criticisms of his work, especially in terms of the lack of attention to detail in his use of historical sources. Nevertheless, as Thompson contends, to disprove his particular reading of this or that theologian is not to render his insights and contribution insignificant. Rather, it is better to adopt the charitable stance Barth took in his early forays into Calvin's theology. He writes:

> I cannot stress too strongly that you should always treat an author with a certain humility on one side and on the other – and this is much the same thing – with a certain free and understanding humor, presuming that the author is always right in some sense even when wrong, so that our only task is to see how far this is always so, perhaps even unintentionally.[4]

My task in this brief final chapter is to see to what extent Gunton was right, or put differently, to outline the successes of his laudable project. I am particularly interested in commending Gunton, especially to those unfamiliar with him or who after reading this volume remain suspicious. To this end I will sketch several emphases in Gunton that are especially noteworthy and stimulating, reflecting first on some features of his overarching approach before pointing out commendable aspects from each of the doctrinal loci introduced throughout this book.

Theology as Conversational and Creative

I mentioned in the introduction that Gunton's theology is forged in the fires of conversation with various figures: Augustine, Barth, Coleridge, Zizioulas, etc. This feature, so obvious in Gunton, seems non-negotiable for any responsible theology. Rowan Williams describes conversation as consisting of two essential features: 'the recognition of an "unfinished" quality in what has been said on either side, and the possibility of correction'. He maintains that theological integrity – speaking well and truthfully about God – is maintained to a large degree through conversation.[5] We see this style of theology to some degree in medieval and Reformation appropriations of Augustine and, in the modern period, in Barth's passionate dialogue with various traditions and writers, to name only a few. Being apprenticed, or at least open, to past masters, even if we end up parting ways, seems a sound path to mastery. The humility Barth called for in the quote above is expressed in one's willingness to take the thought of someone else seriously. I am repeatedly struck when reading Gunton by how one particular insight from one particular theologian set in motion an article, a book, even an entire paradigm shift: his interactions with Zizioulas on persons constituted by relations would form a centre of his theology; his Trinitarian project was animated largely by Coleridge's notion that the Trinity is the basis for all being; his Christology shaped by Irving's concern for the true humanity of Jesus; his pneumatology and eschatology fuelled by Basil's notion that the Spirit is the perfecting cause; and so forth. He recognized the 'unfinished quality' of his theology and was open to the insights and possible correction of others.

One might categorize Gunton's theology as a 'theology of retrieval'. 'For such theologies,' writes John Webster, 'immersion in the texts and habits of thought of earlier (especially pre-modern) theology opens up a wide view of the object of Christian theological reflection, setting before its contemporary practitioners descriptions of the faith unharassed by current anxieties, and enabling a certain liberty in relation to the present.'[6] Theology is most free in dialogue rather than in isolation, just as, to borrow an anthropological insight from Gunton, humans are most free in relation to others. C.S. Lewis, speaking of the need to converse with past theologians, writes: 'They will not flatter us in the errors we are already committing; and their own errors, being now open and palpable, will not endanger us. *Two heads are better than one, not because either is infallible, but because they are unlikely to go wrong in the same direction.*'[7] This was Gunton's *modus operandi*: to listen to and debate with past teachers, not because they were 'cleverer then than we are now' (to borrow again from Lewis), but because they had the potential to liberate us from our present situation and present selves.

His conversations were not limited to particular theologians of the past. In his concern to provide responses to the central problems of modern culture, he extended his dialogues to include the purveyors and main ideas of modernity: Locke, Hume, Kant and Berkeley factor among the key figures; individualism, collectivism, autonomy and freedom among the critical issues. Gunton in most instances embodied the humility, the 'free and understanding humor', that enabled him to be so creative and constructive a theologian (more on this in my second point). Williams captures well this type of dialogical disposition:

> Honest discourse permits response and continuation; it invites collaboration by showing that it does not claim to be, in and of itself, final. It does not seek to prescribe the tone, the direction, or even the vocabulary of a response . . . [I]t makes clear that it accepts, even within its own terms of reference, that there are ways in which it may be questioned and criticized.[8]

In his willingness to appropriate controversial and non-conventional figures (e.g. Irving and Coleridge), non-Protestant traditions (e.g. Orthodoxy through Zizioulas) and non-theologians (e.g. Polanyi), Gunton displayed an openness to correction and change. As a result, he also points to the possibility of fruitful future conversations, not only across time and traditions, and through disciplinary and ideological divides, but across geographical boundaries within the global church. His conversational instinct did not lead him to much by way of global dialogues *per se*, possibly because his concern was primarily the ills of *Western* culture; but no doubt conversations with Asian, African and Latin American theologians could have birthed some insights that might have helped fund his project. Perhaps it is a work for those students inspired by Gunton to bring his theology into conversation with what we might style 'global theology'.

Gunton's belief that the Christian faith had the intellectual resources and coherence to answer questions both theological and cultural freed him to be creative in his approach to theology. In order to better understand what is meant here by 'creative', let us place theologies into two very broad categories: *conservative* and *constructive*. The former, of which most of my formal training consisted, is concerned primarily to articulate and defend the faith as it has been handed down. In this approach there is little concern for, even a suspicion of, novelty. The latter approach views the faith as not merely something to defend but rather something to wield; it provides the substantive resources for addressing important issues within and without the church. Most of Gunton's work fits comfortably in this second category. This is not to suggest that theological novelty is desirable, nor that one style of theology is better than the other, but rather to commend a form of *obedient creativity* in theology: obedience to the teaching of Scripture and its creedal appropriations, creativity in extending its implications. We see historical examples of this approach, for instance, in the marshalling of Christology to address medieval questions regarding images and Reformation debates concerning the Lord's Supper. In the latter case, Lutherans and Reformed extended the insights of fundamentally Chalcedonian Christologies into a current ecclesial controversy. Similar potential exists for extra-ecclesial matters, and Gunton has aptly demonstrated this in *Enlightenment and Alienation, The One, the Three and the Many, The Triune Creator, Act and Being* and his many volumes of collected essays. Conversations for him – centring on the doctrines of the Trinity and creation – produced a certain theological stoutness out of which creative and constructive insights emerged. He could be a free theologian, engaging in the 'happy science' (to echo a phrase from Barth), because his conversations kept him unfettered to the present and its fashions; his attentiveness to other voices liberated him from the status quo. The Christian past was not seen as a problem to be overcome, but as a fount of inspiration for the present day; it was a palliative cure, 'the clean sea breeze of the centuries blowing through our minds', as Lewis writes.[9] Gunton is made confident through conversation, and thus enabled and emboldened to use his theological imagination to offer penetrating diagnoses of and potential solutions to cultural and churchly challenges. Theology need not be merely defensive, having its way determined by alien modes of thought. Rather, positive dogmatics and apologetic concerns may lie peacefully together since creative appropriation of the former may be the answer to the latter – even if these solutions remain tentative and only 'towards', as is often the case with Gunton.

Theological High Points

I ended each doctrinal chapter of this book with some questions and criticisms of Gunton's proposals, not giving as much attention to highlighting distinctive and commendable features. As this volume comes to a close, I will enumerate briefly some elements of his theology that merit consideration if not praise. If one happens to read this chapter before embarking on the book as a whole, perhaps this laudatory synopsis will provide further impetus to read the other chapters as well.

God

Gunton rightly placed the Trinity at the centre of his theological programme. Several features of his doctrine of God are worthy of mention. First, his emphasis that God's being and attributes must be understood *a posteriori* rather than *a priori* is a truth that theology needs to be called back to regularly. We cannot speak of God apart from his revelation through his actions. When we speak of him as love, for example, we recognize that 'love' is circumscribed; it is given definition by God's specific action towards us in Jesus. This must be true also of other, more abstract, attributes like aseity, immutability, simplicity, and so forth. Second, Paul Molnar comments that 'among contemporary theologians, Colin Gunton sees the positive meaning of a proper doctrine of the immanent Trinity with clarity and consistency'.[10] In the face of 'suffering God' theologies and other immanentizing tendencies, Gunton helpfully reasserts the indispensability of the immanent Trinity for maintaining both divine and human freedom. He writes: 'It is because God is a communion of love *prior to and in independence of* the creation that God can enable the creation to be itself.'[11] The doctrine of the immanent Trinity is the foundation for the relative independence and freedom of the world. In this way, Gunton does not oppose divine and human freedom, as if the former undermines the latter. Rather, the latter finds its being in the former. Finally, he rightly pushes us to think about the particular actions of the persons of the Trinity. While this does not necessitate a departure from the dictum regarding the indivisible works of the Trinity, it does move us to think more carefully about what indivisibility looks like while maintaining distinctions in operations. The creeds suggest that worship of the Trinitarian persons is tied to our understanding of their distinct actions *ad extra*.

Creation

Gunton's attempt at a theology of creation is to me his great achievement. Five emphases stand out. First, creation has a purpose as God's project. Thus, from the very beginning creation had an eschatological orientation, which is now being brought to completion through the work of the Son and Spirit. This emphasis in Gunton complements neo-Calvinist teaching on the cultural mandate and recent work in biblical studies highlighting humanity's royal-priestly responsibility to steward the world towards its perfection. Even in its fallen state, God not only sustains the world, but continues to direct it towards the fulfilment of its original purpose. Second, Gunton's teaching on the freedom and relative independence of the world underscores the significance of our actions. We are not part of God, subsumed in his being; rather, we have our own being. This validates human enterprise as the very living out of our freedom. Third, although the world and God are relatively independent realities, God maintains close relations with the world through his 'two hands'. Thus, the transcendent God further confers goodness on the created order by entering into it and sustaining it from within, so to speak. Fourth, what does it mean for the heavens and all creation to 'declare the glory of God'? This lies at the heart of Gunton's search for Trinitarian transcendentals. Are we really to remain agnostic or allergic to the idea that the created order somehow reflects the divine being? Gunton affirms (I think rightly) an *analogia trinitatis* as a form of *analogia entis*. It is difficult to imagine the world not displaying some marks of God's being in its own being. What these marks are remains an open question. Finally, Gunton is correct to emphasize the relational dimension of our human constitution, even if our humanity should not be reduced to relationality. I agree with Mark Thompson when he writes, 'My relations are critical, indispensible elements of my identity, but they aren't quite the sole determinants of my identity. It is almost true that I am constituted by my relations – almost, but not quite.'[12] Nevertheless, Gunton is correct that we neglect the relational dimensions of our being only to our collective detriment.

Reason and revelation

The knowledge of God, according to Gunton, is (1) relational, (2) intellectual, (3) contingent, (4) unique and (5) communal. By this he means that it is received in a relationship with God, contains true, coherent cognitive content, but only comes to us from God through the agency of the incarnate Son and revealing Spirit, and mediated by the Christian community. This is Gunton's skilful way of moving beyond the false 'either/or's of modern theories of knowledge. There is a confidence here that God can be known because he has actually made himself known in Jesus Christ and to the church. Furthermore, Gunton helpfully stresses the humanity of Jesus as revelatory of God.

It is as this particular man that Jesus mediates the knowledge of God. This suggests to Gunton that creaturely realities do not merely obscure God, but are actually his way of disclosing himself.

Jesus Christ

In many ways Gunton's Christology is traditional: he affirms Chalcedon, the two-natures doctrine and the eternal begottenness of the Son. An aspect of his most controversial teaching is probably his most notable contribution. What I have in mind is his emphasis on the true humanity of Jesus and its corollary, the work of the Spirit in Jesus' life. Gunton is correct in noting docetic tendencies in historical treatments of Christ. He has a humanity, we have often affirmed explicitly, but one not truly like our own. All the great deeds he performed were, we often think, because he was the incarnate God. But to reiterate a point made in the chapter on Christology, the miraculous events of Jesus' life – conception, resurrection, ascension – must be seen as central to his *human* history, not merely as signs of his deity. Even if we do not follow Gunton in affirming the fallenness of Jesus' human nature (and I do not), he is surely correct in bringing to the fore the true humanity of Jesus' life and career. In fact, one conservative theologian has recently followed suit in underlining the humanity of the Son of God.[13] By doing so, Jesus can truly be seen as our brother.

The work of Christ

Gunton's aim in his most important writing on the atonement was to show the rationality of atonement metaphors and how they disclose rather than obscure the reality of the work of Christ. While it would have been preferable for Gunton to have sought to find the thread(s) unifying the metaphors, he models what it might look like to trace each metaphor and allow them to speak distinctly about the work of Christ, without (or at least before) subsuming them under a unifying motif. Moreover, what is most stimulating about Gunton's treatment is his placement of atonement within its cosmic context, by closely associating it with God's project of creation. This is reminiscent of Athanasius, who writes at the beginning of *On the Incarnation*:

> We will begin, then, with the creation of the world and with God its Maker, for the first fact that you must grasp is this: the renewal of creation has been wrought by the Self-same Word Who made it in the beginning. There is thus no inconsistency between creation and salvation; for the One Father has employed the same Agent for both works, effecting the salvation of the world through the same Word Who made it in the beginning.[14]

In this arrangement, the atonement is ultimately about moving creation towards the order and perfection envisioned for it at the very beginning, rather than solely about saving people from hell.

The church

Although Gunton rejects particular notions of an 'invisible church', his ecclesiology may still be viewed as an attempt to mediate between conceptions of the church as visible and invisible, present and eschatological, particular and universal, imperfect and perfect, and its reality versus its ideal existence. He innovatively posits that what is needed for a healthy ecclesiology is a *pneumatic* Christology and a *christocentric* pneumatology. The former highlights the humanity of Christ by underscoring his dependence on the Holy Spirit during his earthly life. Although one need not follow Gunton in attributing fallenness to Christ's humanity, a consequence for ecclesiology of emphasizing Christ's Spirit-dependent humanity is a stress on the humanity of the church. The church is the 'body' of a Christ who lived a human life in full reliance on the Spirit. The church is not the kingdom, but rather a human community dependent on the Spirit to grant it the kind of life it is intended to live. The latter – christocentric pneumatology

– emphasizes the Spirit's function of bringing about the 'not-yet' aspects of Christ's redemptive work, which includes conforming the church to Christ's likeness. The incompleteness of the Spirit's christocentric and christomorphic work again highlights the church's humanity. Christology and pneumatology framed this way then create space for a properly eschatological perspective on the church. The church is *simul iustus et peccator*, but oriented towards its future perfection. At one and the same time the church can think quite highly and rather soberly about itself. It is a gathering of those who belong to the God and Father of Jesus Christ, yet who display the marks of citizens of the City of Humanity.

The Holy Spirit

One popular writer speaks of the Spirit as the 'forgotten God', a sentiment with which Gunton would probably agree.[15] What Gunton would mean is not that the Spirit has been altogether forgotten in the church's consciousness, but that the particularity of his person and work has not been fully appreciated nor carefully articulated, especially in the West. In fact, he argued that the Western Church produced its fair share of pneumatologies, but they tend to internalize and immanentize the Spirit within the human person or culture generally. What Gunton contends is echoed in a comment made by Barth in the epilogue to his theology of Schleiermacher (and it is worth quoting at length):

> I would like to reckon with the possibility of a theology of the Holy Spirit, a theology of which Schleiermacher was scarcely conscious, but which might actually have been the legitimate concern dominating even his theological activity. And not his alone! I would also like to apply this supposition in favor of the pietists and (!) rationalists who preceded him, and, of course, in favor of the 'Moravians of a lower order' of the eighteenth century, and beyond that in favor of the 'Enthusiasts' who were so one-sidedly and badly treated by the Reformers, and still further

back, in favor of all those agitated and contemplative souls, spiritualists and mystics of the Middle Ages. Could it not be that so many things which for us were said in an unacceptable way about the church and about Mary in Eastern and Western Catholicism might be vindicated to the extent that they actually intended the reality, the coming, and the work of the Holy Spirit, and that on that basis they might emerge in a positive-critical light?[16]

Gunton would probably agree with this assessment and even Barth's recommendation of charity towards these theologies. However, though these *are* implicit and explicit pneumatologies, a grasping at the reality, they are inadequate. While trying to make some sense of the Spirit, they supplant him in the end. As a welcome corrective, then, Gunton presents the Spirit as transcendent, rather than immanent. In and because of his transcendent freedom from the created order, the Spirit has the distinct work of carrying creation to its perfected end. Surely more can be said of the Spirit's work, but this is an improvement on internalizing doctrines of the Spirit, not least because it ties the Spirit more tightly to God's purposes for all of creation, and not solely to the 'heart' of the believer or the activities of the church.

Recommended Reading

The industry of works evaluating and engaging Gunton is still in its early stages, but is gaining momentum. Assessments vary from severely critical to effusive in praise. It is up to the reader, however, to decide how far Gunton was right, even if he or she does not follow him all the way. It was C.S. Lewis who remarked that a primary source is often more intelligible than any commentary on it. To that end, the following represent recommended and important starting places for those wishing to read Gunton profitably and without undue refraction.[1]

- *Becoming and Being*: This is Gunton's revised dissertation on the doctrine of God in Charles Hartshorne and Karl Barth. It is the best place to start if one wants to catch a glimpse of the early Gunton and some of the key themes that become central in his theology.
- *Christ and Creation*: This is the second of Gunton's two major works on Christology.[2] He brings together major themes in Christology (incarnation, hypostatic union, resurrection) with creation and redemption, addressing how the humanity and divinity of Christ respectively uphold and perfect the creation. This is an early account of Gunton's doctrine of mediation.
- *The Promise of Trinitarian Theology*: This is his most important collection of essays on Trinitarian theology, including agenda-setting chapters on Augustine, creation, personhood, the image of God, the church and the atonement. For one wanting a one-stop overview of Gunton's constructive 'project', this is the best place to start.
- *The One, the Three and the Many*: Widely recognized as Gunton's most important constructive work, this is the published version of

the prestigious Bampton Lectures at Oxford. Gunton traces the decline of Western culture to a lack of Trinitarian consciousness and looks to the doctrine of the Trinity to find the resources to remedy the loss of meaning, truth, personhood and freedom.
- *The Christian Faith*: This is the only 'full' systematic theology Gunton produced. It is more of a brief textbook-like introduction to Christian doctrine, devoting small sections to most of the standard loci and following the main divisions of the creed.
- *Act and Being*: This is the final monograph produced by Gunton before his death. It is worth reading as the only full-length working out of how a doctrine – in this case, the divine attributes – looks differently in the light of the Trinity. The volume goes a long way in answering the 'so what?' of all the talk about Trinitarian theology.

Gunton was so prolific an author that these represent just a small sampling of his important works. However, because his main themes tended to show up everywhere, starting with any of these works will give the reader a sufficient taste of his theology. I close with this, again from Lewis: 'It has always therefore been one of my main endeavours as a teacher to persuade the young that first-hand knowledge is not only more worth acquiring than second-hand knowledge, but is usually much easier and more delightful to acquire.'[3]

May the reader find delight in first-hand conversation with Colin Gunton.

Bibliography

Alston, William P. 'Substance and the Trinity'. Pages 179–201 in *The Trinity* (ed. Stephen T. Davis, Daniel Kendall and Gerald O'Collins; Oxford: Oxford University Press, 1999).

Aquinas, Thomas. *Summa Theologiae* (trans. Fathers of the English Dominican Province; Scotts Valley, CA: Novantiqua, repr. 2008–).

Athanasius. *On the Incarnation* (ed. and trans. A Religious of CSMV; Crestwood, NY: St Vladimir's Seminary Press, 2002).

Augustine. *Enchiridion: On Faith, Hope, and Love.* Library of Christian Classics (ed. and trans. Albert C. Outler; Philadelphia: Westminster Press, 1955).

———. *Sermons 273–305A*. The Works of Saint Augustine III/8 (ed. John E. Rotelle; trans. Edmund Hill; Hyde Park, NY: New City Press, 1994).

———. *The Trinity*. The Works of Saint Augustine I/5 (ed. John E. Rotelle; trans. Edmund Hill; Hyde Park, NY: New City Press, 2012).

Ayres, Lewis. 'Augustine, the Trinity and Modernity'. *Augustinian Studies* 26.2 (1995): pp. 127–33.

———. Review of Colin E. Gunton, *The Promise of Trinitarian Theology*, in *Journal of Theological Studies* 43 (1992): pp. 780–82.

Barnes, Michel René. 'Rereading Augustine's Theology of the Trinity'. Pages 145–78 in *The Trinity: An Interdisciplinary Symposium on the Trinity* (ed. Stephen T. Davis, Daniel Kendall and Gerald O'Collins; Oxford: Oxford University Press, 2002).

Barth, Karl. *Church Dogmatics* (4 vols; ed. and trans. G.W. Bromiley and T.F. Torrance; London: T&T Clark, 2009).

———. *The Göttingen Dogmatics: Instruction in the Christian Religion*, vol. 1 (ed. Hannelotte Reiffen; trans. Geoffrey W. Bromiley; Grand Rapids: Eerdmans, 1991).

———. *The Theology of Calvin* (trans. Geoffrey Bromiley; Grand Rapids: Eerdmans, 1999).

———. *The Theology of Schleiermacher: Lectures at Göttingen, Winter Semester of 1923/24* (ed. Dietrich Ritschl; trans. Geoffrey W. Bromiley; Grand Rapids: Eerdmans, 1982).

Basil. *Letter 38*. Nicene and Post-Nicene Fathers, Second Series, vol. 8 (trans. Blomfield Jackson; ed. Philip Schaff and Henry Wace; Buffalo, NY: Christian Literature Publishing Co., 1895).

———. *On the Holy Spirit*. Popular Patristics Series 42 (trans. Stephen Hildebrand; Yonkers, NY: St Vladimir's Seminary Press, 2011).

Bavinck, Herman. *Reformed Dogmatics: Holy Spirit, Church, and New Creation*, vol. 4 (ed. John Bolt; trans. John Vriend; Grand Rapids: Baker Academic, 2008).

Blocher, Henri. 'Biblical Metaphors and the Doctrine of the Atonement'. *Journal of the Evangelical Theological Society* 47 (2004): pp. 629–45.

Bonaventure. *Breviloquium*, Works of St Bonaventure 9 (ed. and trans. Dominic V. Monti; New York: Franciscan Institute, 2005).

Brunner, Emil. *The Mediator: A Study of the Central Doctrine of the Christian Faith* (trans. Olive Wyon; Philadelphia: Westminster Press, 1947).

Calvin, John. *Institutes of the Christian Religion* (trans. John T. McNeill. Louisville: Westminster John Knox Press, 2006).

Campbell, Cynthia McCall. 'Response to Colin Gunton'. *Theology Today* 43 (1986): p. 332.

Chan, Francis. *Forgotten God: Reversing Our Tragic Neglect of the Holy Spirit* (Colorado Springs: David C. Cook, 2009).

Chia, Roland. 'Trinity and Ontology: Colin Gunton's Ecclesiology'. *International Journal of Systematic Theology* 9 (2007): pp. 552–68.

Coakley, Sarah. '"Persons" in the "Social" Doctrine of the Trinity: A Critique of Current Analytic Discussion'. Pages 123–44 in *The Trinity: An Interdisciplinary Symposium on the Trinity* (ed. Stephen

T. Davis, Daniel Kendall and Gerald O'Collins; Oxford: Oxford University Press, 2002).

Colwell, John E. 'Provisionality and Promise: Avoiding Ecclesiastical Nestorianism?' Pages 100–15 in *The Theology of Colin Gunton* (ed. Lincoln Harvey; London: T&T Clark, 2010).

Congar, Yves. *L'Église: De saint Augustin à l'époque moderne* (Paris: Cerf, 1997).

Crisp, Oliver D. 'Did Christ Have a *Fallen* Human Nature?' *International Journal of Systematic Theology* 6 (2004): pp. 270–88.

———. *Divinity and Humanity: The Incarnation Reconsidered* (Cambridge: Cambridge University Press, 2007).

Cumin, Paul. 'The Taste of Cake: Relation and Otherness with Colin Gunton and the Strong Second Hand of God'. Pages 65–85 in *The Theology of Colin Gunton* (ed. Lincoln Harvey; London: T&T Clark, 2010).

Cunningham, David S. *These Three Are One: The Practice of Trinitarian Theology*. Challenges in Contemporary Theology (Oxford: Blackwell, 1998).

Dale, R.W. *The Atonement: The Congregational Union Lecture for 1875* (London: Congregational Union of England and Wales, 1904).

Egan, John P. 'Toward Trinitarian *Perichoresis*: Saint Gregory the Theologian, *Oration* 31.14'. *Greek Orthodox Theological Review* 39.1 (1994): pp. 83–93.

Ferguson, Everett. *Baptism in the Early Church: History, Theology, and Liturgy in the First Five Centuries* (Grand Rapids: Eerdmans, 2009).

Fermer, Richard M. 'The Limits of Trinitarian Theology as a Methodological Paradigm'. *Neue Zeitschrift für Systematische Theologie und Religionsphilosophie* 41.2 (1999): pp. 158–86.

Green, Bradley G. *Colin Gunton and the Failure of Augustine: The Theology of Colin Gunton in Light of Augustine*. Distinguished Dissertations in Christian Theology 4 (Eugene, OR: Pickwick Press, 2011).

Gunton, Colin. *A Brief Theology of Revelation: The 1993 Warfield Lectures* (London: T&T Clark, 2005).

———. 'A Far-off Gleam of the Gospel: Salvation in Tolkien's *The Lord of the Rings*'. *King's Theological Review* 12 (1989): pp. 6–10.

———. *Act and Being: Towards a Theology of the Divine Attributes* (Grand Rapids: Eerdmans, 2003).

———. *The Actuality of Atonement: A Study of Metaphor, Rationality and the Christian Tradition* (Edinburgh: T&T Clark, 1988).

———. 'All Flesh Is As Grass: Towards an Eschatology of the Human Person'. Pages 22–37 in *Beyond Mere Health: Theology and Health Care in a Secular Society* (ed. Hilary D. Regan and Rodney B. Horsfield; Melbourne: Australian Theological Forum, 1996).

———. 'Atonement', in *Routledge Encyclopedia of Philosophy* (ed. Edward Craig; London: Routledge, 1998) http://www.rep.routledge.com/article/K003SECT2 (accessed 9 May 2014).

———. 'Atonement and the Project of Creation: An Interpretation of Colossians 1:15–23'. *Dialog* 35.1 (1996): pp. 35–41.

———. 'Barth, the Trinity and Human Freedom'. *Theology Today* 43.3 (1986): pp. 316–30.

———. *The Barth Lectures* (ed. P.H. Brazier; London: T&T Clark, 2007).

———. *Becoming and Being: The Doctrine of God in Charles Hartshorne and Karl Barth* (London: SCM Press, 2nd edn, 2001).

———. 'Between Allegory and Myth: The Legacy of the Spiritualising of Genesis'. Pages 47–62 in *The Doctrine of Creation: Essays in Dogmatics, History and Philosophy* (ed. Colin E. Gunton; Edinburgh: T&T Clark, 1997).

———. *Christ and Creation* (Grand Rapids: Eerdmans, 1992).

———. 'Christ the Sacrifice: Aspects of the Language and Imagery of the Bible'. Pages 229–38 in *The Glory of Christ in the New Testament: Studies in Christology in Memory of George Bradford Caird* (ed. L.D. Hurst and N.T. Wright; Oxford: Clarendon Press, 1987).

———. *The Christian Faith: An Introduction to Christian Doctrine* (Malden, MA: Blackwell, 2002).

———. '*Christus Victor* Revisited: A Study in Metaphor and Transformation of Meaning'. *Journal of Theological Studies* 36 (1985): pp. 129–45.

———. 'The Church on Earth: The Roots of Community'. Pages 48–80 in *On Being the Church: Essays on the Christian Community* (ed. Colin E. Gunton and Daniel W. Hardy; Edinburgh: T&T Clark, 1989).

———. 'Creation and Mediation in the Theology of Robert W. Jenson: An Encounter and a Convergence'. Pages 80–93 in *Trinity, Time and Church: A Response to the Theology of Robert W. Jenson* (ed. Colin E. Gunton; Grand Rapids: Eerdmans, 2000).

———. 'Creeds and Confessions, Introductory Essay'. Pages 101–5 in *The Practice of Theology: A Reader* (ed. Colin E. Gunton, Stephen R. Holmes and Murray A. Rae; London: SCM Press, 2001).

———. 'David Ford: Barth and God's Story'. *Scottish Journal of Theology* 37.3 (1984): pp. 375–80.

———. 'The Doctrine of Creation'. Pages 141–57 in *The Cambridge Companion to Christian Doctrine* (ed. Colin E. Gunton; Cambridge: Cambridge University Press, 1997).

———. 'Dogmatic Theses on Eschatology: Conference Paper'. Pages 139–43 in *The Future as God's Gift: Explorations in Christian Eschatology* (ed. David Fergusson and Marcel Sarot; Edinburgh: T&T Clark, 2000).

———. 'Election and Ecclesiology in the Post-Constantinian Church'. *Scottish Journal of Theology* 53.2 (May 2000): pp. 212–27.

———. *Enlightenment and Alienation: An Essay towards a Trinitarian Theology* (Grand Rapids: Eerdmans, 1985).

———. *Father, Son and Holy Spirit: Toward a Fully Trinitarian Theology* (London: T&T Clark, 2003).

———. 'Foreword', in Jeremy Begbie, *Voicing Creation's Praise: Towards a Theology of the Arts* (London: T&T Clark, 1991).

———. 'Foreword', in Thomas Weinandy, *In the Likeness of Sinful Flesh: An Essay on the Humanity of Christ* (London: T&T Clark, 1993).

———. 'God, Grace and Freedom'. Pages 119–33 in *God and Freedom: Essays in Historical and Systematic Theology* (ed. Colin E. Gunton; Edinburgh: T&T Clark, 1995).

———. 'The God of Jesus Christ'. *Theology Today* 54.3 (1997): pp. 325–34.

———. 'Historical and Systematic Theology'. Pages 3–20 in *The Cambridge Companion to Christian Doctrine* (ed. Colin E. Gunton; Cambridge: Cambridge University Press, 1997).

———. 'Holy Spirit'. Pages 304–6 in *The Oxford Companion to Christian Thought* (ed. Adrian Hastings, Alistair Mason and Hugh Pyper (Oxford: Oxford University Press, 2000).

———. 'The Indispensability of Theological Understanding: Theology in the University'. Pages 266–77 in *Essentials of Christian Community: Essays for Daniel Hardy* (ed. David Ford and Dennis L. Stamps; Edinburgh: T&T Clark, 1996).

———. 'Indispensable Opponent: The Relations of Systematic Theology and the Philosophy of Religion'. *Neue Zeitschrift für Systematische Theologie und Religionsphilosophie* 38.3 (January 1996): pp. 298–306.

———. *Intellect and Action: Elucidations on Christian Theology and the Life of Faith* (Edinburgh: T&T Clark, 2000).

———. 'Introduction'. Pages 1–12 in *The Theology of Reconciliation: Essays in Biblical and Systematic Theology* (ed. Colin E. Gunton; London: T&T Clark, 2003).

———. 'Karl Barth and the Development of Christian Doctrine'. *Scottish Journal of Theology* 25.2 (May 1972): pp. 171–80.

———. 'Karl Barth and the Western Intellectual Tradition: Towards a Theology after Christendom'. Pages 285–301 in *Theology Beyond Christendom: Essays on the Centenary of the Birth of Karl Barth, May 10, 1886* (ed. John Thompson; Allison Park, PA: Pickwick Press, 1986).

———. 'Karl Barth's Doctrine of Election as Part of His Doctrine of God'. *Journal of Theological Studies* 25.2 (1974): pp. 381–92.

———. 'Knowledge and Culture: Towards an Epistemology of the Concrete'. Pages 84–102 in *The Gospel and Contemporary Culture* (ed. Hugh Montefiore; London: Mowbray, 1992).

———. 'The Knowledge of God According to Two Process Theologians: A Twentieth-Century Gnosticism'. *Religious Studies* 11 (1975): pp. 87–97.

———. 'One Mediator... the Man Jesus Christ: Reconciliation, Mediation and Life in Community'. *Pro ecclesia* 11 (2000): pp. 146–58.

———. *The One, the Three and the Many: God, Creation and the Culture of Modernity: The 1992 Bampton Lectures* (Cambridge: Cambridge University Press, 1993).

———. 'Persons'. Pages 638–41 in *Dictionary of Ethics, Theology and Society* (ed. Paul A.B. Clarke and Andrew Linzey; London: Routledge, 1996).

———. 'Persons and Particularity'. Pages 97–107 in *Theology of John Zizioulas: Personhood and the Church* (ed. Douglas H. Knight; Burlington, VT: Ashgate, 2007).

———. 'The Place of Reason in Theology'. Pages 149–53 in *The Practice of Theology: A Reader* (ed. Colin E. Gunton, Stephen R. Holmes and Murray A. Rae; London: SCM Press, 2001).

———. 'The Playwright as Theologian: Peter Shaffer's *Amadeus*'. *King's Theological Review* 10 (1987): pp. 1–5.

———. 'Process Theology: A Reply'. *Expository Times* 85.7 (1974): p. 215.

———. 'Process Theology's Concept of God: An Outline and Assessment'. *Expository Times* 84.10 (1973): pp. 292–6.

———. *The Promise of Trinitarian Theology* (Edinburgh: T&T Clark, 2nd edn, 1997).

———. 'Proteus and Procrustes: A Study in the Dialectic of Language in Disagreement with Sallie McFague'. Pages 65–80 in *Speaking the Christian God: The Holy Trinity and the Challenge of Feminism* (ed. Alvin F. Kimel, Jr; Grand Rapids: Eerdmans, 1992).

———. *Revelation and Reason: Prolegomena to Systematic Theology* (ed. P.H. Brazier. London: T&T Clark, 2008).

———. Review of Maurice Wiles, *The Remaking of Christian Doctrine*, in *Theology* 77 (1974): pp. 619–24.

———. 'Rudolf Bultmann and the Location of Language about God'. *Theology* 75 (1972): pp. 535–9.

———. 'Salvation'. Pages 143–58 in *The Cambridge Companion to Karl Barth* (ed. John Webster; Cambridge: Cambridge University Press, 2007).

———. 'The Spirit as Lord: Christianity, Modernity and Freedom'. Pages 169–82 in *Different Gospels* (ed. Andrew Walker; London: Hodder & Stoughton, 1988).

———. 'The Spirit in the Trinity'. Pages 123–35 in *The Forgotten Trinity: A Selection of Papers Presented to the BCC Study Commission on Trinitarian Doctrine Today 3* (ed. Alasdair I.C. Heron; London: BCC/CCBI, 1991).

———. 'The Theologian and the Biologist'. *Theology* 77 (1974): p. 526–8.

———. *The Theologian as Preacher: Further Sermons from Colin E. Gunton* (ed. Sarah J. Gunton and John E. Colwell; London: T&T Clark, 2007).

———. 'Theology in Communion'. Pages 31–6 in *Shaping the Theological Mind: Theological Context and Methodology* (ed. Darren C. Marks; Burlington, VT: Ashgate, 2002).

———. *Theology through Preaching: Sermons for Brentwood* (Edinburgh: T&T Clark, 2001).

———. *Theology through the Theologians: Selected Essays 1972–1995* (Edinburgh: T&T Clark, 1996).

———. 'Time, Eternity and the Doctrine of the Incarnation'. *Dialog* 21 (1982): pp. 263–8.

———. *The Transcendent Lord: The Spirit and the Church in Calvinist and Cappadocian Fathers* (London: Congregational Memorial Hall Trust, 1988).

———. 'The Trinity in Modern Theology'. Pages 937–57 in *Companion Encyclopedia of Theology* (ed. Peter Byrne and Leslie Houlden; London: Routledge, 1995).

———. *The Triune Creator: A Historical and Systematic Study* (Grand Rapids: Eerdmans, 1998).

———. 'The Truth . . . and the Spirit of Truth: The Trinitarian Shape of Christian Theology.' Pages 341–51 in *Loving God with Our Minds:*

The Pastor as Theologian: Essays in Honour of Wallace M. Alston (ed. Michael Welker and Cynthia A. Jarvis; Grand Rapids: Eerdmans, 2004).

———. 'The Truth of Christology'. Pages 91–107 in *Belief in Science and in Christian Life: The Relevance of Michael Polanyi's Thought for Christian Faith and Life* (ed. Thomas F. Torrance; Edinburgh: Handsel, 1980).

———. 'Towards a Theology of Reconciliation'. Pages 167–74 in *The Theology of Reconciliation: Essays in Biblical and Systematic Theology* (ed. Colin E. Gunton; London: T&T Clark, 2003).

———. 'Transcendence, Metaphor, and the Knowability of God'. *Journal of Theological Studies* 31.2 (1980): pp. 503–16.

———. 'Trinity, Ontology and Anthropology: Towards a Renewal of the Doctrine of the *Imago Dei*'. Pages 47–61 in *Persons, Divine and Human: King's College Essays in Theological Anthropology* (ed. Christoph Schwöbel and Colin E. Gunton; Edinburgh: T&T Clark, 1991).

———. 'Two Dogmas Revisited: Edward Irving's Christology'. *Scottish Journal of Theology* 41 (1988): pp. 359–76.

———. 'Universal and Particular in Atonement Theology'. *Religious Studies* 28 (1992): pp. 453–66.

———. '"Until He Comes": Towards an Eschatology of Church Membership'. *International Journal of Systematic Theology* 3 (2001): pp. 187–200.

———. 'Using and Being Used: Scripture and Systematic Theology'. *Theology Today* 47.3 (October 1990): pp. 248–59.

———. *Yesterday and Today: A Study of Continuities in Christology* (Grand Rapids: Eerdmans, 1983).

Gunton, Colin and Robert W. Jenson. 'The Logos Ensarkos and Reason'. Pages 78–85 in *Reason and the Reasons of Faith*. Theology for the Twenty-First Century (ed. Paul J. Griffiths and Reinhard Hütter; New York: T&T Clark, 2005).

Harrison, Verna. 'Perichoresis in the Greek Fathers'. *St Vladimir's Theological Quarterly* 35.1 (1991): pp. 53–65.

Hohne, David A. *Spirit and Sonship: Colin Gunton's Theology of Particularity and the Holy Spirit* (Burlington, VT: Ashgate, 2010).

Holmes, Stephen R. 'In Memoriam Colin Gunton'. *Shored Fragments* (blog), 6 May 2013 http://steverholmes.org.uk/blog/?p=6973 (accessed 30 July 2015).

———. 'Introduction: The Theologian as Preacher, the Preacher as Theologian'. Pages xiv–xv in *The Theologian as Preacher: Further Sermons from Colin E. Gunton* (ed. Sarah J. Gunton and John E. Colwell; London: T&T Clark, 2007).

———. 'The Rev Prof Colin Gunton'. *The Guardian*, 3 June 2003 http://www.theguardian.com/news/2003/jun/03/guardianobituaries.highereducation (accessed 30 July 2015).

———. 'Towards the *Analogia Personae et Relationis*: Developments in Gunton's Trinitarian Thinking'. Pages 32–48 in *The Theology of Colin Gunton* (ed. Lincoln Harvey; London: T&T Clark, 2010).

Irving, Edward. *The Collected Writings of Edward Irving in Five Volumes*, vol. 5 (ed. G. Carlyle; London: Alexander Strachan, 1865).

Jenson, Robert W. 'A Decision Tree of Colin Gunton's Thinking'. Pages 8–16 in *The Theology of Colin Gunton* (ed. Lincoln Harvey; London: T&T Clark, 2010).

———. 'Afterword'. Pages 217–20 in *Trinitarian Soundings in Systematic Theology* (ed. Paul Louis Metzger; London: T&T Clark, 2005).

———. 'The Holy Spirit'. Pages 101–78 in *Christian Dogmatics* (ed. C.E. Braaten and R.W. Jenson; Philadelphia: Fortress Press, 1984).

———. *Systematic Theology, vol. 1: The Triune God* (New York: Oxford University Press, 1991).

Jüngel, Eberhard. *God's Being Is in Becoming: The Trinitarian Being of God in the Theology of Karl Barth* (trans. John Webster; Grand Rapids: Eerdmans, 2001).

Kapic, Kelly M. 'The Son's Assumption of a Human Nature: A Call for Clarity'. *International Journal of Systematic Theology* 3 (2001): pp. 154–66.

Kilby, Karen. 'Perichoresis and Projection: Problems with Social Doctrines of the Trinity'. *New Blackfriars* 81.957 (2000): pp. 432–45.

Knight, Douglas. 'From Metaphor to Mediation: Colin Gunton and the Concept of Mediation'. *Neue Zeitschrift für Systematische Theologie und Religionsphilosophie* 43 (2001): pp. 118–36.

LaCugna, Catherine Mowry. *God for Us: The Trinity and Christian Life* (New York: HarperCollins, 1991).

Lash, Nicholas. *Believing Three Ways in One God: A Reading of the Apostles' Creed* (London: SCM Press, 1992).

Letham, Robert. *The Work of Christ*. Contours of Christian Theology (Downers Grove, IL: InterVarsity Press, 1993).

Lewis, C.S. 'Introduction', in Athanasius, *On the Incarnation* (ed. and trans. A Religious of CSMV; Crestwood, NY: St Vladimir's Seminary Press, 2002).

Macleod, Donald. *The Person of Christ*. Contours of Christian Theology (Downers Grove, IL: InterVarsity Press, 1998).

McCormack, Bruce L. 'Foreword'. Pages 1–4 in *Trinitarian Soundings in Systematic Theology* (ed. Paul Louis Metzger; London: T&T Clark, 2005).

———. '*The One, the Three and the Many*: In Memory of Colin Gunton'. *Cultural Encounters* 1.2 (Summer 2005): pp. 7–17.

McFarlane, Graham W.P. *Christ and the Spirit: The Doctrine of the Incarnation According to Edward Irving* (Carlisle: Paternoster Press, 1996).

McNall, Joshua. *A Free Corrector: Colin Gunton and the Legacy of Augustine*. Emerging Scholars (Minneapolis: Fortress Press, 2015).

Metzger, Paul Louis. 'Response to Bruce L. McCormack's Tribute'. *Cultural Encounters* 1.2 (Summer 2005): p. 20.

Molnar, Paul D. 'Becoming and Being'. *International Journal of Systematic Theology* 5.1 (2003): pp. 80–84.

———. *Divine Freedom and the Doctrine of the Immanent Trinity: In Dialogue with Karl Barth and Contemporary Theology* (London: T&T Clark, 2005).

———. 'The Promise of Trinitarian Theology'. *Theological Studies* 53.2 (1992): pp. 560–61.

———. Review of Colin E. Gunton, *Father, Son and Holy Spirit: Toward a Fully Trinitarian Theology*, in *Pro ecclesia* 14.4 (2005): pp. 494–6.

Moltmann, Jürgen. *The Crucified God* (trans. R.A. Wilson; Minneapolis: Fortress Press, 1993).

———. *The Trinity and the Kingdom* (trans. Margaret Kohl. Minneapolis: Fortress Press, 1993).

Muller, Richard A. *Post-Reformation Reformed Dogmatics: The Rise and Development of Reformed Orthodoxy, ca. 1520 to ca. 1725*, vol. 2 (Grand Rapids: Baker Academic, 2nd edn, 2006).

Nausner, Bernhard. 'The Failure of a Laudable Project: Gunton, the Trinity and Human Self-Understanding'. *Scottish Journal of Theology* 62.4 (2009): pp. 403–20.

O'Brien, P.T. 'The Church as a Heavenly and Eschatological Entity'. Pages 88–119 in *The Church in the Bible and the World* (ed. D.A. Carson; Grand Rapids: Baker, 1987).

Ogden, Schubert M. 'Christian Theology and Neoclassical Theism'. *Journal of Religion* 60.2 (1980): pp. 205–9.

Ormerod, Neil. 'Augustine and the Trinity: Whose Crisis?' *Pacifica* 16.1 (February 2003): pp. 17–32.

Owen, John. *An Enquiry into the Original Name, Institution, Power, Order, and Communion of Evangelical Churches*. Works of John Owen 15 (ed. William H. Goold; Carlisle, PA: Banner of Truth Trust, 1976).

———. *The True Nature of a Gospel Church*. Works of John Owen 16 (ed. William H. Goold; Carlisle, PA: Banner of Truth Trust, 1976).

Pfleiderer, Georg. 'The Atonement'. Pages 127–38 in *Trinitarian Soundings in Systematic Theology* (ed. Paul Louis Metzger; London: T&T Clark, 2005).

Polanyi, Michael. *Personal Knowledge: Towards a Post-Critical Philosophy* (New York: Harper & Row, 1964).

———. *The Tacit Dimension* (Chicago: University of Chicago Press, 2009).

———. 'Tacit Knowing: Its Bearing on Some Problems in Philosophy'. *Reviews of Modern Physics* 34 (1962): pp. 601–16.

Pseudo-Dionysius. 'The Divine Names'. Pages 47–132 in *Pseudo-Dionysius: The Complete Works*. The Classics of Western Spirituality (trans. Colm Luibheid; Mahwah, NJ: Paulist Press, 1987).

Rauser, Randal. 'Can There Be Theology without Necessity?' *Heythrop Journal* 44 (2003): pp. 131–46.

Reed, Esther D. 'Revelation and Natural Rights: Notes on Colin E. Gunton's Theology of Nature'. Pages 203–15 in *Trinitarian Soundings in Systematic Theology* (ed. Paul Louis Metzger; London: T&T Clark, 2005).

Santmire, H. Paul. 'So That He Might Fill All Things: Comprehending the Cosmic Love of Christ'. *Dialog* 42.3 (2003): pp. 257–78.

Schaeffer, Hans. *Createdness and Ethics: The Doctrine of Creation and Theological Ethics in the Theology of Colin E. Gunton and Oswald Bayer* (Berlin: Walter de Gruyter, 2006).

Schwöbel, Christoph. 'A Tribute to Colin Gunton'. Pages 13–18 in *The Person of Christ* (ed. Stephen R. Holmes and Murray A. Rae; London: T&T Clark, 2005).

———. 'The Shape of Colin Gunton's Theology: On the Way towards a Fully Trinitarian Theology'. Pages 182–208 in *The Theology of Colin Gunton* (ed. Lincoln Harvey; London: T&T Clark, 2010).

Sonderegger, Katherine. 'Barth and the Divine Perfections'. *Scottish Journal of Theology* 67.4 (2014): pp. 450–63.

Spence, Alan. 'Christ's Humanity and Ours'. Pages 74–97 in *Persons, Divine and Human: King's College Essays in Theological Anthropology* (ed. Christoph Schwöbel and Colin E. Gunton; Edinburgh: T&T Clark, 1991).

———. 'The Person as Willing Agent: Classifying Gunton's Christology'. Pages 49–64 in *The Theology of Colin Gunton* (ed. Lincoln Harvey; London: T&T Clark, 2010).

Stramara, Jr, Daniel F. 'Gregory of Nyssa's Terminology for Trinitarian Perichoresis'. *Vigiliae christianae* 52 (1998): pp. 257–63.

Studer, Basil. *Trinity and Incarnation: The Faith of the Early Church* (ed. Andrew Louth; trans. Matthias Westerhoff; Collegeville, MN: Liturgical Press, 1993).

Terry, Justyn. 'Colin Gunton's Doctrine of Atonement: Transcending Rationalism by Metaphor'. Pages 130–45 in *The Theology of Colin Gunton* (ed. Lincoln Harvey; London: T&T Clark, 2010).

———. *The Justifying Judgement of God: A Reassessment of the Place of Judgement in the Saving Work of Christ* (Milton Keynes: Paternoster Press, 2007).

Thompson, Mark. 'Has Colin Gunton's Theological Project Really Failed?' *Theological Theology* (blog), 1 December 2009 http://markdthompson.blogspot.com/2009/12/has-colin-guntons-theological-project.html (accessed 1 August 2015).

Tibbs, Paraskevè. 'Created for Action: Colin Gunton's Relational Anthropology'. Pages 116–29 in *The Theology of Colin Gunton* (ed. Lincoln Harvey; London: T&T Clark, 2010).

Tidball, Derek. *The Message of the Cross*. The Bible Speaks Today (Downers Grove, IL: InterVarsity Press, 2001).

van Bavel, Tarsicius J. 'Church'. Pages 169–76 in *Augustine through the Ages: An Encyclopedia* (ed. Allan D. Fitzgerald; Grand Rapids: Eerdmans, 1999).

Vanhoozer, Kevin J. 'The Atonement in Postmodernity: Guilt, Goats and Gifts'. Pages 367–404 in *The Glory of the Atonement: Biblical, Historical and Practical Perspectives: Essays in Honor of Roger Nicole* (ed. Charles E. Hill, Roger R. Nicole and Frank A. James III; Downers Grove, IL: InterVarsity Press, 2004).

Ware, Bruce A. *The Man Christ Jesus: Theological Reflections on the Humanity of Christ* (Wheaton, IL: Crossway, 2012).

Warfield, B.B. 'The Biblical Idea of Inspiration'. Pages 77–112 in *The Works of B.B. Warfield*, vol. 1 (Grand Rapids: Baker, 2003).

Webster, John. 'Gunton and Barth'. Pages 17–31 in *The Theology of Colin Gunton* (ed. Lincoln Harvey; London: T&T Clark, 2010).

———.'Systematic Theology after Barth: Jüngel, Jenson, and Gunton'. Pages 249–64 in *The Modern Theologians: An Introduction to Christian Theology since 1918* (ed. David F. Ford and Rachel Muers; Malden, MA: Blackwell, 3rd edn, 2005).

———.'Theologies of Retrieval'. Pages 583–99 in *The Oxford Handbook of Systematic Theology* (ed. John Webster, Kathryn Tanner and Iain Torrance; Oxford: Oxford University Press, 2007).

Whitney, William B. 'The Correlation between Creation and Culture in the Theology of Abraham Kuyper and Colin E. Gunton'. Pages 76–93 in *The Kuyper Center Review, vol. 3: Calvinism and Culture* (ed. Gordon Graham; Grand Rapids: Eerdmans, 2013).

———. *Problem and Promise in Colin E. Gunton's Doctrine of Creation*. Studies in Reformed Theology 26 (Leiden: Brill, 2013).

Williams, Rowan. *On Christian Theology*. Challenges in Contemporary Theology (Malden, MA: Blackwell, 2000).

Wright, Terry J. 'Colin Gunton on Providence: Critical Commentaries'. Pages 146–64 in *The Theology of Colin Gunton* (ed. Lincoln Harvey; London: T&T Clark, 2010).

Zizioulas, John D. *Being as Communion: Studies in Personhood and the Church* (Crestwood, NY: St Vladimir's Seminary Press, 1985).

Zuckerkandl, Victor. *Sound and Symbol: Music and the External World* (trans. Willard R. Trask; Princeton: Princeton University Press, 1969).

Endnotes

1. Theology and the Theologian: An Introduction

[1] Stephen R. Holmes, 'The Rev Prof Colin Gunton,' *The Guardian*, 3 June 2003 http://www.theguardian.com/news/2003/jun/03/guardianobituaries.highereducation (accessed 30 July 2015).

[2] Much of the subsequent biographical information is taken from a few sources, chiefly: Colin E. Gunton, 'Theology in Communion', in *Shaping the Theological Mind: Theological Context and Methodology* (ed. Darren C. Marks; Burlington, VT: Ashgate, 2002), pp. 31–6; Christoph Schwöbel, 'A Tribute to Colin Gunton', in *The Person of Christ* (ed. Stephen R. Holmes and Murray A. Rae; London: T&T Clark, 2005), pp. 13–18; Holmes, 'Rev Prof Colin Gunton'; Bruce L. McCormack, 'Foreword', and Robert W. Jenson, 'Afterword', in *Trinitarian Soundings in Systematic Theology* (ed. Paul Louis Metzger; London: T&T Clark, 2005), pp. 1–4 and 217–20. Only direct quotes will be cited specifically. For more details of Gunton's life, along with personal reminiscences, I refer the reader to these works.

[3] Gunton, 'Theology in Communion', p. 32.

[4] The dissertation would eventually be published as Colin E. Gunton, *Becoming and Being: The Doctrine of God in Charles Hartshorne and Karl Barth* (Oxford: OUP, 1978). The second edition was published by SCM Press in 2001 with the addition of a new preface and an epilogue. This is the edition to which I will refer throughout this volume. Also note that Jenson was the initial supervisor of the thesis. After he returned to the United States, supervisory duties were taken over first by John Marsh and finally by John Macquarrie (Gunton, *Becoming and Being*, p. ix).

[5] *Persons, Divine and Human: King's College Essays in Theological Anthropology* (1992); *The Doctrine of Creation: Essays in Dogmatics, History and Philosophy* (1997); *Trinitarian Theology Today: Essays on Divine Being and Act* (2000); *God and Freedom* (2001); and *The Theology of Reconciliation* (2003).

6 See Stephen R. Holmes, 'Introduction: The Theologian as Preacher, the Preacher as Theologian', in *The Theologian as Preacher: Further Sermons from Colin E. Gunton* (ed. Sarah J. Gunton and John E. Colwell; London: T&T Clark, 2007), pp. xiv–xv, for Holmes' recollections of Gunton's comments on the matter of Scripture in the church's worship.

7 See Colin E. Gunton, *Intellect and Action: Elucidations on Christian Theology and the Life of Faith* (Edinburgh: T&T Clark, 2000), pp. 139–55. Also published as 'Election and Ecclesiology in the Post-Constantinian Church', *SJT* 53 (2000).

8 For this and other reflections on the non-Reformed character of Gunton's commitments, see Bruce L. McCormack, '*The One, the Three and the Many*: In Memory of Colin Gunton', *Cultural Encounters* (Summer 2005): pp. 13–15. Paul Louis Metzger, in a response to McCormack's tribute, retorts: 'Although I would agree with him that it is difficult "to make a case for the 'Reformed' character of Colin's theology" – a point to which I will return – nonetheless, I find that Colin's work champions, in new ways, certain classic Reformed theological emphases. Such championing includes the respect he pays to propositions as it pertains to revelation in *A Brief Theology of Revelation* and the honor he awards to creation as the theater of redemption in so many of his books. Could one not find as strong a theology of creation in Calvin as one finds in Irenaeus? Then there is the particular concern he shows for safeguarding the distinction between the divine and human natures in the divine Person of the Word in *Act and Being* and the defense he makes of judicial themes concerning Christ's atoning work in *Actuality and Atonement* [sic].' Paul Louis Metzger, 'Response to Bruce L. McCormack's Tribute', *Cultural Encounters* (Summer 2005): p. 20.

9 Holmes, 'Introduction', p. xi. Some of Gunton's sermons are collected in *Theology through Preaching: Sermons for Brentwood* (Edinburgh: T&T Clark, 2001) and *The Theologian as Preacher* (ed. S. Gunton and Colwell).

10 Read Holmes' personal recollections of the events leading up to news of Gunton's death (Stephen Holmes, 'In Memoriam Colin Gunton', *Shored Fragments* (blog) http://steverholmes.org.uk/blog/?p=6973 (accessed 30 July 2015).

11 Holmes, 'In Memoriam'.

12 Jenson, 'Afterword', pp. 218–19.

13 Colin E. Gunton, *Theology through the Theologians: Selected Essays, 1972–1995* (London: T&T Clark, 1996), p. 5.

14 Elsewhere he defines systematic theology as 'that discipline whose responsibility is to articulate the truth and coherence of the view of the

whole implicit in the Bible or a consequence of its message' (Colin Gunton, 'Indispensable Opponent: The Relations of Systematic Theology and the Philosophy of Religion', *NZSTh* 38 [1996]: p. 305).

15 Colin Gunton, 'Historical and Systematic Theology', in *The Cambridge Companion to Christian Doctrine* (Cambridge: CUP, 1997), p. 3.

16 Colin Gunton, 'The Truth . . . and the Spirit of Truth: The Trinitarian Shape of Christian Theology', in *Loving God with Our Minds: The Pastor as Theologian: Essays in Honor of Wallace M. Alston* (Grand Rapids: Eerdmans, 2004), pp. 344–5.

17 Gunton, *Theology through the Theologians*, p. 7. While being cautious about being overly systematic, he does charge the likes of Newman with being too unsystematic. See Gunton, *Theology through the Theologians*, p. 26.

18 Gunton, *Theology through the Theologians*, pp. 7–8; Colin E. Gunton, *Intellect and Action: Elucidations on Christian Theology and the Life of Faith* (Edinburgh: T&T Clark, 2000), p. 21. Being a part of culture, theology shares in culture's fragmentation caused by sin (Colin Gunton, 'Foreword', in Jeremy Begbie, *Voicing Creation's Praise: Towards a Theology of the Arts* [London: T&T Clark, 1991], p. xi).

19 Both quotes derive from Emil Brunner, *The Mediator: A Study of the Central Doctrine of the Christian Faith* (trans. Olive Wyon; Philadephia: Westminster Press, 1947), p. 262, in Gunton, *Theology through the Theologians*, p. 8.

20 Colin Gunton, 'Using and Being Used: Scripture and Systematic Theology', *Theology Today* 47 (1990): p. 251.

21 Gunton, 'Historical and Systematic Theology', p. 11.

22 Gunton, 'Using and Being Used', p. 257.

23 Gunton, 'Using and Being Used', pp. 258–9.

24 Gunton, 'Using and Being Used', pp. 253–5.

25 Gunton indeed speaks of both processes – the formation of Scripture and its use in theology – as two kinds of 'inspiration'. He concludes a piece on what theologians can learn from playwright Peter Shaffer and his *Amadeus*, writing: 'The obvious, if rather banal point, is that theologians, too, need the inspiration of the Spirit if we are to escape from the prisons in which our expectations and presuppositions so often encase us' (Colin Gunton, 'The Playwright as Theologian: Peter Shaffer's *Amadeus*', *King's Theological Review* 10 [1987]: p. 4).

26 Gunton, *Intellect and Action*, p. 1.

27 Gunton tries to make a subtle distinction between formal (e.g. ecumenical creeds) and less formal (e.g. confessions of faith). The point remains that dogmas are authoritative summaries of the church's understanding

of the Christian faith. Gunton, *Intellect and Action*, pp. 3–7. Cf. Colin E. Gunton, 'Creeds and Confessions, Introductory Essay', in *The Practice of Theology: A Reader* (ed. Colin E. Gunton, Stephen R. Holmes and Murray A. Rae; London: SCM Press, 2001), pp. 101–5.

28 Gunton, *Intellect and Action*, pp. 11–12. He offers another definition of dogma: 'rules for safeguarding the gracious character of God's work in Israel and Christ' (Gunton, *Intellect and Action*, p. 16).

29 Gunton, *Intellect and Action*, p. 12.

30 Gunton, *Intellect and Action*, p. 11.

31 Gunton, *Theology through the Theologians*, p. 37. This essay (in a slightly different form) was originally published in 1972 as 'Karl Barth and the Development of Christian Doctrine', *SJT* 25 (1972): pp. 171–80. It appears to be the earliest of Gunton's published academic writings.

32 Gunton, *Theology through the Theologians*, p. 38.

33 Gunton, *Theology through the Theologians*, p. 40.

34 Gunton, *Theology through the Theologians*, p. 42.

35 This particular dimension of the Spirit's person and work will be discussed in detail in Chapter 8.

36 Gunton, *Theology through the Theologians*, pp. 42–5.

37 Gunton, *Theology through the Theologians*, pp. 45–8.

38 See Gunton, 'The Truth . . . and the Spirit of Truth', p. 342.

39 Gunton, 'Indispensable Opponent', pp. 300–1.

40 Gunton, 'Indispensable Opponent', pp. 305–6. Gunton softens Barth's setting up of dogmatics over against apologetics. According to Gunton, the latter is the responsibility of the former and the former arises because of the latter. In fact, an openness to apologetic concerns is what keeps theology fresh. See Gunton, 'Karl Barth and the Development of Christian Doctrine', p. 180.

41 The theology undergirding early modern science – e.g. in Faraday and Newton – is commonly cited by Gunton as an example of this truth. Colin Gunton, 'The Indispensability of Theological Understanding: Theology in the University', in *Essentials of Christian Community* (ed. Daniel W. Hardy, David Ford and Dennis L. Stamps; Edinburgh: T&T Clark, 1996), pp. 269–71.

42 For example, John Owen and John Locke. See Gunton, 'Indispensability of Theological Understanding', pp. 271, 274–5.

43 Gunton, 'Indispensability of Theological Understanding', pp. 275–7.

44 Thus Gunton's chief critique of Maurice Wiles' *The Remaking of Christian Doctrine* is that it does not answer the question of whether theology is concerned for truth or merely expressing in words one's own faith

tradition. Colin Gunton, review of *The Remaking of Christian Doctrine*, in *Theology* 77 (1974): pp. 621–2.
45 Of course, many essays and other books might have been listed under each of those categories.
46 Bernhard Nausner, 'The Failure of a Laudable Project: Gunton, the Trinity and Human Self-Understanding', *SJT* 62 (2009): p. 403.
47 These are the subtitles of *Enlightenment and Alienation*, a chapter from *The One, the Three and the Many*, *Act and Being* and *Father, Son and Holy Spirit* respectively. Full bibliographic information for all of the books named above is found in subsequent chapters.
48 Taken from Gunton's transcribed lectures published as *The Barth Lectures* (ed. P.H. Brazier; T&T Clark, 2007), p. 10 (emphasis added).
49 For a thorough account of Gunton's complex relation to Barth, see John Webster, 'Gunton and Barth', in *The Theology of Colin Gunton* (ed. Lincoln Harvey; London: T&T Clark, 2010), pp. 17–31. Webster is not convinced of Gunton's reading of Barth, largely attributing the former's shortcomings to his limited interaction with Barth's work outside of the *Church Dogmatics* and *Romans* commentary. Gunton got the broad outline correct but was less than precise concerning the details of Barth's theology (Webster, 'Gunton and Barth', pp. 27–8).
50 See, e.g., Gunton's exposition of Coleridge's contribution to the question of human perception in Colin Gunton, *Enlightenment and Alienation: An Essay towards a Trinitarian Theology* (Grand Rapids: Eerdmans, 1985), pp. 30–36. This is also one of the earliest (if not the earliest) references to Coleridge in Gunton's published works.
51 See Colin E. Gunton, *The Promise of Trinitarian Theology* (Edinburgh: T&T Clark, 2nd edn, 1997), pp. 96–7.
52 Gunton, *Promise of Trinitarian Theology*, p. 24.
53 On what Gunton means by system, see the previous section on prolegomena.
54 Gunton writes in his unfinished and unpublished projected dogmatics: 'Augustine's chief weakness is that he asked the wrong question . . . about how to reconcile the absolute simplicity of God with the apparent plurality of the persons, rather than seeking a concept of divine unity on the basis of the economy.' Quoted in Robert W. Jenson, 'A Decision Tree of Colin Gunton's Thinking', in *The Theology of Colin Gunton* (ed. Harvey), p. 10.
55 Jenson, 'A Decision Tree', pp. 8–16.
56 Schwöbel, in his tribute to Gunton, remarks: 'If we still followed the ancient custom of venerating the great doctors of the church by a particular

title, Colin Gunton would have to be the *doctor particularitatis*, the teacher of the significance of the particular who was never content with abstract generalities' (Schwöbel, 'Tribute', p. 14).

57 See Jenson, 'Afterword', p. 219. No doubt this book would be strengthened by the inclusion of material from this proposed dogmatics. However, try though I did, the extant rough draft of the first volume was unavailable to me.

2. Persons in Communion: The Triune God and the Divine Attributes

1 According to Gunton, the classical concept of God holds to the following: first, there is a commitment to 'supernaturalism' that is commonly expressed in the form of a negative theology: God is *not* like the natural world. We define God primarily in terms of what he is not. Second, God is held to be timelessly eternal, relating to the created order in a timeless fashion. Third, and related, the classical concept depends on a hierarchy of being, with God at the summit and everything else by degrees lower and different from him. In a world of motion and change, God is the unmoved Mover and changeless One (Colin E. Gunton, *Becoming and Being: The Doctrine of God in Charles Hartshorne and Karl Barth* [London: SCM Press, 2nd edn, 2001], pp. 2–4).

2 Gunton, *Becoming and Being*, pp. 2–5.

3 Colin Gunton, 'Process Theology's Concept of God: An Outline and Assessment', *Expository Times* 84 (1973): p. 292.

4 Gunton, *Becoming and Being*, pp. 12–14.

5 For example, on the moral front, Hartshorne accuses the classical doctrine of depicting a God who is unconcerned with the affairs of the world. If God is eternal, unchanging, necessary and perfect, then he is not affected by the created order, thus calling into question the overall value of the world. If God is unchanged no matter what we do, then it makes no difference whether we perform one act rather than another (Gunton, *Becoming and Being*, p. 20).

6 Gunton, *Becoming and Being*, p. 31. According to Hartshorne, God is the 'Creator-and-the-Whole-of-what-he-has-created' (quoted in Gunton, *Becoming and Being*, p. 29).

7 Gunton, 'Process Theology's Concept of God', p. 294.

8 Gunton, *Becoming and Being*, p. 42.

9. Gunton, 'Process Theology's Concept of God', p. 294.
10. Gunton, *Becoming and Being*, p. 39.
11. Gunton, 'Process Theology's Concept of God', p. 295. Cf. Gunton, *Becoming and Being*, p. 52.
12. Gunton, *Becoming and Being*, pp. 78–9. Cf. Colin Gunton, 'Process Theology: A Reply', *Expository Times* 85 (1974): p. 215.
13. Gunton, *Becoming and Being*, pp. 74–5.
14. In his later writing, Gunton charges Ted Peters and Catherine Mowry LaCugna with the similar problem of diminishing divine and human freedom resulting from an overemphasis on the economy of salvation. See Colin Gunton, 'The God of Jesus Christ', *Theology Today* 54 (1997): pp. 328–9. We will take up this issue later in this chapter.
15. Gunton, 'Process Theology's Concept of God', p. 296.
16. Gunton, *Becoming and Being*, pp. 128–9, 137. It is interesting to note that much of Gunton's foregoing discussion of Barth is dependent on Eberhard Jüngel's *Gottes Sein ist im Werden*, translated as *God's Being Is in Becoming: The Trinitarian Being of God in the Theology of Karl Barth* (trans. John Webster; Grand Rapids: Eerdmans, 2001) and various works from Robert W. Jenson.
17. Gunton, *Becoming and Being*, p. 167.
18. Gunton, *Becoming and Being*, p. 191. At least one further similarity remains, namely, their contention that unity consists in multiplicity and plurality (e.g. Gunton, *Becoming and Being*, pp. 138, 203).
19. Gunton, *Becoming and Being*, p. 149. Gunton elsewhere asserts: 'The place taken by the Son in Barth's doctrine of God is taken by the world in neoclassical theism' (*Becoming and Being*, p. 160).
20. This difference can also be expressed in terms of differing conceptions of transcendence and immanence. In Hartshorne, God is transcendent immanence, which amounts to total immanence and transcendence only in the abstract (as the totality of temporal events). In Barth, 'God is transcendent in that he is able *to become* immanent in Jesus Christ.' Therefore, transcendence is seen in terms of freedom rather than spatial otherness (see Colin Gunton, 'Transcendence, Metaphor, and the Knowability of God', *JTS* 31 (1980): pp. 510–14.
21. Gunton, *Becoming and Being*, pp. 147–8.
22. Gunton, *Becoming and Being*, p. 148.
23. Gunton, *Becoming and Being*, p. 163.
24. Gunton, *Becoming and Being*, p. 194.
25. Gunton, *Becoming and Being*, p. 206.

26 Gunton, *Becoming and Being*, p. 209. It should be mentioned that Schubert Ogden, noted process theologian, takes Gunton to task on his reading of Hartshorne. In his review of *Becoming and Being*, he complains that Gunton's rendering of Hartshorne bears only a 'faint resemblance' and his analysis and interpretation are 'so full of misunderstanding that one is at a loss to account for them'. Schubert M. Ogden, 'Christian Theology and Neoclassical Theism', *Journal of Religion* 60 (1980): p. 206.

27 For example, while both theologians affirm a theology of the cross, only Barth can account for the cross as a loving act. Hartshorne's God passively endures suffering, while Barth's actively receives suffering as an act of grace (Gunton, *Becoming and Being*, p. 212). Interesting enough, this is precisely where Ogden places the failure of Gunton's book. He charges that the God advocated by Gunton through Barth cannot be both free (in their sense) and loving, or rather, is really free but not loving. He concludes: 'The theological significance of neoclassical theism, it seems to me, is to have powerfully raised the question of whether any such understanding of the freedom and love of God can still be supposed appropriate to the Christian witness. But if this is so, the deeper reason for the failure of Gunton's book is its unqualified success in suppressing this question' (Ogden, 'Christian Theology and Neoclassical Theism': p. 209).

28 This is a repeated critique Gunton will make of Barth, probably deriving somewhat from Robert Jenson. For one exposition of this critique in Jenson, see Robert W. Jenson, *Systematic Theology, vol. 1: The Triune God* (New York: OUP, 1991), pp. 153–5.

29 See Gunton, *Becoming and Being*, pp. 182–5, for five criticisms along these lines. It should also be noted that Gunton (at the time of writing) is generally positive about Barth's doctrine of election, remarking after his exposition of Barth: 'It becomes clear that in his doctrine of election Barth has given rational expression to the distinctive character of the Christian God that is possibly without equal in power, comprehensiveness, and originality' (Colin Gunton, 'Karl Barth's Doctrine of Election as Part of His Doctrine of God', *JTS* 25 [1974]: p. 392). See also his brief positive defence of Barth a decade later in Colin Gunton, 'David Ford: Barth and God's Story', *SJT* 37 (1984): pp. 378–9.

30 Gunton, *Becoming and Being*, p. 164.

31 Gunton, *Becoming and Being*, p. 218.

32 Gunton, *Becoming and Being*, p. 218. In the second edition of *Becoming and Being*, published over twenty years later, Gunton is more critical of Barth's Trinitarianism. Chief among his critiques are Barth's

inadequate use of 'person' language, his acceptance of the *filioque*, and the lack of eschatology in his treatment of the Spirit (*Becoming and Being*, pp. 225–45).

33 We see this even after his account in *Becoming and Being* in, for example, his 1980 essay on the transcendence of God (Gunton, 'Transcendence, Metaphor, and the Knowability of God', pp. 503–8).

34 He earlier (1984) points briefly to Augustine as the source of the Western suspicion of materiality and its consequences for how we understand God's relation to the world and our coming to know God (see Gunton, 'David Ford', p. 375). Gunton is not alone in this assessment of Augustine. See Bradley G. Green, *Colin Gunton and the Failure of Augustine: The Theology of Colin Gunton in Light of Augustine*, Distinguished Dissertations (Eugene, OR: Pickwick, 2011), pp. 19–29, for an exploration of Gunton's counterparts, Rahner, Moltmann, Pannenberg and Zizioulas.

35 Colin Gunton, 'The One, the Three, and the Many: An Inaugural Lecture in the Chair of Christian Doctrine, 1985', published in revised form as Chapter 5 in Colin E. Gunton, *The Promise of Trinitarian Theology* (Edinburgh: T&T Clark, 2nd edn, 1997). A similar critique is lodged in Colin E. Gunton, 'Barth, the Trinity and Human Freedom', *Theology Today* 43 (1986): pp. 325–6.

36 Gunton, *Promise of Trinitarian Theology*, p. 31. This lecture is published under the same title as Chapter 3 of this volume. Since many of Gunton's occasional pieces and articles were later published in edited volumes, throughout this book I have most often simply indicated the page number in the edited volume without reference to the title of the essay either in the volume or in its original form.

37 Gunton, *Promise of Trinitarian Theology*, pp. 33–4.

38 Gunton, *Promise of Trinitarian Theology*, p. 35.

39 Gunton, *Promise of Trinitarian Theology*, p. 36.

40 Gunton, *Promise of Trinitarian Theology*, p. 36.

41 Gunton, *Promise of Trinitarian Theology*, p. 37.

42 Another translation has him calling the distinction 'rather obscure'. Augustine, *The Trinity*, Works of Saint Augustine I/5 (ed. John E. Rotelle; trans. Edmund Hill; New York: New City, 2012), V.10.

43 Gunton, *Promise of Trinitarian Theology*, pp. 39–40.

44 Gunton, *Promise of Trinitarian Theology*, pp. 41–2 (italics original). Gunton elsewhere sums up the problem well: 'Theologically speaking, Augustine deprived the concept [of relations] of theological power by treating relation as ontologically intermediate between substance and accident, thus (1) identifying – or initiating the process which

eventually identified – the person and the relation: the person, in God at any rate, *is* an eternal relation; and (2) rendering person subordinate to being in the reality of God. By reifying relations in that way, he made the concept effectively redundant' (Gunton, *Promise of Trinitarian Theology*, p. 152).

45 Ayres cautions that Augustine's use of substance language is logical and analogical; he uses substance language as a way to relate biblical and philosophical understandings of the Trinity, rather than as specifying some fourth thing underlying the Godhead. Lewis Ayres, 'Augustine, the Trinity and Modernity', *Augustinian Studies* 26 (1995): p. 130.
46 Gunton, *Promise of Trinitarian Theology*, p. 42.
47 Gunton, *Promise of Trinitarian Theology*, p. 43.
48 Gunton, *Promise of Trinitarian Theology*, pp. 44–5.
49 Augustine, *The Trinity*, XIV.8.
50 Gunton, *Promise of Trinitarian Theology*, pp. 46–8.
51 Gunton, *Promise of Trinitarian Theology*, pp. 49–50.
52 Gunton expands on the issue of the depersonalizing of culture arising from Augustine (and others), most notably, in Colin E. Gunton, *The One, the Three and the Many: God, Creation and the Culture of Modernity: The 1992 Bampton Lectures* (Cambridge: CUP, 1993).
53 One scholar refers negatively to these criticisms as Gunton's 'historical scapegoating'. See David S. Cunningham, *These Three Are One: The Practice of Trinitarian Theology*, Challenges in Contemporary Theology (Oxford: Blackwell, 1998), pp. 33, 40–41. Many writers oppose this reading of Augustine. Among the most notable is Michel René Barnes, 'Rereading Augustine's Theology of the Trinity', in *The Trinity: An Interdisciplinary Symposium on the Trinity* (ed. Stephen T. Davis, Daniel Kendall and Gerald O'Collins; Oxford: OUP, 2002), pp. 145–76. Barnes has convincingly argued that the main reason for this typical misreading of Augustine is that many fail to take into account a number of important contextual factors, the chief of which are Augustine's other Trinitarian writings as well as the fourth- and fifth-century Latin 'catholic' (Nicene) Trinitarian theology within which Augustine developed his own theology. See also Basil Studer, *Trinity and Incarnation: The Faith of the Early Church* (ed. Andrew Louth; trans. Matthias Westerhoff; Collegeville, MN: Liturgical Press, 1993), pp. 167–85. With specific regard to Gunton's reading of Augustine, see Green, *Colin Gunton and the Failure of Augustine*; and Neil Ormerod, 'Augustine and the Trinity: Whose Crisis?' *Pacifica* 16.1 (2003): pp. 17–32. Robert Jenson, however, defends Gunton's reading in Jenson, 'A Decision Tree', pp. 10–12. For an attempt to

both confirm and oppose Gunton's reading of Augustine and his legacy, see Joshua McNall, *A Free Corrector: Colin Gunton and the Legacy of Augustine*, Emerging Scholars (Minneapolis: Fortress Press, 2015).
54 Again, at least the second factor can be traced back to Augustine. See Gunton, *Promise of Trinitarian Theology*, pp. 2–4.
55 Colin E. Gunton, *Father, Son and Holy Spirit: Toward a Fully Trinitarian Theology* (London: T&T Clark, 2003), pp. 11–12.
56 'Irenaeus' analogy is with the hands: when our hands do something, we ourselves do it. So, when the Son and the Spirit act in time and history, their acts are the acts of God the Father performed through them' (Colin Gunton, *The Christian Faith: An Introduction to Christian Doctrine* [Malden, MA: Blackwell, 2002], p. 181).
57 See Gunton, *Father, Son and Holy Spirit*, pp. 12–17.
58 Gunton, *Father, Son and Holy Spirit*, p. 12.
59 See Gunton, *Promise of Trinitarian Theology*, p. 47.
60 Gunton, *Father, Son and Holy Spirit*, pp. 17–18.
61 See esp. Jürgen Moltmann's *The Crucified God* and *The Trinity and the Kingdom*, and LaCugna's *God for Us*. Gunton also includes Ted Peters' *God as Trinity* in some of his discussions. For examples of his critiques of these trends in Trinitarian theology, see Gunton, 'God of Jesus Christ', pp. 327–9; Gunton, *Promise of Trinitarian Theology*, pp. xvii–xviii, 20–23.
62 Gunton, 'God of Jesus Christ', pp. 328–9.
63 Although Gunton often gives deference to the Eastern Trinitarian tradition, he does lodge a complaint against the doctrine of divine energies, a later development in Eastern thought. For example, he writes: 'In effect, it may be glossed, the energies crowded out the persons of the Son and the Spirit as the mediators of divine action in and towards the world, so that the implications of the relational ontology became submerged' (Colin Gunton, 'The Trinity in Modern Theology', in *Companion Encyclopedia of Theology* [ed. Peter Byrne and Leslie Houlden; London: Routledge, 1995], p. 940).
64 I am referring to 'The One, the Three, and the Many' (1985) and 'Augustine, the Trinity and the Theological Crisis of the West' (1988).
65 Colin E. Gunton, 'Persons', in *Dictionary of Ethics, Theology and Society* (ed. Paul A.B. Clarke and Andrew Linzey; London: Routledge, 1996), p. 638.
66 Gunton, 'Persons', p. 638. It is noteworthy that Gunton rejects the oversimplification that Eastern theology, when speaking of God, begins with the three, while the West begins with the one. The difference is one of 'weighting': the West overweights the one, so that the threeness – the particularity – of persons is obscured. See Gunton, *Promise of Trinitarian Theology*, pp. 43–4.

67 Gunton, 'Persons', p. 638.
68 Gunton, 'Persons', p. 639.
69 Gunton, *The One, the Three and the Many*, pp. 152, 163–6. Cf. Gunton, *Promise of Trinitarian Theology*, p. 152.
70 Colin Gunton, 'Trinity, Ontology and Anthropology: Towards a Renewal of the Doctrine of the *Imago Dei*', in *Persons, Divine and Human: King's College Essays in Theological Anthropology* (ed. Christoph Schwöbel and Colin E. Gunton; Edinburgh: T&T Clark, 1991), p. 56. He writes similarly: 'The central point about the concept [of perichoresis] is that it enables theology to preserve both the one and the many in dynamic interrelations. It implies that the three persons of the Trinity exist only in reciprocal eternal relatedness. God is not God apart from the way in which Father, Son and Spirit in eternity give to and receive from each other what they essentially are. The three do not merely coinhere, but dynamically constitute one another's being' (Gunton, *The One, the Three and the Many*, pp. 163–4).
71 Gunton, *Father, Son and Holy Spirit*, p. 16.
72 'It should be objected that in their anxiety to expel all traces of Arianism from the scene, theologians like Athanasius and Cyril have stressed too strongly the absolute equality of the three persons of the Trinity, and in so doing have divorced theology, what is called the immanent Trinity, from economy, the biblical account of God's action in the world. For scripture, as for Irenaeus, the economy is very much the economy of the Father, and the Son and the Spirit are its economically subordinate mediators . . . They are indeed "perfect, coequal, coeternal" but some articulations of that are in danger of subverting the economy, of divorcing theology from economy' (Colin Gunton, 'Persons and Particularity', in *Theology of John Zizioulas: Personhood and the Church* [ed. Douglas H. Knight; Burlington, VT: Ashgate, 2007], p. 98).
73 John Calvin, *Institutes* I.13.18, quoted in Gunton, 'God of Jesus Christ', p. 332.
74 See, e.g., Gunton, 'God of Jesus Christ', p. 333.
75 Gunton concludes: 'The Spirit's distinctive mode of action in both time and eternity, economy and essence, consists in the constituting and realization of particularity' (Gunton, *The One, the Three and the Many*, p. 190).
76 To speak more precisely, personhood is most basic and the 'open transcendentals' of perichoresis (the mutual indwelling and constituting action of particular persons), substantiality (constituted by the particular persons) and relationality flow from it. See Gunton, *The One, the Three and the Many*, chs 5–7.

77 Christoph Schwöbel, 'The Shape of Colin Gunton's Theology: On the Way towards a Fully Trinitarian Theology', in *The Theology of Colin Gunton* (ed. Lincoln Harvey; London: T&T Clark, 2010), p. 196.
78 For a brief summary of how the Trinity might shape the doctrine of the attributes, see Gunton, *Christian Faith*, pp. 188–91.
79 Colin E. Gunton, *Act and Being: Towards a Theology of the Divine Attributes* (Grand Rapids: Eerdmans), p. 3.
80 Pseudo-Dionysius, 'The Divine Names' 817C–817D, in *Pseudo-Dionysius: The Complete Works*, The Classics of Western Spirituality (trans. Colm Luibheid; Mahwah, NJ: Paulist Press, 1987), p. 98; quoted in Gunton, *Act and Being*, p. 16.
81 Gunton, *Act and Being*, p. 16.
82 Gunton, *Act and Being*, pp. 17–18.
83 John of Damascus, *On the Divine Images* I.2, quoted in Gunton, *Act and Being*, p. 46 (parenthetical insertion added by Gunton).
84 Gunton, *Act and Being*, pp. 46–7.
85 Gunton, *Act and Being*, pp. 49–52.
86 Gunton, *Act and Being*, pp. 53–4.
87 Gunton, *Act and Being*, p. 70.
88 Gunton, *Act and Being*, pp. 70–74.
89 Gunton, *Act and Being*, p. 77.
90 Irenaeus, *Against Heresies* 4.6.4, quoted in Gunton, *Act and Being*, p. 80.
91 Irenaeus, *Against Heresies* 4.6.6, quoted in Gunton, *Act and Being*, p. 80.
92 Gunton, *Act and Being*, p. 122.
93 Gunton applies this line of thinking to the metaphysical attributes: 'Aseity provides a necessary defence of God's ontological self-sufficiency; simplicity a defence of the indivisibility of his action, immutability of his utter constancy and consistency, impassibility of the indefectibility of his purposes for the perfection of his creation, and omnipotence of the guarantee that what God began in creation he will complete' (Gunton, *Act and Being*, p. 133).
94 Gunton, *Act and Being*, pp. 124–5.
95 Gunton, *Act and Being*, pp. 138–40.
96 One writer argues that Gunton's account of the mediation of creation is 'asymmetrical': 'Formal considerations aside, his default view of the mediation of creation by the hands of God is that, once Christ has been resurrected by the Spirit, God becomes functionally one-handed. Thenceforth the Spirit basically runs the show.' H. Paul Santmire, 'So That He Might Fill All Things: Comprehending the Cosmic Love of Christ', *Dialog* 42 (2003): p. 262.

97 Gunton, *Act and Being*, pp. 140–46.
98 Gunton, *Act and Being*, p. 147.
99 Gunton, *Becoming and Being*, p. 228.
100 This is a question repeatedly raised by Paul Molnar. See his interactions with Gunton in his *Divine Freedom and the Doctrine of the Immanent Trinity: In Dialogue with Karl Barth and Contemporary Theology* (London: T&T Clark, 2002), pp. 317–30. These criticisms are repeated in his reviews of *Becoming and Being* in *IJST* 5 (2003): pp. 80–84, and *The Promise of Trinitarian Theology* in *Theological Studies* 53 (1992): pp. 560–61.
101 Richard M. Fermer, 'The Limits of Trinitarian Theology as a Methodological Paradigm', *NZSTh* 41 (1999): p. 167.
102 Lewis Ayres, review of Colin E. Gunton, *The Promise of Trinitarian Theology*, in *JTS* 43 (1992): pp. 781–2. For a critical appraisal of Gunton's use of Trinitarian language, see Nausner, 'The Failure of a Laudable Project', esp. pp. 413–20. One could also add that Gunton may have overly relied on Zizioulas' reading of the Cappadocians.
103 Such were the perspectives of Gregory of Nyssa, Gregory Nazianzus, Pseudo-Cyril and John of Damascus. For helpful overviews of these matters see William P. Alston, 'Substance and the Trinity', in *The Trinity* (ed. Stephen T. Davis, Daniel Kendall and Gerald O'Collins; Oxford: OUP, 1999), pp. 189–93; Verna Harrison, 'Perichoresis in the Greek Fathers', *St Vladimir's Theological Quarterly* 35 (1991): pp. 53–65; John P. Egan, 'Toward Trinitarian *Perichoresis*: Saint Gregory the Theologian, *Oration* 31.14', *Greek Orthodox Theological Review* 39 (1994): pp. 83–93; Daniel F. Stramara, Jr, 'Gregory of Nyssa's Terminology for Trinitarian Perichoresis', *Vigiliae christianae* 52 (1998): pp. 257–63.
104 Bruce L. McCormack, '*The One, the Three and the Many*: In Memory of Colin Gunton', *Cultural Encounters* (Summer 2005): p. 15.
105 Though I do not agree with the entirety of Kilby's paper, her argument here, which I outline, seems to capture the situation accurately. Karen Kilby, 'Perichoresis and Projection: Problems with Social Doctrines of the Trinity', *New Blackfriars* 81.957 (2000): pp. 432–45.
106 This is to reduce the divine being to perichoresis, something not done by the Cappadocians. See Nausner, 'The Failure of a Laudable Project', pp. 413–14.
107 These are the kinds of questions posed to Gunton at the end of Stephen Holmes' essay entitled 'Towards the *Analogia Personae et Relationis*: Developments in Gunton's Trinitarian Thinking', in *The Theology of Colin Gunton* (ed. Harvey), p. 44.

108 Katherine Sonderegger, 'Barth and the Divine Perfections', *SJT* 67 (2014): pp. 462–3.

109 See Paul D. Molnar, review of Colin E. Gunton, *Father, Son and Holy Spirit: Toward a Fully Trinitarian Theology*, in *Pro ecclesia* 14 (2005): p. 496. See also Molnar, *Divine Freedom*, pp. 320, 329.

110 Fermer, 'Limits of Trinitarian Theology', p. 174. 'Gunton and Zizioulas, unlike the Cappadocians before them, by their identification of the *essence or* being of God with communion of the Father, Son and Spirit, have trespassed on the limits of *cataphatic* theology. Given the fact that we do not have *sub specia aeternitatis*, how can we say what constitutes the Divine *ousia?*' (Fermer, 'Limits of Trinitarian Theology', p. 175).

111 See, e.g., Gunton, *Promise of Trinitarian Theology*, pp. 7, 28.

3. 'It Is Very Good': Creation, Providence and Human Personhood

1 He calls it a 'sterile debate' (see Colin Gunton, 'The Theologian and the Biologist', *Theology* 77 [1974]: p. 527). Cf. Colin E. Gunton, *The Triune Creator: A Historical and Systematic Study* (Grand Rapids: Eerdmans, 1998), p. 15.

2 Gunton, *Triune Creator*, pp. 25–7. This contrast between Heraclitus (the philosopher of the 'many') and Parmenides (the philosopher of the 'one') is foundational to Gunton's seminal account of the decline of Western culture in Colin E. Gunton, *The One, the Three and the Many: God, Creation and the Culture of Modernity: The 1992 Bampton Lectures* (Cambridge: CUP, 1993); see esp. ch. 1.

3 Gunton, *Triune Creator*, pp. 28–9. Below the material representations are artistic representations of material objects.

4 Gunton, *Triune Creator*, p. 29.

5 Gunton, *Triune Creator*, pp. 30–31.

6 Gunton, *Triune Creator*, p. 31.

7 Gunton, *Triune Creator*, pp. 33–6.

8 Gunton, *Triune Creator*, pp. 52–6.

9 Exceptions include Athanasius and Basil. The former argued that because the Father eternally relates to the Son and Spirit, he is not bound to create, but rather freely wills to create. The latter held to what Gunton calls the 'ontological homogeneity' of creation, which denotes that if God is the creator of everything, every created thing has the same ontological status. There are no degrees of being. See Gunton, *Triune Creator*, pp. 66–71.

10. Gunton, *Triune Creator*, pp. 57–9. For more on Gunton's reading of the tradition of spiritualizing the early chapters of Genesis, see Colin E. Gunton, 'Between Allegory and Myth: The Legacy of the Spiritualising of Genesis', in *The Doctrine of Creation: Essays in Dogmatics, History and Philosophy* (ed. Colin E. Gunton; Edinburgh: T&T Clark, 1997), pp. 47–62. I will elaborate on this issue in the discussion of Augustine ahead.
11. Gunton, *Triune Creator*, pp. 60–61.
12. Gunton, *Triune Creator*, p. 75.
13. Gunton, *Triune Creator*, p. 76.
14. This 'embarrassment' regarding literal days is already found in Philo (Gunton, *Triune Creator*, p. 77).
15. Augustine, *Confessions* 12.7, quoted in Gunton, *Triune Creator*, pp. 77–8.
16. Gunton, *Triune Creator*, pp. 83–4.
17. Gunton, *Triune Creator*, p. 84.
18. Colin E. Gunton, *Theology through the Theologians: Selected Essays, 1972–1995* (London: T&T Clark, 1996), p. 133.
19. Gunton, *Theology through the Theologians*, pp. 130–31.
20. Gunton, *Triune Creator*, pp. 99–102.
21. Gunton, *Triune Creator*, pp. 118–21.
22. Gunton, *Triune Creator*, pp. 121–4.
23. Gunton, *Triune Creator*, pp. 148–9.
24. Gunton, *Triune Creator*, p. 153.
25. Gunton, *Triune Creator*, p. 153. Of course there were problems in the Reformers' treatments of the doctrine, such as the failure to more carefully spell out the Trinitarian patterns of mediation in creation, as well as reconciliation and redemption (see Gunton, *Triune Creator*, pp. 153–4).
26. Colin Gunton, 'The Doctrine of Creation', in *The Cambridge Companion to Christian Doctrine* (ed. Colin E. Gunton; Cambridge: CUP, 1997), p. 141.
27. Gunton, 'Doctrine of Creation', pp. 141–2; Colin Gunton, *The Christian Faith: An Introduction to Christian Doctrine* (Malden, MA: Blackwell, 2002), p. 18. Cf. Colin E. Gunton, *Christ and Creation* (Grand Rapids: Eerdmans, 1992), p. 44.
28. Gunton, *Christian Faith*, p. 18.
29. Gunton, *Christian Faith*, pp. 10–11.
30. Gunton, *Theology through the Theologians*, p. 135; Gunton, 'Doctrine of Creation', p. 142.
31. Gunton, *Christian Faith*, pp. 5–8.
32. Gunton, *Christian Faith*, p. 10. Gunton argues that one's construal of the divine and human relation in Christ is the key to understanding the relationship between Creator and creature. The chief difference between him and his *Doktorvater*, Robert Jenson, for example, is that the latter's

Christology tends in a monophysite direction, and thus conceives of the Creator–creature relation as one in which the creature is effectively enveloped by the Creator, as the human would in the hypostatic union. The world's *Selbständigkeit* – its own independent reality – is compromised in this configuration, as creation is taken somewhat into the being of God. The 'without confusion' of Chalcedon must be taken seriously in order to yield a Christology that could fund a proper account of the God–world relation. See Colin Gunton, 'Creation and Mediation in the Theology of Robert W. Jenson: An Encounter and a Convergence', in *Trinity, Time and Church: A Response to the Theology of Robert W. Jenson* (ed. Colin E. Gunton; Grand Rapids: Eerdmans, 2000), pp. 80–93.

33 Gunton, *Christ and Creation*, p. 45.

34 Colin Gunton, 'Atonement and the Project of Creation: An Interpretation of Colossians 1:15–23', *Dialog* 35 (1996): p. 36.

35 Gunton, 'Atonement and the Project of Creation', p. 38. This emphasis on creation's goodness and eschatological perfection, according to one scholar, is helpful for a theology of culture. See William Baltmanis Whitney, 'The Correlation between Creation and Culture in the Theology of Abraham Kuyper and Colin E. Gunton', in *The Kuyper Center Review, vol. 3: Calvinism and Culture* (ed. Gordon Graham; Grand Rapids: Eerdmans, 2013).

36 Gunton, *Christian Faith*, p. 19. Elsewhere, in his earlier work, he describes God's purpose in this way: 'That all things may through being perfected praise the one who made them' (Gunton, *Christ and Creation*, p. 96).

37 'Corresponding to the creator's gift of the creation is the creature's glad and willing praise of the creator's goodness in a sacrifice of praise and thanksgiving' (Gunton, 'Atonement and the Project of Creation' p. 39).

38 Gunton, *The One, the Three and the Many*, p. 142.

39 Gunton, *The One, the Three and the Many*, pp. 142–3.

40 Gunton, *The One, the Three and the Many*, pp. 144–5. Coleridge spoke of the Trinity as the *Idea Idearum*, through which we could understand our being (see Colin E. Gunton, *The Promise of Trinitarian Theology* [Edinburgh: T&T Clark, 2nd edn, 1997], p. 28). Moreover, Gunton by no means considers the world the image of God, as such a position is fraught with problems. First, it blurs the distinction between the creation generally and human beings in particular. The image of God is personal, and thus a mark of human being in contrast to the world. Second, the other side of the coin is that the character of the non-human creation is then difficult to conceive. See Gunton, *Promise of Trinitarian Theology*, p. 141.

41 Richard M. Fermer, 'The Limits of Trinitarian Theology as a Methodological Paradigm', *NZSTh* 41 (1999): p. 170.
42 In an earlier essay, Gunton briefly explores freedom, relation and energy as potential candidates for Trinity-shaped transcendentals. See Gunton, *Promise of Trinitarian Theology*, pp. 139–45.
43 Gunton, *The One, the Three and the Many*, p. 164.
44 Gunton, *The One, the Three and the Many*, pp. 165–6.
45 Gunton, *The One, the Three and the Many*, pp. 168–72.
46 Gunton, *The One, the Three and the Many*, p. 189.
47 Gunton, *The One, the Three and the Many*, p. 190.
48 Gunton, *The One, the Three and the Many*, p. 191.
49 Gunton, *The One, the Three and the Many*, p. 225.
50 Gunton, *The One, the Three and the Many*, p. 229. Gunton prefers the term *relationality* to *sociality* because the latter is only true of personal relationships, in which love and freedom are possibilities. This is not true of non-personal entities.
51 Some writers, speaking from the Calvinist tradition, find this treatment too speculative. See, e.g., Craig Bartholomew, 'The Healing of Modernity: A Trinitarian Remedy? A Critical Dialogue with Colin Gunton's *The One, the Three and the Many: God, Creation and the Culture of Modernity*', *European Journal of Theology* 6 (1997): pp. 111–30.
52 Gunton contrasts the garden with paradise: 'In paradise, the fruits simply fall off the trees on to our tables; in a garden, trees have to be tended' (Gunton, *Triune Creator*, p. 197).
53 Gunton, *Christian Faith*, pp. 28–31. In a pithy way, he defines providence as 'conservation in eschatological perspective' (Gunton, *Christian Faith*, p. 36).
54 Gunton, *Christian Faith*, p. 35.
55 Gunton, *Triune Creator*, pp. 176–7.
56 Gunton, 'Atonement and the Project of Creation', pp. 37–8.
57 Gunton, *Triune Creator*, p. 182–3.
58 Gunton, *Triune Creator*, p. 177–8.
59 A third aspect could be added, namely, that the Spirit upholds the world, particularly by keeping it in Christ, in whom, through whom and for whom all things were made (Gunton, *Triune Creator*, p. 177).
60 Gunton, *Triune Creator*, p. 192.
61 'We are able to use the concept of the person about human beings *because* we know something of the nature of a personal God.' Colin Gunton, 'Knowledge and Culture: Towards an Epistemology of the Concrete', in *The Gospel and Contemporary Culture* (ed. Hugh Montefiore; London: Mowbray, 1992), p. 95 (emphasis added).

62 Since the theology underlying human personhood was taken up in Chapter 2, the present discussion will be kept brief.
63 Gunton, *Christian Faith*, pp. 41–2.
64 Gunton, *Christian Faith*, pp. 45–6.
65 Gunton, *Promise of Trinitarian Theology*, p. 113.
66 Gunton, *Promise of Trinitarian Theology*, pp. 100–2.
67 Gunton, *Triune Creator*, p. 205.
68 Gunton, *Promise of Trinitarian Theology*, pp. 111–12.
69 Gunton, *Christ and Creation*, p. 102. One scholar mistakenly contends that Gunton has 'somewhat conflicting opinions' on the functional view because in one place he identifies it as inadequate ('too restrictive') and in a slightly later work says the image has 'something to do' with presenting the creation to God perfected. There is no conflict here, just further elaboration on what would make a functional view more adequate (but still insufficient). See Paraskevè Tibbs, 'Created for Action: Colin Gunton's Relational Anthropology', in *The Theology of Colin Gunton* (ed. Lincoln Harvey; London: T&T Clark, 2010), pp. 121–2.
70 He also argues that this version of the relational view is too anthropocentric, not giving any space to the non-human creation and its place in the covenant (Gunton, *Promise of Trinitarian Theology*, p. 112).
71 Gunton, *Christ and Creation*, p. 101.
72 Gunton, *Christ and Creation*, pp. 102–3.
73 Gunton, *Christ and Creation*, p. 100.
74 Gunton, *Christ and Creation*, pp. 103–5. Gunton in several writings comments that there is often too much hysteria concerning the so-called ecological crisis. In one place he provides a sober starting point to discussions of ecology: '[A]ll human dominion of the earth will involve the alteration of the balance of things, and . . . no human behaviour, however well-intentioned, will be free from problematic consequences. There is therefore no natural cure, no solution to be read off nature, of the problems caused by human relatedness with the rest of the created order, so that there will always be an ecological problem' (Gunton, *Christ and Creation*, p. 105 [see also pp. 33–4]).
75 Gunton, *Christ and Creation*, p. 101.
76 Gunton, *Christ and Creation*, pp. 108–12.
77 Of course the theme of creation's freedom is already present in *Becoming and Being*, as we have seen.
78 Kant is the key exemplar of this perspective, according to Gunton. Colin Gunton, *Enlightenment and Alienation: An Essay towards a Trinitarian Theology* (Grand Rapids: Eerdmans, 1985), pp. 57–68.

[79] Gunton, *Enlightenment and Alienation*, p. 93.
[80] Paul's picture of Christ's self-emptying is also another stark example of the harmony of authority and obedience (Gunton, *Enlightenment and Alienation*, pp. 94–5).
[81] Gunton, *Enlightenment and Alienation*, p. 99. The basic form of this treatment of freedom is already found in Barth. See Colin E. Gunton, 'Barth, the Trinity and Human Freedom', *Theology Today* 43 (1986): pp. 321–8.
[82] Gunton, *Enlightenment and Alienation*, p. 103.
[83] Gunton, *Enlightenment and Alienation*, p. 105.
[84] Colin E. Gunton, 'God, Grace and Freedom', in *God and Freedom: Essays in Historical and Systematic Theology* (ed. Colin E. Gunton; Edinburgh: T&T Clark, 1995), p. 122.
[85] For an extended engagement with Gunton's theology of particularity as it relates to the Spirit's role in Jesus' life, see David A. Hohne, *Spirit and Sonship: Colin Gunton's Theology of Particularity and the Holy Spirit* (Burlington, VT: Ashgate, 2010).
[86] Gunton, 'God, Grace and Freedom', pp. 130–31. One writer suggests (incorrectly, I believe) that Gunton's account of freedom is not Trinitarian enough. Rather than seeing the Spirit as the source of human freedom, Gunton should have grounded it in the triunity of God. See Cynthia McCall Campbell, 'Response to Colin Gunton', *Theology Today* 43 (1986): p. 332. It is unclear to me, however, how Gunton's connection of Father, Son and Spirit above is anything but a Trinitarian sourcing of freedom.
[87] Gunton, *Christian Faith*, p. 61.
[88] He employs a gardening (of which I hear he was quite fond) metaphor to elucidate: 'But it remains the case that our social being is the compost within which our historically transmitted fallenness is nourished and grows' (Gunton, *Christian Faith*, p. 61).
[89] Gunton denies Adam as historical, claiming such a view requires 'a naïve and literalist reading'. He is more ambivalent about a historical fall. See Gunton, *Christian Faith*, pp. 61–2.
[90] For a helpful and highly favourable study of Gunton's theology of creation, consult William B. Whitney, *Problem and Promise in Colin E. Gunton's Doctrine of Creation*, Studies in Reformed Theology 26 (Leiden: Brill, 2013). Whitney sees Gunton's treatment of the role of Greek thought on Christian theology as 'relatively uncontroversial' (Whitney, *Problem and Promise*, p. 38).
[91] John Webster, 'Systematic Theology after Barth: Jüngel, Jenson, and Gunton', in *The Modern Theologians: An Introduction to Christian*

Theology since 1918 (ed. David F. Ford and Rachel Muers [Malden, MA: Blackwell, 3rd edn, 2005], p. 261.

92. Nicholas Lash, *Believing Three Ways in One God: A Reading of the Apostles' Creed* (London: SCM Press, 1992), p. 32, quoted in Fermer, 'Limits of Trinitarian Theology', pp. 176–7.

93. Fermer, 'Limits of Trinitarian Theology', p. 178.

94. Fermer, 'Limits of Trinitarian Theology', p. 180.

95. Fermer, 'Limits of Trinitarian Theology', p. 181.

96. Fermer, 'Limits of Trinitarian Theology', p. 182.

97. Bernhard Nausner, 'The Failure of a Laudable Project': Gunton, the Trinity and Human Self-Understanding', *SJT* 62 (2009): p. 415. Perhaps one might nuance Fermer and Nausner and concede that there is a sense in which numerical identity *is* constituted by relations. For example, one's relationships to God as Creator and one's parents as biological sources determine (as sources), in differing degrees, our numerical identity. I owe this point to my colleague, Matt Jenson.

98. Nausner, 'The Failure of a Laudable Project', p. 418. Cf. Fermer, 'Limits of Trinitarian Theology', p. 182.

99. For example, in his introduction to Christian doctrine, *The Christian Faith*, he devotes about five pages (out of roughly 200) to a direct treatment of sin. Though agreeing generally with this accusation, Whitney comes to Gunton's rescue by offering four reasons why Gunton's treatment of sin is limited and structured the way it is. See Whitney, *Problem and Promise*, pp. 126–37.

100. See Tibbs, 'Created for Action', p. 124. Remarking on Rom. 1, Green writes, 'It appears that Paul's argument is that a culture must not simply have the right *ideas* of God, that culture must also glorify God and give thanks to Him, and this latter emphasis is missing in Gunton' (Bradley G. Green, *Colin Gunton and the Failure of Augustine: The Theology of Colin Gunton in Light of Augustine*, Distinguished Dissertations [Eugene, OR: Pickwick, 2011], p. 173). From an entirely different angle, Douglas Knight questions whether Gunton's account of sin is sufficiently theologically and eschatologically determined: 'One question that could be asked of Gunton is whether he is entirely successful in keeping the concept of sin theologically determined. Sin is not a natural category . . . A thoroughly theological definition measures sin from the telos, against what the people of God will become.' Douglas Knight, 'From Metaphor to Mediation: Colin Gunton and the Concept of Mediation', *NZSTh* 43 (2001): p. 125.

[101] Paul D. Molnar, *Divine Freedom and the Doctrine of the Immanent Trinity: In Dialogue with Karl Barth and Contemporary Theology* (London: T&T Clark, 2002), p. 296.

[102] Hans Schaeffer, *Createdness and Ethics: The Doctrine of Creation and Theological Ethics in the Theology of Colin E. Gunton and Oswald Bayer* (Berlin: Walter de Gruyter, 2006), p. 237.

[103] Whitney, *Problem and Promise*, p. 103.

[104] Another author questions whether Gunton's model makes the fall necessary. He writes: 'The question that must now be asked is this: if redemption is the Spirit-inspired, Christ-structured movement of creation towards a greater end than its beginning, is the fallenness of the world *necessary* to implement the eschatological perfecting of creation?' (Terry J. Wright, 'Colin Gunton on Providence: Critical Commentaries', in *The Theology of Colin Gunton* [ed. Lincoln Harvey; London: T&T Clark, 2010], p. 151). Gunton is not explicit on this exact issue. However, he would state that Christ would have come even if there were no fall (Gunton, *Christ and Creation*, p. 96).

4. The Knowledge of Faith: Reason, Revelation and Scripture

[1] Colin E. Gunton, 'The Place of Reason in Theology', in *The Practice of Theology: A Reader* (ed. Colin E. Gunton, Stephen R. Holmes and Murray A. Rae; London: SCM Press, 2001), pp. 149–50.

[2] Colin Gunton, 'Karl Barth and the Western Intellectual Tradition: Towards a Theology after Christendom', in *Theology Beyond Christendom: Essays on the Centenary of the Birth of Karl Barth, May 10, 1886* (ed. John Thompson; Allison Park, PA: Pickwick, 1986), pp. 286–8.

[3] Gunton, 'The Place of Reason', p. 150. Cf. Gunton, 'Karl Barth and the Western Intellectual Tradition', p. 288.

[4] Gunton, 'The Place of Reason', p. 150.

[5] Luther, Calvin and Turretin are presented as those who stressed the fallenness of the whole human person, including their reason. Thus redemption precedes the proper use of the faculties. See Gunton, 'The Place of Reason', pp. 150–51.

[6] Gunton, 'Karl Barth and the Western Intellectual Tradition', p. 289.

[7] Colin E. Gunton, *Theology through the Theologians: Selected Essays, 1972– 1995* (London: T&T Clark, 1996), p. 51.

[8] Gunton, *Theology through the Theologians*, pp. 51–2. This may be seen as another dualism generated by reason's new relation to faith – that between

objectivism and subjectivism. Whether in the form of Descartes' rationalism, British empiricism or Kant's idealism, there developed a divide between knower and known. In Descartes, for instance, the stress was on the knowing subject over against the object to be known. In Kant we find the separation between pure and practical reason, as well as objective knowledge and subjective belief. These shifts betray an increased confidence in the capacities of reason to offer a full account of reality. See Colin E. Gunton, 'The Truth of Christology', in *Belief in Science and in Christian Life: The Relevance of Michael Polanyi's Thought for Christian Faith and Life* (ed. Thomas F. Torrance; Edinburgh: Handsel, 1980), pp. 95–6.

[9] Gunton, *Theology through the Theologians*, pp. 52–3.

[10] Michael Polanyi, *The Tacit Dimension* (Chicago: University of Chicago Press, 2009), p. 4. Cf. Michael Polanyi, *Personal Knowledge: Towards a Post-Critical Philosophy* (New York: Harper & Row, 1964), pp. 69–70, where he introduced these concepts. He distinguishes between two types of knowledge: 'There is (1) knowing a thing *by attending to it*, in the way we attend to an entity as a whole and (2) knowing a thing *by relying on our awareness of it for the purpose of attending to an entity to which it contributes*. The latter knowledge can be said to be *tacit*, so far as we cannot tell what the particulars are, on the awareness of which we rely for attending to the entity comprising them' (Michael Polanyi, 'Tacit Knowing: Its Bearing on Some Problems in Philosophy', *Reviews of Modern Physics* 34 [1962]: p. 601).

[11] Gunton, 'The Truth of Christology', pp. 96–7 (italics original).

[12] Polanyi, 'Tacit Knowing', p. 606.

[13] On presuppositions as indwelt tools, see Polanyi, *Personal Knowledge*, p. 60.

[14] Colin Gunton, *Enlightenment and Alienation: An Essay towards a Trinitarian Theology* (Grand Rapids: Eerdmans, 1985), p. 40.

[15] Gunton, *Theology through the Theologians*, p. 54. Elsewhere he writes: 'Indwelling presupposes a real relation of mind and body, person and world, concept and reality, and is illustrated at its highest level by the relation between mathematical theory and the universe' (Gunton, 'The Truth of Christology', p. 99).

[16] Gunton, *Theology through the Theologians*, pp. 55–6. Cf. Colin Gunton, 'Knowledge and Culture: Towards an Epistemology of the Concrete', in *The Gospel and Contemporary Culture* (ed. Hugh Montefiore; London: Mowbray, 1992), pp. 97–9.

[17] Gunton, 'Karl Barth and the Western Intellectual Tradition', pp. 291–4.

[18] Gunton, 'Karl Barth and the Western Intellectual Tradition', pp. 295–7.

[19] Gunton, 'Karl Barth and the Western Intellectual Tradition', p. 298.

20 Gunton, 'Karl Barth and the Western Intellectual Tradition', pp. 298–9. Another way of putting the matter could be found in an essay co-written with Robert Jenson, where they argue that since Jesus Christ is the Logos – *the* rational principle of all things – 'there can be no reliable tracing of the logos of things in general that does not in fact conform . . . to the story of Jesus' life, death, and resurrection'. They say again: 'Theology must therefore claim to be a universal discourse, in the sense that any discourse must be irrational that cannot be interpreted by the church's discourse about Jesus the Christ.' The basic point is that knowledge of God and everything else is mediated through the incarnate Word. See Colin Gunton and Robert W. Jenson, 'The Logos Ensarkos and Reason', in *Reason and the Reasons of Faith*, Theology for the Twenty-First Century (ed. Paul J. Griffiths and Reinhard Hütter; New York: T&T Clark, 2005), pp. 78–85. Gunton early in his career charges Rudolf Bultmann and process theology with committing the very same error of making Jesus Christ irrelevant in matters epistemological. See Colin Gunton, 'Rudolf Bultmann and the Location of Language about God', *Theology* 75 (1972): pp. 537–8, and 'The Knowledge of God According to Two Process Theologians: A Twentieth-Century Gnosticism', *Religious Studies* 11 (1975): pp. 95–6.

21 He is referring to Barth's statements in *CD* II/1, p. 21: 'Certainly we have God as an object, but not in the same way as we have other objects . . . We have all other objects as they are determined by the pre-arranged disposition and pre-arranged mode of our own existence.' See Gunton, *Theology through the Theologians*, p. 67.

22 Gunton, *Theology through the Theologians*, p. 67.

23 Colin E. Gunton, *Intellect and Action: Elucidations on Christian Theology and the Life of Faith* (Edinburgh: T&T Clark, 2000), pp. 55–64.

24 Colin E. Gunton, *A Brief Theology of Revelation: The 1993 Warfield Lectures* (London: T&T Clark, 2005), pp. 3–4. For a very helpful and moderately critical overview of Gunton's relationship to Barth, see John Webster, 'Gunton and Barth', in *The Theology of Colin Gunton* (ed. Lincoln Harvey; London: T&T Clark, 2010), pp. 17–31. I benefited greatly from some of Webster's analysis.

25 Gunton hints at agreement with the charge that Barth's theory of revelation evinces an over-realized eschatology: revelation is here and now, direct and full. He contrasts Barth's with Pannenberg's view that full revelation is solely eschatological and presently indirect. See Colin E. Gunton, *Revelation and Reason: Prolegomena to Systematic Theology* (ed. P.H. Brazier; London: T&T Clark, 2008), pp. 68–9.

26 Colin Gunton, *The Christian Faith: An Introduction to Christian Doctrine* (Malden, MA: Blackwell, 2002), p. 5.

27 Colin E. Gunton, *Act and Being: Towards a Theology of the Divine Attributes* (Grand Rapids: Eerdmans), p. 77. This theology of mediation was often developed through the use of Irenaeus' image of the Son and Spirit as the Father's 'two hands'. See, e.g., Colin E. Gunton, *Christ and Creation* (Grand Rapids: Eerdmans, 1992), p. 75.

28 Gunton, *Brief Theology of Revelation*, p. 5. This argument Gunton borrows from Alan Spence, 'Christ's Humanity and Ours', in *Persons, Divine and Human: King's College Essays in Theological Anthropology* (ed. Christoph Schwöbel and Colin E. Gunton; Edinburgh: T&T Clark, 1991), esp. pp. 88–93.

29 Gunton, *Act and Being*, pp. 77–8.

30 Gunton might characterize this as an example of Barth's capitulation to the Augustinian heritage of placing a radical disjunction between God and the created order. For an example of Gunton's critique of Augustine's doctrine of creation, see Colin E. Gunton, *Triune Creator: A Historical and Systematic Study* (Grand Rapids: Eerdmans, 1998), pp. 76–7. This is also discussed in Chapter 3 of the present volume.

31 Gunton, *Brief Theology of Revelation*, p. 123.

32 This failure may be a symptom of a larger problem Gunton finds in Barth's theology, namely, the 'swallowing up' of the humanity of the Son by the divinity. He writes: 'Because the humanity of Christ is for Barth the humanity of God, everything that happens is for Barth the act of God. That is right, but raises the question: in what sense is everything that happens also the action and passion of a man?' (Gunton, *Christ and Creation*, p. 48). Elsewhere he charges that Barth 'orders' the priesthood of Christ to his divinity, therefore diminishing the human character of his priestly work (Colin Gunton, 'Salvation', in *The Cambridge Companion to Karl Barth* [ed. John Webster; Cambridge: CUP, 2007], p. 157).

33 Gunton, *Brief Theology of Revelation*, p. 122. This failure to specify patterns of mediation might be a result of what Gunton recurrently charges as Western theology's resistance to further distinguish the particular *ad intra* and *ad extra* operations of the Trinitarian persons, as well as its inability to ascribe real personhood and meaningful agency to the Holy Spirit. See, e.g., Colin Gunton, 'The Spirit in the Trinity', in *The Forgotten Trinity: A Selection of Papers Presented to the BCC Study Commission on Trinitarian Doctrine Today 3* (ed. Alisdair I.C. Heron; London: BCC/CCBI, 1991), pp. 123–35; Colin E. Gunton, *The Promise of Trinitarian Theology* (Edinburgh: T&T Clark, 2nd edn, 1997), pp. 30–55; and

Gunton, *The One, the Three and the Many: God, Creation and the Culture of Modernity: The 1992 Bampton Lectures* (Cambridge: CUP, 1993), pp. 188–92.

34 Gunton, *Brief Theology of Revelation*, pp. 22–30.
35 Gunton, *Brief Theology of Revelation*, pp. 32–5.
36 Gunton blames this development on the ontological dualism handed down from Augustine's neoplatonic cosmology (Gunton, *Brief Theology of Revelation*, pp. 44–5).
37 Here he follows Calvin's discussion of general revelation and natural theology in the *Institutes* I.5–6.
38 'A theology of nature is the gift of biblical revelation, for it teaches us that the unity of things is upheld by . . . the incarnate Lord whose work on earth was achieved in the power of the Spirit and in weakness. It follows that it is because we have a theology of creation derived from revelation – that is, biblically mediated revelation – that we can seek for the glory of God in the things that have been made.' One can hear Barth in the background: 'The doctrine of general revelation is not therefore something that operates in parallel with biblical revelation, but is derived from it.' Gunton, *Brief Theology of Revelation*, pp. 59, 61. For a treatment of Gunton's theology of nature applied to 'natural rights', see Esther D. Reed, 'Revelation and Natural Rights: Notes on Colin E. Gunton's Theology of Nature', in *Trinitarian Soundings in Systematic Theology* (ed. Paul Louis Metzger; London: T&T Clark, 2005), pp. 203–15.
39 Gunton, *Brief Theology of Revelation*, pp. 109, 113, 125.
40 Gunton, *Brief Theology of Revelation*, p. 106.
41 Gunton, *Intellect and Action*, p. 52.
42 Gunton, *Intellect and Action*, pp. 53–4.
43 Gunton, *Brief Theology of Revelation*, p. 113.
44 On the particularizing role of the Spirit within the Godhead and the created order, see Gunton, *The One, the Three and the Many*, pp. 182–90. Regarding the Spirit's particularizing of Jesus' humanity, Gunton borrows from Edward Irving. See, e.g., Gunton, *Christian Faith*, p. 102; Gunton, *Theology through the Theologians*, pp. 151–68.
45 Gunton, *Christian Faith*, p. 7.
46 He sums up his view of the mediation of revelation thus: 'Revelation is mediated in a number of ways: each way is a different way of revealing something of God and the truth . . . There are a variety of means through which we can gain Revelation' (Gunton, *Revelation and Reason*, pp. 76–7).
47 Colin Gunton, *The Barth Lectures* (ed. P.H. Brazier; London: T&T Clark, 2007), p. 74. Admittedly, comments made in a lecture may be less

guarded than in a publication. However, there was in Gunton dissatisfaction with Barth's treatment of the doctrine.

48 Gunton, *Barth Lectures*, pp. 73–4; cf. Gunton, *Revelation and Reason*, p. 188.
49 It is probably fair to say that Gunton's main point is that Barth *overemphasizes* present 'inspiration' relative to past inspiration. In a response to a question during a lecture, he briefly acknowledges that Barth holds to some view of original inspiration (Gunton, *Revelation and Reason*, p. 81). Yet the brunt of his critique is directed towards the perceived lack of a doctrine of inspiration in Barth.
50 Gunton, *Brief Theology of Revelation*, pp. 76–8.
51 Gunton, *Brief Theology of Revelation*, p. 68.
52 Gunton, *Brief Theology of Revelation*, p. 66.
53 Cited in Gunton, *Brief Theology of Revelation*, p. 66. It appears that Gunton's logic (as he borrows from Coleridge) is thus: (1) revelation equals dictation; (2) inspiration is clearly not dictation; (3) therefore revelation does not equal inspiration. Thus, the traditional assumption that because something is inspired it is revelation apparently falters. See also Gunton, *Revelation and Reason*, p. 72.
54 Gunton, *Brief Theology of Revelation*, p. 66. On the non-problem of fallibility, he notes: 'In so far as God deals with us humanly then there has to be space between the words and God. In one sense you will want to hold to the infallibility of scripture in a broad sense, but there has to be space between the words and the *Word* as Barth would see it, between the words and *God*' (Gunton, *Revelation and Reason*, pp. 83–4).
55 Gunton, *Brief Theology of Revelation*, p. 67. Put differently, Scripture is *revelatory* or *revealing*, not revelation, properly speaking. On this distinction, see also Gunton, *Barth Lectures*, p. 74.
56 Gunton, *Brief Theology of Revelation*, pp. 68, 71–2.
57 Gunton writes: 'The distinct mark of the revelatory character of the Bible is its relation to salvation in Christ the mediator of salvation. The revelatory uniqueness of the Bible derives from its mediation of the life of this man, and particularly his cross and resurrection' (Gunton, *Brief Theology of Revelation*, p. 73). He also writes: 'The particular quality of the Bible's mediation of revelation is derived from its mediation of salvation. It's [sic] uniqueness derives from the uniqueness of the Christ who is mediated and of that which is mediated by Christ' (Gunton, *Brief Theology of Revelation*, p. 74).
58 See, e.g., Gunton, *Theology through the Theologians*, p. 202.
59 Gunton, *Brief Theology of Revelation*, p. 75.
60 Gunton, *Brief Theology of Revelation*, p. 75–6.

61 Gunton, *Brief Theology of Revelation*, p. 77.
62 Gunton, *Brief Theology of Revelation*, p. 78.
63 He writes: 'The form of revelation is not identical to the form of that which it reveals, any more than the form of a scientific theory is identical with the form of the world it makes known, though in both cases there is an intrinsic relation between the two.' Similarly, he concludes: 'Dogma and theology are revisable, scripture is in certain respects open to question, but revelation, mediated through scripture, is not' (Gunton, *Brief Theology of Revelation*, p. 81).
64 Gunton, *Christian Faith*, p. 155.
65 Gunton, *Brief Theology of Revelation*, p. 120.
66 'If God wished to give His people a series of letters like Paul's, He prepared a Paul to write them, and the Paul He brought to the task was a Paul who spontaneously would write just such letters' (B.B. Warfield, 'The Biblical Idea of Inspiration', in *The Works of B.B. Warfield*, vol. 1 [Grand Rapids: Baker, 2003], p. 101).
67 Gunton, *Brief Theology of Revelation*, p. 77.
68 Gunton, *Brief Theology of Revelation*, pp. 77–78.
69 Gunton, *The One, the Three and the Many*, p. 212.
70 Paul D. Molnar, *Divine Freedom and the Doctrine of the Immanent Trinity: In Dialogue with Karl Barth and Contemporary Theology* (London: T&T Clark, 2002), p. 277.
71 Bonaventure, *Breviloquium*, Works of St Bonaventure 9 (ed. and trans. Dominic V. Monti; New York: Franciscan Institute, 2005), prol. 0.2 (italics original).
72 Bonaventure, *Breviloquium*, prol. 4.4.
73 See Richard A. Muller, *Post-Reformation Reformed Dogmatics: The Rise and Development of Reformed Orthodoxy, ca. 1520 to ca. 1725*, vol. 2 (Grand Rapids: Baker Academic, 2nd edn, 2006), pp. 38–47, 243–4.
74 See Aquinas, *Summa Theologiae*, II-II, q. 171, art. 1.
75 B.B. Warfield, 'The Biblical Idea of Inspiration', in *The Works of B.B. Warfield*, 1:106–7.
76 Warfield, 'Inspiration', p. 107.
77 With respect to Barth, Gunton's concern is that an overemphasis on contemporary 'inspiration' leads to a conflation of it with revelation and to an accompanying lack of attention to the Spirit's inspiration of the original authors and community. In response, it might be observed that Barth sought not to separate original and contemporary 'inspiration', nor to elevate the latter over the former. Rather, his aim was to demonstrate the inseparability of the two. It might even be argued that he held to the

priority of the *there* and *then* of inspiration, over the *here* and *now*, since one can only hear God's voice through the voices of the original authors (see Karl Barth, *The Göttingen Dogmatics: Instruction in the Christian Religion*, vol. 1 [ed. Hannelotte Reiffen; trans. Geoffrey W. Bromiley; Grand Rapids: Eerdmans, 1991], pp. 222–6; Barth, *CD* I/2, pp. 504–6). The issue is not, perhaps, whether or not Barth treated original inspiration with some detail, but rather what the relative weighting of it was in his overall account. The emphasis on inspiration (or illumination, or revelation) being a free gift and not a possession may detract from issues regarding original inspiration and reception. Thus Gunton looks to provide something that supplements or moves beyond Barth.

[78] Randal Rauser insists that Gunton's claim for the contingency of all knowledge leads to scepticism. See Randal Rauser, 'Can There Be Theology without Necessity?' *Heythrop Journal* 44 (2003): pp. 131–46 (esp. 133, 143).

5. The Logic of Divine Saving Love: Jesus Christ

[1] Colin E. Gunton, *Yesterday and Today: A Study of Continuities in Christology* (Grand Rapids: Eerdmans, 1983), pp. 5–7.
[2] Gunton, *Yesterday and Today*, p. 5.
[3] Gunton, *Yesterday and Today*, pp. 10–11.
[4] Gunton, *Yesterday and Today*, pp. 11–13.
[5] Gunton, *Yesterday and Today*, p. 15.
[6] Gunton, *Yesterday and Today*, pp. 15–18.
[7] Gunton, *Yesterday and Today*, pp. 18–22.
[8] Gunton, *Yesterday and Today*, p. 22.
[9] Gunton, *Yesterday and Today*, pp. 22–4. This issue will be discussed below.
[10] Gunton, *Yesterday and Today*, p. 28.
[11] Gunton, *Yesterday and Today*, pp. 29–30.
[12] Gunton, *Yesterday and Today*, p. 34.
[13] Gunton, *Yesterday and Today*, pp. 35–8.
[14] Gunton, *Yesterday and Today*, pp. 38–9.
[15] Gunton, *Yesterday and Today*, p. 44.
[16] Gunton, *Yesterday and Today*, p. 45.
[17] Gunton, *Yesterday and Today*, pp. 52–3.
[18] Gunton, *Yesterday and Today*, p. 53.

[19] Gunton, *Yesterday and Today*, p. 52.
[20] Several other problems with the quest are highlighted. See Gunton, *Yesterday and Today*, pp. 58–60.
[21] These comments are directed against those who propose a Hellenizing of primitive Christology (Gunton, *Yesterday and Today*, p. 64). Similar comments are directed against those, like James Dunn, who see too radical a development of Christology within the New Testament itself (see Gunton, *Yesterday and Today*, pp. 72–3).
[22] Colin E. Gunton, 'The Truth of Christology', in *Belief in Science and in Christian Life: The Relevance of Michael Polanyi's Thought for Christian Faith and Life* (ed. Thomas F. Torrance; Edinburgh: Hansel, 1980), p. 105.
[23] 'The second reason for the relatively haphazard nature of the predications lies in the fact that there was little difficulty in ascribing divinity, either, and because of this, moments of revelation of Jesus's divine status are expressed either as arguments in support of some other point or at crucial stages in his story: baptism, Peter's confession, transfiguration, resurrection, etc. This means that the divinity of Jesus was not a problem for the New Testament as it came to be in the earliest Christian systematic theology. As a result, the ascription of some kind of equality with God is often indirect and capable of varying interpretations' (Gunton, *Yesterday and Today*, p. 69).
[24] Gunton, *Yesterday and Today*, pp. 77–80.
[25] Gunton, *Yesterday and Today*, p. 83.
[26] Gunton, *Yesterday and Today*, pp. 114–15.
[27] Here Gunton borrows heavily from Victor Zuckerkandl, *Sound and Symbol: Music and the External World* (trans. Willard R. Trask; Princeton: Princeton University Press, 1969) (Gunton, *Yesterday and Today*, pp. 115–19).
[28] Colin Gunton, 'Time, Eternity and the Doctrine of the Incarnation', *Dialog* 21 (1982): pp. 264–5. On Gunton's use of 'perichoresis' in the context of Christology, see Gunton, *Yesterday and Today*, p. 130.
[29] Gunton, *Yesterday and Today*, p. 125.
[30] Gunton, *Yesterday and Today*, p. 125.
[31] Gunton, *Yesterday and Today*, pp. 129–30; Gunton, 'Time, Eternity and the Doctrine of the Incarnation', p. 267.
[32] He believes many conversations surrounding the communication of attributes focus too narrowly on the relation between the two natures (conceived separately) in Jesus' actions. But natures, he writes, 'are not things but refer to ways in which Jesus is and acts'. See Colin Gunton, *The Christian Faith: An Introduction to Christian Doctrine* (Malden, MA:

Blackwell, 2002), p. 95. Elsewhere he describes his 'lack of enthusiasm' for the *communicatio idiomatum*, as expressed in Lutheran theology, Moltmann and Jungel. See Colin E. Gunton, *Christ and Creation* (Grand Rapids: Eerdmans, 1992), pp. 82–6.

33 Gunton, *Yesterday and Today*, p. 133.
34 Gunton, *Yesterday and Today*, pp. 178–81.
35 Gunton, *Christian Faith*, pp. 86–7.
36 Colin Gunton, 'One Mediator . . . the Man Jesus Christ: Reconciliation, Mediation and Life in Community', *Pro ecclesia* 11 (2000): pp. 150–51. Cf. Calvin, *Institutes* II.12.2.
37 Gunton, *Christian Faith*, p. 88. Similar things are said concerning God's immutability: 'In terms of the doctrine we are discussing [immutability], we must therefore say that such changes as this unique historic act inevitably imply for God can represent only the outworking or expression and not the overturning of God's immutability. It follows that if what happens in Jesus is genuinely God's doing, it is an event in which God is true to his deepest reality, consistently the one who creates and provides' (Gunton, *Christian Faith*, p. 93).
38 Gunton, *Christ and Creation*, p. 83.
39 Colin E. Gunton, *Father, Son and Holy Spirit: Toward a Fully Trinitarian Theology* (London: T&T Clark, 2003), p. 60.
40 Gunton, *Father, Son and Holy Spirit*, p. 61.
41 Gunton, *Father, Son and Holy Spirit*, pp. 69–70.
42 This is Gunton's attempt to stand with the tradition against modern rejections of the immanent Trinity and the related issue of the eternal generation of the Son (Gunton, *Father, Son and Holy Spirit*, pp. 70–71).
43 Gunton, *Father, Son and Holy Spirit*, p. 71.
44 Gunton, *Father, Son and Holy Spirit*, p. 72.
45 Gunton, *Father, Son and Holy Spirit*, pp. 72–3.
46 Gunton, *Father, Son and Holy Spirit*, pp. 73–4.
47 Even theologies intending to remedy this weakness fall prey to the same illness. For example, Robert Jenson, in trying to do justice to the unity of person of Jesus proposes too strong a notion of the *communicatio idiomatum* and, in doing so, confuses the two natures in Christ. Moreover, in seeking to underscore the revelatory and ontological significance of the God-man, he ends up too closely identifying the incarnate with the pre-incarnate Word. See Colin Gunton, 'Creation and Mediation in the Theology of Robert W. Jenson: An Encounter and a Convergence', in *Trinity, Time and Church: A Response to the Theology of Robert W. Jenson* (ed. Colin E. Gunton; Grand Rapids: Eerdmans, 2000), pp. 83–5.

48 Colin E. Gunton, *Theology through the Theologians: Selected Essays, 1972–1995* (London: T&T Clark, 1996), p. 154. Also published as 'Two Dogmas Revisited: Edward Irving's Christology', *SJT* 41 (1988).
49 Gunton, *Christ and Creation*, pp. 41, 43.
50 According to Gunton, *anhypostasia* teaches that Christ's humanity and personhood do not have their sole basis in the way ours do, that is, in this-worldly processes. *Enhypostasia* asserts positively that the person of Christ has its basis in the eternal Son of God. See Gunton, *Christ and Creation*, pp. 47–8. For a recent and detailed discussion of this distinction, see Oliver D. Crisp, *Divinity and Humanity: The Incarnation Reconsidered* (Cambridge: CUP, 2007), ch. 3.
51 Gunton offers Barth and Augustine as exemplars of this tendency. See Gunton, *Christ and Creation*, pp. 48–50.
52 For an in-depth treatment of Irving's Christology, see Graham W.P. McFarlane, *Christ and the Spirit: The Doctrine of the Incarnation According to Edward Irving* (Carlisle: Paternoster Press, 1996), for which Gunton writes the foreword.
53 Edward Irving, *The Collected Writings of Edward Irving in Five Volumes* (ed. G. Carlyle; London: Alexander Strachan, 1865), 5:134, quoted in Gunton, *Theology through the Theologians*, p. 157.
54 Irving, *Collected Writings*, 5:118, quoted in Gunton, *Theology through the Theologians*, p. 158.
55 Gunton, *Theology through the Theologians*, p. 158. Gunton elsewhere cites both Barth and Roman Catholicism as failing to account for the full humanity of Christ. Regarding Barth, he writes: '[H]is uncompromising concentration on divine action in Christ leaves little room for more than the bare assertion of Jesus' sinful humanity.' As for Catholic doctrine, he contends that the notion of an Immaculate Conception militates against any proper conception of Christ's taking on fallen human flesh. See Colin E. Gunton, 'Foreword', in Thomas Weinandy, *In the Likeness of Sinful Flesh: An Essay on the Humanity of Christ* (London: T&T Clark, 1993), pp. x–xi.
56 Gunton, *Theology through the Theologians*, pp. 161–2.
57 Gunton, *Theology through the Theologians*, p. 159.
58 Gunton, *Theology through the Theologians*, p. 160.
59 Gunton, *Theology through the Theologians*, pp. 162–3.
60 Gunton, *Christian Faith*, pp. 105–6.
61 Gunton, *Christian Faith*, pp. 109–10.
62 For Gunton's exposition of the birth, baptism, temptation, death, resurrection and ascension as all pointers to Jesus' humanity, rather than merely his divinity, see Gunton, *Christ and Creation*, pp. 50–67.

63 Gunton, *Father, Son and Holy Spirit*, pp. 153–6.
64 Gunton, *Father, Son and Holy Spirit*, pp. 157–8.
65 Paul D. Molnar, *Divine Freedom and the Doctrine of the Immanent Trinity: In Dialogue with Karl Barth and Contemporary Theology* (London: T&T Clark, 2002), p. 282. John Webster offers a similar critique: 'My judgement is that his criticisms of Barth in this matter [Christology] are in large part misplaced, and rest on a separation of Word and Spirit which gives little room to the Word's continuing activity in the history of the incarnate one' (John Webster, 'Gunton and Barth', in *The Theology of Colin Gunton* [ed. Lincoln Harvey; London: T&T Clark, 2010], p. 28).
66 Molnar, *Divine Freedom*, pp. 286, 290.
67 See, e.g., Gunton, *Christ and Creation*, pp. 58–9.
68 Molnar, *Divine Freedom*, p. 296.
69 Alan Spence, 'The Person as Willing Agent: Classifying Gunton's Christology', in *The Theology of Colin Gunton* (ed. Harvey), pp. 61–2.
70 Emil Brunner, Karl Barth and contemporary Catholic theologian, Thomas Weinandy, are among those making similar claims. See Kelly M. Kapic, 'The Son's Assumption of a Human Nature: A Call for Clarity', *IJST* 3 (2001): pp. 155–6.
71 Donald Macleod, *The Person of Christ*, Contours of Christian Theology (Downers Grove, IL: IVP, 1998), pp. 224–9.
72 Oliver Crisp, 'Did Christ Have a *Fallen* Human Nature?' *IJST* 6 (2004): pp. 284–7.

6. Metaphors and Atonement: The Work of Christ

1 Colin E. Gunton, *The Actuality of Atonement: A Study of Metaphor, Rationality and the Christian Tradition* (Edinburgh: T&T Clark, 1988), pp. 29–30 (italics original).
2 Gunton, *Actuality of Atonement*, p. 31.
3 Gunton, *Actuality of Atonement*, p. 32.
4 Gunton, *Actuality of Atonement*, pp. 34–5.
5 Gunton is cautious about the dangers of metaphorical language as it is used to describe God. He argues that there is always the temptation to project our experience onto God, which betrays a lack of controls on the language we use for God. See Colin Gunton, 'Proteus and Procrustes: A Study in the Dialectic of Language in Disagreement with Sallie McFague', in *Speaking the Christian God: The Holy Trinity and the*

Challenge of Feminism (ed. Alvin F. Kimel, Jr; Grand Rapids: Eerdmans, 1992), pp. 65–80.
6. Gunton, *Actuality of Atonement*, p. 46.
7. Gunton, *Actuality of Atonement*, pp. 48–51.
8. For example, R.W. Dale, a writer with which Gunton would engage, writes: 'These illustrations of the nature and effect of the Death of Christ are illustrations, and nothing more. They are analogous to the transcendent fact only at single points. The fact is absolutely unique.' R.W. Dale, *The Atonement: The Congregational Union Lecture for 1875* (London: Congregational Union of England and Wales, 1904), p. 358.
9. In an article to which I will refer a few times, Henri Blocher observes that many writers, Gunton included, see the reality of biblical metaphors of atonement as militating against the evangelical doctrine of penal substitution. He writes: 'A major attack is being launched against the Reformers' view . . . which has been, through Puritanism and revivals, the hallmark of evangelical preaching and piety. And metaphors are used as missiles.' Henri Blocher, 'Biblical Metaphors and the Doctrine of the Atonement', *Journal of the Evangelical Theological Society* 47 (2004): p. 630.
10. Colin Gunton, 'Atonement', in *Routledge Encyclopedia of Philosophy* (ed. Edward Craig; London: Routledge, 1998) http://www.rep.routledge.com/article/K003SECT2 (accessed 9 May 2014).
11. Gunton, 'Atonement'.
12. Colin Gunton, '*Christus Victor* Revisited: A Study in Metaphor and Transformation of Meaning', *JTS* 36 (1985): pp. 129–30.
13. Gunton, '*Christus Victor* Revisited', p. 130.
14. Gunton, *Actuality of Atonement*, pp. 56–7.
15. Gunton, *Actuality of Atonement*, pp. 58–9.
16. Gunton, *Actuality of Atonement*, pp. 62–4. Elsewhere he writes: 'Only the literal-minded would ask the question to whom was the ransom paid when Christ died on the cross, suggesting that it is usually not the Bible but its interpreters with whom we have to take issue. Similarly, it could be argued that all the patristic and medieval argument about whether the devil had rights over man as the result of the Fall derives from a similar literalism' (Gunton, '*Christus Victor* Revisited', p. 134).
17. Gunton, *Actuality of Atonement*, pp. 65–6 (italics original).
18. Gunton, *Actuality of Atonement*, pp. 66–7.
19. Gunton, *Actuality of Atonement*, pp. 69–71.
20. Gunton, *Actuality of Atonement*, p. 73.
21. Gunton, *Actuality of Atonement*, pp. 76–7.
22. Gunton, *Actuality of Atonement*, pp. 77–81.

23. Here Gunton more or less follows Harnack's interpretation of the development of atonement theology in the West (Gunton, *Actuality of Atonement*, pp. 85–7).
24. Gunton, *Theology through the Theologians*, pp. 172–3; Gunton, *Actuality of Atonement*, p. 87.
25. Gunton, *Actuality of Atonement*, pp. 87–9.
26. Gunton, *Actuality of Atonement*, p. 90.
27. Gunton, 'Atonement'.
28. Gunton, *Actuality of Atonement*, pp. 90–91.
29. Colin E. Gunton, 'Introduction', in *The Theology of Reconciliation: Essays in Biblical and Systematic Theology* (ed. Colin E. Gunton; London: T&T Clark, 2003), p. 2.
30. Gunton, *Actuality of Atonement*, pp. 91–2. Appealing to and even applauding Calvin, Gunton writes: 'But, and this is the key, Christ's work of obedience derives from God's love; it does not establish it . . . It is this which prevents the emergence of crude substitutionary teaching, and provides the essential context for Calvin's treatment of the juridical elements of the atonement . . .' Here the Reformer is seen along similar lines as Anselm, providing an 'unscholastic' account of substitution. See Colin E. Gunton, *Intellect and Action: Elucidations on Christian Theology and the Life of Faith* (Edinburgh: T&T Clark, 2000), p. 127.
31. Gunton, *Actuality of Atonement*, pp. 93–100.
32. Gunton, *Actuality of Atonement*, pp. 101–2. Luther's personal emphasis resulted in 'versions of penal substitution which do appear to attribute to God an excessively punitive character' (Gunton, *Actuality of Atonement*, p. 101).
33. Gunton, *Actuality of Atonement*, p. 103.
34. Gunton, *Actuality of Atonement*, p. 116.
35. Colin Gunton, 'Christ the Sacrifice: Aspects of the Language and Imagery of the Bible', in *The Glory of Christ in the New Testament: Studies in Christology in Memory of George Bradford Caird* (ed. L.D. Hurst and N.T. Wright; Oxford: Clarendon Press, 1987), p. 233.
36. Gunton, *Actuality of Atonement*, p. 119.
37. Gunton, 'Christ the Sacrifice', p. 233.
38. Gunton, *Actuality of Atonement*, p. 121.
39. Gunton, *Actuality of Atonement*, pp. 122–3.
40. Gunton, *Actuality of Atonement*, pp. 123–6.
41. Gunton, *Actuality of Atonement*, p. 126.
42. Edward Irving, *The Collected Writings of Edward Irving in Five Volumes* (ed. G. Carlyle; London: Alexander Strachan, 1865), 5:218, quoted in Gunton, *Actuality of Atonement*, p. 129.

43 Colin E. Gunton, *Father, Son and Holy Spirit: Toward a Fully Trinitarian Theology* (London: T&T Clark, 2003), p. 192.
44 Gunton, *Actuality of Atonement*, p. 132 (emphasis added).
45 Gunton, *Actuality of Atonement*, p. 132.
46 Gunton, *Father, Son and Holy Spirit*, p. 193.
47 See Colin Gunton, 'Universal and Particular in Atonement Theology', *Religious Studies* 28 (1992): p. 464. Cf. Gunton, *Father, Son and Holy Spirit*, p. 185. In an interesting article, Gunton contends that these transcendentals are helpful access points to understanding much literature (especially Tolkien's *The Lord of the Rings*). See Colin Gunton, 'A Far-off Gleam of the Gospel: Salvation in Tolkien's *The Lord of the Rings*', *King's Theological Review* 12 (1989): pp. 6–10.
48 Gunton, *Actuality of Atonement*, pp. 150–52. This discussion resembles the centuries-old question of whether Christ would have appeared if there had been no sin. If creation was always intended to have some close relationship to Christ – to be perfected and united in him – then probably Gunton would respond that Christ would have come even if there were no sin.
49 Gunton, *Actuality of Atonement*, pp. 152–3.
50 Colin Gunton, 'Atonement and the Project of Creation: An Interpretation of Colossians 1:15–23', *Dialog* 35 (1996), p. 39.
51 Gunton, *Actuality of Atonement*, p. 154.
52 Gunton, *Actuality of Atonement*, p. 157.
53 Gunton, *Actuality of Atonement*, p. 158.
54 Gunton, *Actuality of Atonement*, pp. 158–9.
55 Gunton, *Actuality of Atonement*, p. 160.
56 Gunton, 'Universal and Particular', p. 454.
57 Gunton sets up this discussion in terms of overcoming limitations to universality – spatial, temporal and ontological (Gunton, 'Universal and Particular', pp. 455–6).
58 Barth's view is the flipside of the coin, for it stresses the universal over the particular, leading to a virtual universalism, according to Gunton (Gunton, 'Universal and Particular', pp. 457–8).
59 Gunton, 'Universal and Particular', p. 458.
60 Gunton, *Actuality of Atonement*, pp. 161–4.
61 Gunton, *Actuality of Atonement*, p. 165.
62 Here notice that the idea of penalty and wrath is not entirely absent (Gunton, *Intellect and Action*, p. 128). Elsewhere he writes: 'The incarnate Son of God exchanged all this for something else, bearing the human flesh which has so succumbed to corruption and death, enduring

in Gethsemane and on the cross the *wrath* of God' (Colin E. Gunton, 'Towards a Theology of Reconciliation', in *The Theology of Reconciliation*, p. 167 [italics added]).

[63] Gunton, *Actuality of Atonement*, p. 165. Cf. Gunton, *Intellect and Action*, p. 131.

[64] Gunton, *Actuality of Atonement*, pp. 166–7.

[65] Justyn Terry, 'Colin Gunton's Doctrine of Atonement: Transcending Rationalism by Metaphor', in *The Theology of Colin Gunton* (ed. Lincoln Harvey; London: T&T Clark, 2010), pp. 133, 138–9. Another author argues that Gunton furthermore does not integrate his account of atonement with the doctrine of the Trinity. See Georg Pfleiderer, 'The Atonement', in *Trinitarian Soundings in Systematic Theology* (ed. Paul Louis Metzger; London: T&T Clark, 2005), pp. 127–38.

[66] Gunton, *Actuality of Atonement*, p. 141.

[67] Blocher, 'Biblical Metaphors', pp. 640–45. Cf. Terry, 'Colin Gunton's Doctrine of Atonement', p. 139; Justyn Terry, *The Justifying Judgement of God: A Reassessment of the Place of Judgement in the Saving Work of Christ* (Milton Keynes: Paternoster Press, 2007).

[68] Gunton speaks of the penal substitution view as 'stock exchange divinity' (following Irving). Robert Letham responds that such talk is 'simply a coded message; the author means "I don't like it"' (Robert Letham, *The Work of Christ*, Contours of Christian Theology [Downers Grove, IL: IVP, 1993], p. 138). Blocher similarly points out that Gunton does not argue against penal substitution so much as degrade it by the 'frequent occurrence of value-laden, manipulative epithets', such as 'mathematical', 'abstract' and 'grim' (Blocher, 'Biblical Metaphors', p. 633 n. 21).

[69] Calvin, *Institutes* III.11.6.

[70] Blocher, 'Biblical Metaphors', p. 645.

[71] William B. Whitney, *Problem and Promise in Colin E. Gunton's Doctrine of Creation*, Studies in Reformed Theology 26 (Leiden: Brill, 2013), pp. 105–9.

[72] Kevin J. Vanhoozer, 'The Atonement in Postmodernity: Guilt, Goats and Gifts', in *The Glory of the Atonement: Biblical, Historical and Practical Perspectives: Essays in Honor of Roger Nicole* (Downers Grove, IL: IVP, 2004), pp. 380–81.

[73] Terry recounts Barth's treatment of 'The Judge Judged in Our Place' in *Church Dogmatics* as an example of how penal substitution need not have all the negative connotations sometimes ascribed to it (Terry, 'Colin Gunton's Doctrine of Atonement', pp. 139–40).

[74] See Derek Tidball, *The Message of the Cross*, The Bible Speaks Today (Downers Grove, IL: IVP, 2001), p. 251.

75 Terry, 'Colin Gunton's Doctrine of Atonement', p. 136.

7. The Real and Ideal Community: The Church

1 Colin E. Gunton, *The Promise of Trinitarian Theology* (Edinburgh: T&T Clark, 2nd edn, 1997), p. 58. Originally published as 'The Church on Earth: The Roots of Community', in *On Being the Church: Essays on the Christian Community* (ed. Colin E. Gunton and Daniel W. Hardy; Edinburgh: T&T Clark, 1989), pp. 48–80. For a descriptive look at the relationship of the doctrine of the Trinity and ecclesial ontology in Gunton see Roland Chia, 'Trinity and Ontology: Colin Gunton's Ecclesiology', *IJST* 9 (2007): pp. 552–68.
2 Gunton, *Promise of Trinitarian Theology*, p. 61.
3 Gunton, *Promise of Trinitarian Theology*, p. 61.
4 Gunton, *Promise of Trinitarian Theology*, pp. 61–2.
5 Gunton, *Promise of Trinitarian Theology*, p. 72. See also John D. Zizioulas, *Being as Communion: Studies in Personhood and the Church* (Crestwood, NY: St Vladimir's Seminary, 1985), p. 134.
6 Gunton, *Promise of Trinitarian Theology*, p. 73. Herein we find what appears to be Gunton's first reference to perichoresis in ecclesiology, which will play a large role in his ecclesial ontology, as we will see shortly.
7 Gunton, *Promise of Trinitarian Theology*, p. 74.
8 Gunton, *Promise of Trinitarian Theology*, p. 74.
9 Gunton, *Promise of Trinitarian Theology*, pp. 74–5.
10 Colin E. Gunton, *Theology through the Theologians: Selected Essays, 1972–1995* (London: T&T Clark, 1996), p. 198. Previously published as *The Transcendent Lord: The Spirit and the Church in Calvinist and Cappadocian Fathers* (London: Congregational Memorial Hall Trust, 1988).
11 Gunton, *Promise of Trinitarian Theology*, p. 75.
12 Gunton, *Theology through the Theologians*, pp. 193–4.
13 John Owen, *An Enquiry into the Original Name, Institution, Power, Order, and Communion of Evangelical Churches*, Works of John Owen 15 (ed. William H. Goold; Carlisle, PA: Banner of Truth Trust, 1976), p. 262.
14 John Owen, *The True Nature of a Gospel Church*, Works of John Owen 16 (ed. William H. Goold; Carlisle, PA: Banner of Truth Trust, 1976), p. 11.
15 Gunton, *Theology through the Theologians*, pp. 193–4. These reflections appear earlier in an abbreviated form in Gunton. See Gunton, *Promise of Trinitarian Theology*, pp. 75–6.

16. Gunton writes: 'We can agree with [Owen] that the formal cause of the Church – the reason for its being the kind of entity it is – is the "voluntary coalescency" of visible believers into a society. But if that is all that is said, may not the outcome be a kind of ecclesiological Pelagianism, according to which we begin to forget the kind of freedom that we have, and behave as if we do it all ourselves?' (Gunton, *Theology through the Theologians*, pp. 199–200). The specific roles of the Holy Spirit in Gunton's ecclesiology will be given further attention later in this chapter.

17. Gunton, *Theology through the Theologians*, pp. 195–202. Gunton elsewhere notes: '[The church] is like other voluntary organizations in being joined freely; it is unlike them in attributing that joining to the work of God the Spirit and in orienting its life to worship and learning the ways of love' (Colin Gunton, *The Christian Faith: An Introduction to Christian Doctrine* [Malden, MA: Blackwell, 2002], p. 135).

18. Gunton, remember, defines open transcendentals as 'possibilities for thought which are universal in scope yet open in their application.' (See Colin E. Gunton, *The One, the Three and the Many: God, Creation and the Culture of Modernity: The 1992 Bampton Lectures* [Cambridge: CUP, 1993], p. 223.)

19. It should be noted that Gunton develops these concepts in the context of diagnosing and proposing a theological solution to fundamental issues of modernity – overemphasizing the individual at the expense of society and vice versa. I discuss these in more detail in Chapter 3.

20. Gunton, *The One, the Three and the Many*, p. 164.

21. Gunton, *The One, the Three and the Many*, pp. 164–5.

22. Gunton, *The One, the Three and the Many*, p. 191.

23. Gunton, *The One, the Three and the Many*, p. 191.

24. Gunton, *The One, the Three and the Many*, p. 212.

25. Here Gunton departs from the view of 'sociality' as a transcendental because it only takes into account personal beings to the exclusion of non-personal objects. Relationality provides a broader, more inclusive concept that accounts for non-personal objects and the role they play in constituting and being constituted by the other (Gunton, *The One, the Three and the Many*, p. 223).

26. Gunton, *The One, the Three and the Many*, p. 214 n. 4.

27. Elsewhere Gunton affirms: 'The triune God is one whose triune *koinōnia* has overflowed into the creation and redemption of a world he loves, and particularly of those creatures he has made in his image and remade in the image of his Son Jesus. It is for that reason – because God is himself communion – that the worship of the church cannot be disentangled

from its social and political matrix and outcome' (Colin Gunton, '"Until He Comes": Towards an Eschatology of Church Membership', *IJST* 3 [2001]: pp. 187–200, esp. 195–6).

28 Gunton, *Promise of Trinitarian Theology*, p. 82.
29 See Gunton, *Promise of Trinitarian Theology*, p. 83. Gunton envisions an 'ecclesiology of perichoresis' in which there is 'no permanent structure of subordination, but in which there are overlapping patterns of relationships, so that the same person will be sometimes "subordinate" and sometimes "superordinate" according to the gifts and graces being exercised'. He, however, does recognize that this idea may be 'hopelessly idealistic' (Gunton, *Promise of Trinitarian Theology*, pp. 80–81).
30 Gunton, *Theology through the Theologians*, p. 187.
31 Gunton, *Theology through the Theologians*, p. 189. Gunton elsewhere levels a similar charge against modern theologians such as Robert Jenson. One of Jenson's chief ecclesiological weaknesses, according to Gunton, is that he claims too close a relation between God and the church, which may actually lead to clericalism (Gunton, '"Until He Comes"', p. 197).
32 Gunton, *Theology through the Theologians*, pp. 196–7. For Basil's distinctions, see *On the Spirit* 16.38.
33 Gunton, *Theology through the Theologians*, pp. 198–9 (italics original). See Zizioulas, *Being as Communion*, pp. 129–30.
34 Here Gunton is again following Zizioulas (Gunton, *Theology through the Theologians*, p. 199). See Zizioulas, *Being as Communion*, p. 129.
35 Gunton, *Theology through the Theologians*, p. 201.
36 Gunton, *Theology through the Theologians*, p. 201.
37 Gunton, *Theology through the Theologians*, p. 202.
38 Colin E. Gunton, *The Actuality of Atonement: A Study of Metaphor, Rationality and the Christian Tradition* [Edinburgh: T&T Clark, 1988], p. 179.
39 Gunton, *Theology through the Theologians*, p. 202.
40 See John E. Colwell, 'Provisionality and Promise: Avoiding Ecclesiastical Nestorianism?' in *The Theology of Colin Gunton* (ed. Lincoln Harvey; London: T&T Clark, 2010), pp. 100–15. Colwell does a fine job in tracing this theme throughout Gunton's writings, beginning in *The Actuality of Atonement* (1988) through his later works.
41 Gunton, *Theology through the Theologians*, p. 203.
42 Although I am seeking to isolate the various strands of Gunton's Trinitarian ecclesiology, his writings are at many junctures attempts to do quite the opposite. This qualification, as we will see, is necessary as we turn to the role of the Son in his doctrine of the church.
43 Gunton, *Promise of Trinitarian Theology*, p. 66.

44 Gunton, *Promise of Trinitarian Theology*, p. 66.
45 Gunton, *Promise of Trinitarian Theology*, p. 67.
46 Thus a christological problem is at once a pneumatological problem (see Gunton, *Promise of Trinitarian Theology*, pp. 67–8).
47 Gunton, *Promise of Trinitarian Theology*, pp. 69–70. Although Gunton's ecclesiological proposals make little mention of Edward Irving, his Spirit-Christology is much indebted to Irving. See, e.g., Colin Gunton, 'Two Dogmas Revisited: Edward Irving's Christology', *SJT* 41(1988): pp. 359–76. For a helpful summary and critique of Irving's Spirit-Christology, see Donald Macleod, *The Person of Christ*, Contours of Christian Theology (Downers Grove, IL: IVP, 1998), pp. 221–30.
48 Gunton, *Promise of Trinitarian Theology*, p. 70.
49 This 'balance' is missing from proposals like John Howard Yoder's in that he only deals with the humanity of Jesus in his ecclesiology and does not take the crucial step towards articulating the role of the Holy Spirit in the constitution of the community. His perspective falls short of a *Trinitarian* ontology of the church (Gunton, *Promise of Trinitarian Theology*, pp. 70–71).
50 Providing some reasons for the evil that still exists in the church, Gunton notes that the church stands between the times and is not immune to the evils of the world. Moreover, the contemporary church is what it is because of poor decisions made in the early centuries by its predecessors. 'It is now battered with inherited ills which it is not yet able to transcend' (Gunton, *Actuality of Atonement*, p. 175).
51 Gunton, '"Until He Comes"', p. 188.
52 Here Gunton makes reference to some in the Anabaptist tradition like Stanley Hauerwas and John Howard Yoder (Gunton, '"Until He Comes"', pp. 188–9).
53 Colin E. Gunton, *Intellect and Action: Elucidations on Christian Theology and the Life of Faith* (Edinburgh: T&T Clark, 2000), pp. 101–20.
54 Gunton, *Intellect and Action*, pp. 103–5. In the end, two things must always be kept in tension in any ecclesiology: the church's relation to the triune being of God and the church as a finite, creaturely entity (see Gunton, *Promise of Trinitarian Theology*, p. 78).
55 Gunton, *Intellect and Action*, p. 106. See also his discussion of the Spirit's eschatological work in Gunton, *Christian Faith*, pp. 155–6.
56 Gunton, *Intellect and Action*, p. 107.
57 Gunton, *Intellect and Action*, p. 109.
58 Gunton, *Intellect and Action*, p. 109.
59 Gunton, *Intellect and Action*, p. 112.

[60] Gunton, *Intellect and Action*, p. 113.
[61] Gunton, *Intellect and Action*, pp. 119–20.
[62] Gunton, '"Until He Comes"', p. 190.
[63] Gunton, '"Until He Comes"', p. 193 (see pp. 191–200 for his extensive treatment of 1 Corinthians regarding the church as an eschatological entity). In Scripture there are two poles in this discussion. On the one hand, there is the near identification of the church with Christ himself. On the other hand, there is an 'equally strong movement to distinguish himself from the members of the church' (Gunton, *Christian Faith*, p. 132).
[64] Gunton, '"Until He Comes"', p. 193.
[65] Gunton, '"Until He Comes"', p. 200.
[66] Gunton, *Christian Faith*, pp. 129–30.
[67] Gunton, *Christian Faith*, p. 130.
[68] Colin E. Gunton, *Father, Son and Holy Spirit: Toward a Fully Trinitarian Theology* (London: T&T Clark, 2003), p. 203 (italics original).
[69] Gunton, *Father, Son and Holy Spirit*, p. 203 (italics original).
[70] Gunton, *Father, Son and Holy Spirit*, pp. 204–5.
[71] Gunton, *Father, Son and Holy Spirit*, p. 206. 'As I have already suggested, such a question cannot be answered simply by proofs of whether or not children were baptized in the early Church, partly because all such debate is inconclusive' (Gunton, *Father, Son and Holy Spirit*, p. 211). On the conclusive historical data against infant baptism, see, e.g., Everett Ferguson, *Baptism in the Early Church: History, Theology, and Liturgy in the First Five Centuries* (Grand Rapids: Eerdmans, 2009).
[72] Gunton, *Father, Son and Holy Spirit*, p. 206.
[73] Gunton, *Father, Son and Holy Spirit*, p. 207. 'Water is a natural substance, that which at once maintains life, cleanses it and can destroy it by drowning, so that Jesus' baptism in the Jordan, and consequently the new life of the Christian, constitutes the end of the old world, the world in which life is swallowed up by death, by the acceptance of eschatological judgement on the world' (Gunton, '"Until He Comes"', p. 199).
[74] Gunton, *Father, Son and Holy Spirit*, pp. 208–9.
[75] In making his case, he asks, 'Are we going to deny that the children of Christian people are members of the covenant community? And what of the mentally handicapped and those who will never reach an "age of reason" that enables them to make the prior decision upon which baptism is supposedly to depend?' (Gunton, *Father, Son and Holy Spirit*, p. 211). Of course it could be argued that Gunton oversimplifies or caricatures 'experience' and 'decision', not allowing for a more robust understanding of the Spirit's work in enabling faith.

76 Gunton, *Father, Son and Holy Spirit*, pp. 211–14. Ultimately, it is children of active Christian parents who are to be baptized. This is Gunton's way of guarding against the charge that infant baptisms have been too indiscriminately undertaken, thus contributing to the development of Christendom.

77 Gunton, *Christian Faith*, p. 133. 'The Supper falls when the members of the community fail to adopt a due orientation to God's redeeming action in Christ, and especially his death, as that is mediated by the Word and the Spirit in the life of the community' (Gunton, *Christian Faith*, p. 132).

78 Gunton, '"Until He Comes"', p. 195.

79 Gunton, *Christian Faith*, p. 133.

80 Gunton, '"Until He Comes"', p. 195; Gunton, *Actuality of Atonement*, pp. 199–200.

81 Gunton, *Christian Faith*, p. 134.

82 Augustine, *Enchiridion* 56. Cf. Tarsicius J. van Bavel, 'The Church', in *Augustine through the Ages: An Encyclopedia* (ed. Allan D. Fitzgerald; Grand Rapids: Eerdmans, 1999), p. 170. I received much help from this article and follow it closely in the subsequent discussion.

83 See Augustine, *Sermons* 300.1. It could indeed be argued that Augustine does not use the term 'church' here to refer to God's people of the pre-Christian age.

84 Van Bavel, 'The Church', p. 170.

85 Augustine, *Sermons* 272; cf. van Bavel, 'The Church', p. 171.

86 Augustine, *Sermons* 341.1.

87 Augustine, *Sermons* 10.7.

88 With reference to this so-called 'double concept' of the church in Augustine, Yves Congar is certainly correct to point out that this problem is not unique to Augustine, but one inherent in all ecclesiologies (Yves Congar, *L'Église: De saint Augustin à l'époque moderne* [Paris: Cerf, 1997], p. 21).

89 For a detailed study of the heavenly and eschatological dimensions of the church, see P.T. O'Brien, 'The Church as a Heavenly and Eschatological Entity', in *The Church in the Bible and the World* (ed. D.A. Carson; Grand Rapids: Baker, 1987), pp. 88–119.

90 See the above section on Gunton's ecclesial ontology.

91 E.g. Basil, *Letters* 38.4–5. This letter was originally ascribed to Basil. See the helpful discussion in Sarah Coakley, '"Persons" in the "Social" Doctrine of the Trinity: A Critique of Current Analytic Discussion', in *The Trinity: An Interdisciplinary Symposium on the Trinity* (ed. Stephen T. Davis, Daniel Kendall and Gerald O'Collins; Oxford: OUP, 2002), pp. 123–44 (esp. 131).

92 Richard M. Fermer, 'The Limits of Trinitarian Theology, as a Methodological Paradigm', *NZSTh* 41 (1999): p. 165. He points out that *koinōnia* in the Cappadocians' writings most often refers to a 'community' of essence or nature. Cf. Bernhard Nausner, 'The Failure of a Laudable Project': Gunton, the Trinity and Human Self-Understanding', *SJT* 62 (2009): p. 414.
93 Coakley, '"Persons" in the "Social" Doctrine of the Trinity', p. 137.
94 For example, see Gunton, *Promise of Trinitarian Theology*, p. 79, and '"Until he Comes"', pp. 262–3.
95 Colwell, 'Provisionality and Promise', pp. 105–6.
96 Colwell, 'Provisionality and Promise', p. 110 (italics original).

8. Perfecting Cause and Perfected End: The Spirit and Last Things

1 Colin Gunton, *The Transcendent Lord: The Spirit and the Church in Calvinist and Cappadocian Fathers* (London: Congregational Memorial Hall Trust, 1988), pp. 4, 6; Colin E. Gunton, *Theology through the Theologians: Selected Essays, 1972–1995* (London: T&T Clark, 1996), pp. 105–11. On Eastern weaknesses see Colin Gunton, 'The Spirit in the Trinity', in *The Forgotten Trinity: A Selection of Papers Presented to the BCC Study Commission on Trinitarian Doctrine Today 3* (ed. Alasdair I.C. Heron; London: BCC/CCBI, 1991), pp. 125, 132.
2 Gunton, *Transcendent Lord*, pp. 4–5, quoting Robert W. Jenson, 'The Holy Spirit', in *Christian Dogmatics* (ed. C.E. Braaten and R.W. Jenson; Philadelphia: Fortress Press, 1984), p. 126.
3 On the need for a unified conception of God's action, and the Spirit's part therein, see Colin E. Gunton, *Father, Son and Holy Spirit: Toward a Fully Trinitarian Theology* (London: T&T Clark, 2003), p. 79.
4 Gunton, *Transcendent Lord*, p. 5. Although he focuses on modern examples, Gunton acknowledges that this is also a pre-modern phenomenon. See Colin E. Gunton, 'The Spirit as Lord: Christianity, Modernity and Freedom', in *Different Gospels* (ed. Andrew Walker; London: Hodder & Stoughton, 1988), p. 177.
5 Gunton, *Theology through the Theologians*, pp. 105–6.
6 Gunton, *Theology through the Theologians*, pp. 106–7. It is noteworthy that Gunton appears to leave it open that the Spirit may be referred to as an 'it' or a 'he'. In one essay he writes: 'It is here worth observing that

one recent treatise did suggest reasons why it might be appropriate to characterise the Spirit as "it", and if we are to identify the Spirit as personal or as a person we must be aware of the fact that the attribution is not so obvious as in the case of the other persons of the Trinity.' He adds: '[R]eason has also been given to show why it is not altogether inappropriate sometimes to speak of the Spirit in impersonal or subpersonal terms, as a power or force. The suggestions of mysterious and unpredictable power, the freedom of the Spirit in relation to the created order, make it quite understandable that his work should be described in metaphors suggesting materiality' (Gunton, *Theology through the Theologians*, pp. 107, 118). However, elsewhere he is emphatic that 'the Spirit is a person – not an it, but a you'. See Colin Gunton, *Theology through Preaching: Sermons for Brentwood* (Edinburgh: T&T Clark, 2001), p. 111.

[7] Gunton, *Theology through the Theologians*, pp. 107–8.
[8] Gunton, *Theology through the Theologians*, pp. 109–10.
[9] Gunton, *Theology through the Theologians*, pp. 110–11. In fact, Gunton observes, it is the Son rather than the Spirit who primarily represents God's immanence in history. See Gunton, *Transcendent Lord*, p. 13. Cf. Gunton, *Theology through the Theologians*, p. 119, where he nuances that account of the Son's and Spirit's distinct actions.
[10] Gunton, *Father, Son and Holy Spirit*, pp. 114–15. He similarly contends that one of the failures of Pentecostalism is its limiting of the Spirit's work to the human sphere. See Colin Gunton, 'Holy Spirit', in *The Oxford Companion to Christian Thought* (ed. Adrian Hastings, Alistair Mason and Hugh Pyper; Oxford: OUP, 2000), p. 306.
[11] Gunton, *Father, Son and Holy Spirit*, pp. 108–11.
[12] Gunton, *Father, Son and Holy Spirit*, p. 113. Another failure of Pentecostalism is its lack of explicit connection between the Spirit's work and Christ's. See Gunton, 'Holy Spirit', p. 306.
[13] Gunton, *Father, Son and Holy Spirit*, p. 114.
[14] Gunton, *Father, Son and Holy Spirit*, pp. 116–17.
[15] Gunton, *Father, Son and Holy Spirit*, p. 117.
[16] Gunton, *Father, Son and Holy Spirit*, p. 118.
[17] Gunton, 'The Spirit as Lord', p. 177.
[18] Gunton, 'The Spirit as Lord', p. 181.
[19] Gunton, however, acknowledges that any cultural good done by even unbelievers, particularly in the arts, is attributable to the Spirit. See, e.g. Gunton, *Father, Son and Holy Spirit*, p. 123, and *Theology through the Theologians*, p. 121.
[20] Gunton, 'The Spirit as Lord', p. 181–2 (italics original).

21 Gunton, 'The Spirit as Lord', p. 182.
22 Gunton, 'The Spirit in the Trinity', p. 128; Gunton, *Theology through the Theologians*, p. 121.
23 Colin E. Gunton, *The Theologian as Preacher: Further Sermons from Colin E. Gunton* (ed. Sarah J. Gunton and John E. Colwell; London: T&T Clark, 2007), pp. 128–30.
24 Gunton, *Father, Son and Holy Spirit*, pp. 120–21.
25 Gunton, 'The Spirit in the Trinity', pp. 131–2.
26 Gunton finds John Owen helpful in affirming the need to make distinctions within God without falling into error. See Gunton, *Transcendent Lord*, pp. 6–7.
27 Gunton, 'The Spirit in the Trinity', p. 132.
28 Gunton, *Theology through the Theologians*, pp. 126–7. This does not mean that (1) God must necessarily create an other, or (2) being self-satisfied, God has no internal reason for creating. See Gunton, *Theology through the Theologians*, pp. 127–8.
29 Gunton, *Theology through the Theologians*, p. 128.
30 Gunton, *Father, Son and Holy Spirit*, p. 53.
31 Gunton, *Father, Son and Holy Spirit*, pp. 55–6.
32 Cumin cites Gunton's unpublished manuscript (A Christian Dogmatic Theology: Volume One) as demonstrating a shift in Gunton's view on this matter. Earlier the Father was only seen as economically prior, but in later work as ontologically prior. See Paul Cumin, 'The Taste of Cake: Relation and Otherness with Colin Gunton and the Strong Second Hand of God', in *The Theology of Colin Gunton* (ed. Lincoln Harvey; London: T&T Clark, 2010), p. 77.
33 See his entire sermon on the Holy Spirit in Gunton, *Theology through Preaching*, pp. 109–15.
34 Gunton, *Theology through Preaching*, pp. 111–13. Cf. Gunton, *Father, Son and Holy Spirit*, p. 80.
35 Colin Gunton, 'Dogmatic Theses on Eschatology: Conference Paper', in *The Future as God's Gift: Explorations in Christian Eschatology* (ed. David Fergusson and Marcel Sarot; Edinburgh: T&T Clark, 2000), p. 139. Cf. Colin Gunton, *The Christian Faith: An Introduction to Christian Doctrine* (Malden, MA: Blackwell, 2002), pp. 157–8.
36 Gunton, *Christian Faith*, p. 160.
37 Gunton, *Theologian as Preacher*, p. 105. This is surely a form of the view known as 'soul sleep'.
38 Similarly he writes: 'You do not fly up to heaven when you die; you rot and await the resurrection in God's due time' (Gunton, *Theologian*

as Preacher, pp. 102–3). Gunton contends that the only positive value in speaking of 'heaven' is that it prompts us to look forward to the resurrection and thus view death positively. Heaven, however, is not the destination of dead believers. See Gunton, *Theologian as Preacher*, pp. 105–6.

39. Gunton, *Christian Faith*, pp. 159–60. Cf. Colin Gunton, 'All Flesh Is As Grass: Towards an Eschatology of the Human Person', in *Beyond Mere Health: Theology and Health Care in a Secular Society* (ed. Hilary D. Regan and Rodney B. Horsfield; Melbourne: Australian Theological Forum, 1996), p. 36.
40. Gunton, *Christian Faith*, p. 159; Gunton, 'Dogmatic Theses', p. 140; Gunton, 'All Flesh Is As Grass', p. 36.
41. Gunton, *Christian Faith*, pp. 152–3.
42. Colin E. Gunton, *Theology through Preaching: Sermons for Brentwood* (Edinburgh: T&T Clark, 2001), p. 120.
43. Gunton, *Christian Faith*, pp. 153–4, 169–70.
44. Gunton, *Christian Faith*, p. 161.
45. He qualifies things somewhat: 'The old doctrine of hell had, and perhaps has, a measure of justice in it. It does seem fair that those who have been unrepentantly wicked should meet with punishment in the end . . . The punishment of the wicked is a kind of justice' (Gunton, *Theologian as Preacher*, p. 78). He does allow punishment to have some place in judgement.
46. Gunton, *Christian Faith*, p. 161.
47. Gunton, *Christian Faith*, p. 164 (italics original).
48. Gunton concludes his discussion of universalism with the rather prosaic statement: '[W]hether any will receive final condemnation must be left to the merciful justice of God.' In framing the matter this way, however, he reverses the traditional manner of thinking on the issue.
49. Gunton, *Theologian as Preacher*, pp. 78–9.
50. Gunton, *Christian Faith*, pp. 165–6.
51. An image he uses on more than one occasion.
52. Gunton, *Christian Faith*, p. 171.
53. Cumin, 'The Taste of Cake', p. 79.
54. This is a charge Molnar brings against Gunton. See, e.g., Paul D. Molnar, *Divine Freedom and the Doctrine of the Immanent Trinity: In Dialogue with Karl Barth and Contemporary Theology* (London: T&T Clark, 2002), pp. 278, 320.
55. The language of a 'strong second hand' is borrowed from Cumin in 'The Taste of Cake'.

56 Herman Bavinck, *Reformed Dogmatics: Holy Spirit, Church, and New Creation*, vol. 4 (ed. John Bolt; trans. John Vriend; Grand Rapids: Baker Academic, 2008), p. 711. See his whole treatment of universalism on pp. 704–14.

9. A Concluding Commendation

1. Bernhard Nausner, 'The Failure of a Laudable Project: Gunton, the Trinity and Human Self-Understanding', *SJT* 62 (2009).
2. Richard M. Fermer, 'The Limits of Trinitarian Theology as a Methodological Paradigm', *NZSTh* 41 (1999).
3. Mark Thompson, 'Has Colin's Gunton's Theological Project Really Failed?' *Theological Theology* (blog) http://markdthompson.blogspot.com/2009/12/has-colin-guntons-theological-project.html (accessed 1 Dec. 2009).
4. Karl Barth, *The Theology of Calvin* (trans. Geoffrey Bromiley; Grand Rapids: Eerdmans, 1999), p. 6.
5. Rowan Williams, *On Christian Theology*, Challenges in Contemporary Theology (Malden, MA: Blackwell, 2000), p. 4.
6. John Webster, 'Theologies of Retrieval', in *The Oxford Handbook of Systematic Theology* (ed. John Webster, Kathryn Tanner, and Iain Torrance; Oxford: OUP, 2007), pp. 584–5. For the chief commonalities of such theologies, see 'Theologies of Retrieval', p. 584.
7. C.S. Lewis, 'Introduction', in Athanasius, *On the Incarnation* (trans. and ed. A Religious of CSMV; Crestwood, NY: St Vladimir's Seminary Press, 2002), p. 5 (emphasis added).
8. Williams, *On Christian Theology*, p. 5.
9. Lewis, 'Introduction', p. 5. Though, as a colleague points out, 'his singular dismissal of Augustine casts a long shadow here'.
10. Paul D. Molnar, *Divine Freedom and the Doctrine of the Immanent Trinity: In Dialogue with Karl Barth and Contemporary Theology* (London: T&T Clark, 2002), p. 273.
11. Colin Gunton, 'The God of Jesus Christ', *Theology Today* 54 (1997), pp. 328–9 (emphasis added).
12. Thompson, 'Has Colin's Gunton's Theological Project Really Failed?'
13. Bruce A. Ware, *The Man Christ Jesus: Theological Reflections on the Humanity of Christ* (Wheaton, IL: Crossway, 2012).
14. Athanasius, *On the Incarnation* I.1, p. 26.
15. Francis Chan, *Forgotten God: Reversing Our Tragic Neglect of the Holy Spirit* (Colorado Springs: David C. Cook, 2009).

16 Karl Barth, *The Theology of Schleiermacher: Lectures at Göttingen, Winter Semester of 1923/24* (ed. Dietrich Ritschl; trans. Geoffrey W. Bromiley; Grand Rapids: Eerdmans, 1982), p. 278.

Recommended Reading

1 For an extensive bibliography of Gunton's works (though not including most book reviews written by him), see Colin E. Gunton, *Revelation and Reason: Prolegomena to Systematic Theology* (ed. P.H. Brazier; London: T&T Clark, 2008), pp. 208–18. I am much indebted to editor Paul Brazier for compiling this list.
2 The first is *Yesterday and Today*.
3 C.S. Lewis, 'Introduction', in Athanasius, *On the Incarnation* (trans. and ed. A Religious of CSMV; Crestwood, NY: St Vladimir's Seminary Press, 2002), p. 3.

We trust you enjoyed reading this book for Paternoster. If you want to be informed of any new titles from this author and other releases you can sign up to the Paternoster newsletter by contacting us:

By post:
Paternoster
PO Box 6326
Bletchley
Milton Keynes
MK1 9GG

E-mail
paternoster@authenticmedia.co.uk

Follow us:

Leon Morris

One Man's Fight for Love and Truth

Neil Bach

Leon Morris's story needs to be told. In this unique and long-awaited work Neil Bach shows Leon Morris as a prodigious and original thinker from the wrong side of the world who restored the credibility of evangelical scholarship and the centrality of the cross. Many of us have been nurtured by his enormously helpful books on the cross, but few know about the obstacles that had to be overcome. The author gives us a life of Leon Morris which is true to the man, unflinching in its evaluation of his work and inspiring in its conclusions. The book claims what evangelicals have widely acknowledged: Leon Morris was, and remains, Australia's most influential international scholar and pastor.

978-1-84227-986-1

The Big Picture

Building Blocks of a Christian World View

Brian Harris

The Big Picture is an accessible and stimulating exploration of the big building blocks of the Christian faith. Harris's take on the big building blocks of Christian faith is refreshing and will be appreciated by all who would like to think through different ways to follow Jesus the Christ in an ever-changing context.

'Skilfully bringing together biblically-informed theology and the everyday world, Brian Harris unpacks themes of grace, creation and Christian hope in an engaging conversational manner. The result is a book that empowers us to live out our faith wherever we are.'
Stephen Garner, Laidlaw College, Auckland, New Zealand

978-1-84227-856-7

www.ingramcontent.com/pod-product-compliance
Lightning Source LLC
Chambersburg PA
CBHW050841230426
43667CB00012B/2098